THE OLD LIGHTHOUSE

The Story of the
Pacific Garden Mission

THE OLD LIGHTHOUSE

The Story of the Pacific Garden Mission

By

JAMES R. ADAIR

PACIFIC GARDEN MISSION

CHICAGO

Printed in the United States of America

DEDICATION

To those of God's people
who regularly give and pray
to keep the
Old Lighthouse shining

"The dayspring from on high hath visited us, to give light to them that sit in darkness and in the shadow of death" (Luke 1:78-79).

TABLE OF CONTENTS

CHAPTER PAGE

1. Skid Row, Chicago 11
2. The Old Lighthouse 23
3. Telegram from the Rockies 31
4. Colonel and "Mother" Clarke's Children 37
5. Kid in the Sage-Green Suit 44
6. The Reign of Harry Monroe 50
7. Barefoot Walk on Suicide Road 55
8. Pa and Ma to Skid Row 62
9. God's Electrician 70
10. Saulnier, the Man 80
11. Good-bye, Skid Row! 91
12. Called to Serve 98
13. A Haven for Women 108
14. Welcome, GI! 118
15. Filming the PGM Story 129
16. Drama on the Airwaves 137
17. Doctoring Skid Row Ills 148
18. Keeping the Lower Lights Burning 153

ACKNOWLEDGMENTS

I'M GLAD for the day in 1948 when Ken Anderson, the widely known author of Christian books and producer of gospel films, took a trip to the Orient. It was then that Harry Saulnier, superintendent of Pacific Garden Mission, called to ask me to take over temporarily the editing of the *Pacific Garden Mission News,* a job Ken had been handling. As it turned out, Ken became so involved with books and films on his return to the States that I continued editing the *News.*

It has been a joy working with Harry Saulnier over the years. I have come to love him as a Christian brother and to admire him as a master soul winner. Thus, writing this book about the Mission and the miracles God has wrought at the Old Lighthouse has been a task I have thoroughly enjoyed.

Today, as I was writing this, I received a letter from a man who has strange ideas about the Christian faith. I hope this book will help convince even such skeptics as he that God is still very much in the business of transforming lives broken by sin. The letter writer commented sarcastically, "By and large, the 20th century is a world full of entirely different people, who cannot be helped to live in this world by trying to apply the outmoded, culturally determined, heretical 'old-time religion' you peddle [through Scripture Press and *Power* Magazine]."

If only this man could meet and talk to some of the people whose lives have been transformed at the Mission by the power of the gospel! A great many are 20th century people, very much alive today, living entirely different lives from those they once knew. Fortunately, they applied the "heretical 'old-time religion'" before it was too late.

I acknowledge with thanks the help of many people who worked with me to make this book possible. Harry Saulnier, of course, gave many hours of his time. His secretary, Helen Koester, worked long hours on several occasions as she dug out needed material. Others on the Mission staff were gracious in helping me obtain information. I'm deeply indebted to Jack Odell and his "Unshackled!" staff for details relating to many converts of the Harry Saulnier era. Certain parts of early chapters of this book, particularly material relating to Harry Monroe and the Taylors, are based by permission on Carl Henry's Mission history, *A Doorway to Heaven,* published in 1942.

JAMES R. ADAIR

Chapter 1

SKID ROW, CHICAGO

DARKNESS WAS SETTLING softly over Chicago's Loop as I hurried from a restaurant on Wabash Avenue. A biting December wind, the kind that plays tag with you at every corner in Chicago, made me appreciate again the hot meal I had eaten. An el train clattered on the tracks above, and traffic on the street threaded its way by the steel beams supporting the el structure. From the corner of my eye I noticed a man move toward me from the shadows, and I turned instinctively. A thin wisp of a man, bent with sin more than with years, he fitted the role of a panhandler: gray stubble on his face; bleary eyes; threadbare, filthy clothes. I guessed he was in his 50's, though he looked older.

"Help me, Bud," he begged. "It's cold. I've got nowhere to go, and I haven't eaten today." He pulled his thin coat about him, hunching inside it, and looked up pathetically into my face.

Smelling whiskey on his breath, I shook my head. "Sorry, friend, but money isn't the solution to your problem. You'd only spend it on drink. You need to know Jesus Christ."

White anger flashed in the man's gaunt face. "Why, I bet I know more about the Bible than you do!" he said hotly, beginning to quote the account of the creation of man from Genesis.

"Fine," I told him, "but your knowledge is evidently in your head. When it gets in your heart, a change comes into your life."

Recommending a place where he could get help if he really wanted food and shelter, I turned to go. "Friend," I said, "I have a night class at Northwestern University. I must hurry on."

I stepped back as his expression suddenly changed. With a faraway look in his eyes, he muttered, "*Northwestern.* Why, I graduated from there." Then he named a prominent Chicago physician who he said was one of his classmates.

For a moment I looked at him. This derelict a university graduate? An M.D.? "But what happened?"

"Malpractice. An illegal operation. I was barred from practice—"

"—and then you took to drink," I added.

Sadness filled his eyes as I laid my hand on his bony shoulder. "There's no use being bitter," I said. "I know you're cold and hungry." Again I told him where he could get help. On an impulse, I took out a business card and scribbled on it, "Fix this man up." He, of course, didn't need the card to be received at the place, but I felt he'd appreciate it.

I walked north whispering a prayer against the wind that through a miracle old Doc would make a comeback and once again find a useful place in society. I had known of others who had. It could happen to Doc. I glanced back over my shoulder. He was shuffling south and turning the corner toward South State Street, clutching the card I had given him.

This episode occurred in the early 1950's, but I remember it well since it opened the door to Skid Row in a new way for me. Until I met Doc, I knew little or nothing of the anxiety and despair gnawing at the souls of these social outcasts. I had made my choices in life; they had made theirs. I was here; they were there. I had my world; they had theirs. We were worlds apart.

Yes, I was acquainted with the physical aspects of Chicago's vast Skid Row area. On occasion I had walked hurriedly through this twilight world, detouring around panhandlers if possible, always breathing a sigh of relief when I came again to sunshine.

Skid Row, Chicago, isn't all in one place; and it isn't always connected, though many derelicts wander from one Skid Row area to another. West Madison Street, North Clark, South State, and a few neighboring areas, all within a mile or two of the "world's busiest corner," State and Madison, look alike. You leave the business district with its towering buildings, banks, the stock exchange, and such famous name stores as Marshall Field's, Carsons, Wards, and Sears; and suddenly you are in this mysterious twilight world where Satan is paymaster.

Every third or fourth establishment seems to be a smelly, dark tavern blaring suggestive music and featuring beer on tap for 15 cents. Greasy restaurants and cafeterias vie for the Skid Row dollar with such signs as, "CHILI—LARGEST BOWL IN TOWN! 15¢" and "FULL SHOT AND A BEER, 25¢." Flophouses, posing as comfortable hotels, ask anywhere from 50 to 85 cents a night for chicken-wire cubicles. Your flesh crawls as you think of cockroaches, lice, and bedbugs. You quicken your step. Pawnshops offer to buy, sell, or exchange, and you instinctively know that many men have shuffled across the threshold to hock items they have found or stolen in order to get cash for more drink or dope. Employment agencies, called "slave markets" by the men, advertise for workers to come by at 6 A.M. for spot jobs. They boast that "everyday is payday."

On South State Street, just south of the elevated tracks, you enter an area called "Hell's Half Acre" before the turn of the century. Here for some years following the 1871 Chicago fire, after the city had been rebuilt and people were living it up again, the owner of the Lone Star Saloon got his name into the American common speech. Mickey Finn put his more affluent patrons to sleep before robbing them. Since then a knockout drop has been a "Mickey Finn."

In this area today the twilight world will be brightened by the new $2.5 million, six-story Jones Commercial High School building which was being constructed at the corner of State and Harrison when this book was written. But this is still Skid Row where tattoo parlors, taverns, pawnshops, and flophouses rub elbows with burlesque houses, movie theaters specializing in nudist colony films, and penny arcades with peep shows offering "Parisian movies for adults only." Pictures on the outside of the theaters lure high school boys, servicemen, and others who wander into the area. These pictures feature the feminine form as close to nature as the Municipal Code and the police will allow.

Since the evening I met Doc, the beggar from the shadows, I have sought to find the answers to many questions concerning the shuffling forms of humanity that inhabit Chicago's Skid Row areas. Is it a certain "type" of person who is served by Skid Row? Why do these men choose to live in cheap, vermin-infested flophouses? Why do they slouch for hours in semidark taverns, spending their last dime for beer or cheap wine and listening to a blaring juke box or a painted hussy singing suggestive songs? What has happened to men who, almost in the shadows of such famous hotels as the Palmer House and the Conrad Hilton, sleep under newspapers in an alley or doorway because they haven't even 50 cents for a flophouse bed or because they are too drunk to go farther?

Interviews with many of the men themselves and people who know them, plus other research, refuted any thoughts I had that there is a certain "type" person who frequents Skid Row. Actually, there are many types, and each type has a different combination of reasons for living in this twilight world. Statistics indicate that close to 15,000 homeless men haunt Chicago's Skid Row districts, having arrived by different routes, all victims of problems they couldn't control. Look them over and talk with some of them:

The elderly men watching TV in the lobby of the Ewing Hotel in the 700 block of South State are pensioners whose small monthly check won't allow them better living standards. They are without families, or their children no longer welcome them as members of the family. On Skid Row perhaps they find other men who understand them, and they can talk of the good old days.

Like the pensioner, the physically disabled man feels that Skid Row offers the best means of making his small monthly check meet his need for food, shelter, and clothing. Both he and the elderly pensioner can at least go to a mission if cash runs out before the month does. A lot of times it depends on such things as how often a man visits the taverns as to whether a check lasts a month.

The bewhiskered, dishevelled, bleary-eyed alcoholics, some of them once men of distinction like my friend Doc, find in Skid Row a place where their dollar will give them the maximum number of drinks and at the same time food and shelter. They have been rejected by normal society or have simply withdrawn and are frantically seeking to escape from reality. For some, absenteeism and drinking on the job separated them from well-paying positions.

In addition, you meet unskilled laborers and migrant workers seeking jobs in the slave market; the transient bums who beg for a living and move from place to place; the semisettled or settled panhandlers or other shiftless humanity who are physically able to work but choose not to; and a number of petty thieves, gamblers, confidence men, or other criminals hiding from the police.

To look into the lives of some of the residents of Skid Row, I spent an afternoon interviewing men on South State Street. I squared with each, telling him the purpose of my interview, and assuring him that real names would not be used. I asked each substantially the same questions and recorded their answers in their own words.

First, I interviewed "Bill," a bewhiskered man who smelled of beer and had blood on the front of a once-white shirt. His shirt was partly unbuttoned. Beneath it he wore unwashed long-handled underwear. Bill, who said he used to be a fundamentalist but now believed in reincarnation, told me he was 35; but he looked 45. Here, condensed, are comments he gave in reply to my questions:

"The place where I worked burned down, and I was out of a job. I came to St. Louis first, and somebody told me it was better around Chicago. It took me two days to hitchhike here. The first guy that picked me up was a colored guy. He gave me 50 cents and I got a sandwich with one quarter and beer with the other. Then another guy picked me up and took me about ten miles. I got a bunch of rides after that—I lost count. One guy picked me up and he had some whiskey. He said he was going to visit some cousins and he took me there and I slept the night on the floor.

"Then I got rides in cars and a couple of trucks to get to Chicago. Once a couple girls picked me up too—one was a WAC. I have a job washing dishes now—just enough to keep me going. Last night I stayed at the Eagle Hotel. I pay 80 cents a night there. Some floors have showers and some baths. Some of the fellows I meet are nice, and some are no good ——s. Some are good guys just like me who've been given bad breaks, guys who've tried to be somebody but can't because they can't get their chance."

I pointedly asked Bill why he drank.

"I don't know. I like it. I'm an alcoholic, I know that. It makes me feel good. It builds you up, settles your nerves. I took up the habit of smoking when I was 14. I started drinking back in my teen years but had to sneak around to do it because I wasn't 21. I'm a heavy drinker. I'm a beer drinker—whiskey and wine sometimes. The doctor told me I should drink tap beer if I must drink."

Next I talked with "Charlie," a thickset nervous man who said he was a laborer, 51 years of age:

"My occupation is factory work, cooking, cleaning. I'm a jack-of-all-trades. I live in a small hotel on Clark Street right now. My room isn't wonderful, but it's at least not on the street. It's chicken wire—you can lock it so people don't come in and bother you at night. I live in this area because of my financial situation. I usually work about 14 hours and get 9 dollars.

"I used to live with my brother here in Chicago, but things

didn't work out. I was married and divorced. I brought this situation on myself. I drink now because it's something I can't run away from. I drink mostly beer. After work I drink about a quart and a half."

"Arnold," who told me he was 65, impressed me immediately as a man much more refined and cultured than the other men to whom I had talked. Grandfatherly looking, balding and paunchy, he fumbled nervously through items in his billfold and at last found a paper which he proudly unfolded and showed me. It was an old tattered concert program in which he was featured as violinist. The picture was of a young man, but I could see the resemblance. A biographical sketch said that Arnold had studied in Europe. But why was he on South State Street, in seedy attire, minus his teeth?

"It's been quite a few years since I actually gave a concert. I haven't taught for years. I've had a few jobs but nothing significant."

Arnold revealed that his aged mother had, at his insistence, given him enough money to leave the area to get a fresh start at 65. Then, apparently to block his leaving, she took some of the money and hid it from him. Angry, he argued with her until she locked him out of the house, keeping him from his clothing, false teeth, and all else that he owned. Arnold was checking with a lawyer about filing suit against his mother.

My next interviewee introduced himself as "Clyde." A lanky fellow with sagging shoulders, he gave his age as 33. His front teeth were missing and he walked with a jump. He told me:

"I've been in Chicago since the first of September. I came here [from Indiana] to get a new start. I had an alcoholic problem, ended up in a state hospital, and they advised me to leave the state because I didn't have a chance in my hometown to make a comeback. I'm married and have three children. I'm not divorced, but I don't know where they are. The home got broken up because of drink. I was in the hospital altogether nine months.

"I came up here and it hasn't seemed to help me. When I first came here, I got a job; and I got drunk and messed up my job. I've been taking about one spot job a week. The fellows on Skid Row are nice—I haven't had any trouble with them. But I'd like to get off this area. The thing I want most in the world is to get off this area, I can tell you that. But I haven't got any friends in the world. People treat us like dogs. We'll be standing on the street and people will ride by and stare out the car like we're animals. I hope that I'll get away from here eventually."

"Jim," 54, a coal-black Negro, had an equally hard-luck story:

"St. Louis is my hometown. I've been here two years. I don't like it around here. I don't know why I live here. I came on a freight train with another fellow. He robbed me, or at least he got me robbed. My wife is dead. I stay here because of the missions when I'm not working. I depend mainly on spot jobs I can pick up. I do mostly kitchen work. [Where I live] it's dirty. You can't fasten the doors. I watch TV in the lobby. You can't go in after 10. You can get out at 5 in the morning, but you don't have to go out until 7. When I'm not working, I sit around. I can drink or leave it. I took my last drink a month ago. It doesn't make any difference whether I have anything or not. I think the missions do a lot for the people. If it weren't for the missions I don't know what all these guys would do. I wouldn't know where I was."

"Ed," a light-complexioned Negro with a moustache and bushy hair, told me he was 28, a drifter half his life. His clothing was typical of the street. Polite and conversant, he said:

"My hometown is Philadelphia. I've been drifting from place to place. I had a chance to go to Las Vegas, but I was short of money. My work is generally restaurant. I work sometimes at Goldblatt's. This morning I was five minutes late, so I had to forget all about the Goldblatt's bus. We wash cars for them.

"I'm a light drinker. I drink beer, wine. Beer is 25 cents. In the course of a month I guess I would spend anywhere in the neighborhood of 36 or 39 bucks. The reason I stay around here is because I can get back and forth to work. I don't particularly like the area, but as it stands so far I have no other alternative."

"George," minus three lower teeth, slouched sickly as he talked surlily and nervously rubbed sores on his face:

"I'll be 48 in February. Chicago is my hometown. I have been a chemist by occupation. I was in charge of the research department at ————. The last I worked at my occupation was seven or eight years ago—since my divorce. The divorce threw me for a loop. I turned alcoholic. I never touched a drink or smoked a cigarette either, even though my father had a tavern. My problem was gambling. Gambling broke up my home. Then I began to rely more and more on liquor. I can outdrink 16 men. I drink Scotch, whiskey, beer, wine. I'm a compulsive drinker. I'm an escapist, trying to escape from reality, you see. I try to escape my problems and forget my past. I drink and drink until I get so sick I can't look at the stuff. Then I got to lay off of it; I can't eat; I can't hold water. It's a vicious circle.

"I couldn't even count what I spend a month on liquor. My grandfather left me 175,000 dollars, and I ran through that in two years just in gambling. I get to the point where money doesn't mean anything. I always had anything I wanted, new cars and all.

"There are a lot of hotels around here that have the cages. You run into bed bugs and conditions of that short. Misery loves company, and that's the first thing I like about this area. When you're miserable you like to find a fellow as miserable as you are.

"Naturally, the missions are needed. I don't get tired of hearing the messages. I have read the Bible over several times. I had six courses of religion in Loyola University. We had to go to communion every Friday or we were fined one dollar. I was a Catholic, but my wife was German Lutheran."

One drifter I talked with had an ugly gash in his forehead

that had just begun to heal. A short, balding man who had the marks of being more than the 39 years he claimed, "Fred" said he was a painter, that Racine, Wisconsin, was his hometown. As we talked, I ultimately learned how he had suffered the head injury:

"The rooms at the flophouse I live in are like a birdcage—screen on the top. I think the reason this place is quieter is because most of the men work in the slave markets or labor pools, and they're tired; and the hotel don't allow too much rough housing. I've been depending on the slave markets mainly in the past few weeks. But I find it pretty hard getting a job now when they see this gash on my head.

"I was a victim of circumstances. I couldn't sleep one night for the bedbugs, so I just started walking the street. I had been drinking the night before. I was sitting in Sophie's Restaurant down State Street. This was a week ago this morning. I was sitting there drinking coffee looking through the mirror at this guy who had his girl friend with him. He figured I was eyeing her up. So he clobbered me with a stool. I went to the hospital and they took X rays and taped it up. The cops took me there.

"I started drinking when I was in World War II. I couldn't really say why I drink. I was married and we had a divorce, and I guess I just kept on drinking. I'd go on a binge and then lose a good job. I'd stay off it for a couple, three weeks and then be back at it. It's a vicious cycle. I just keep on going one day to the next. I drink mostly beer, whiskey, and when you get broke you start on cheap wine. This is about 50 cents a pint. I'm a heavy drinker. I know I spend 40 to 50 dollars a month on liquor."

I talked to "Tim," who has been around Skid Row for many years and asked about crime and evil conditions in general in the area, particularly along South State. Among other things, he said:

"Shove a dollar bill over the counter in a tavern, and you'll get your head split open for the change. You see a lot of jack-rolling. They get you around the neck, hold your arms in back, and go through your pockets. It's usually two guys working together. Sometimes somebody will pick a fight to get at you. Maybe a bartender points out a guy with money because he's going to get a percentage. I've seen them rob guys on the street in broad daylight. After dark, guys usually will walk right on the curb to stay away from the buildings because they'll pull you into a doorway so fast, one on each side and one behind you with a knife."

"I learned about these things the hard way," another man, "Jake," told me. "I was a merchant marine, and when I came to Chicago two years ago I had two big checks on me. I ate my breakfast in a restaurant and cashed a check for about 150 dollars. On North Clark Street I walked into the King's Palace and sat there drinking. When I walked outside, I felt myself getting dizzy and sick; and all I know is the lights went out. When I woke up, my money, wallet, identification papers, and all were gone. Another time on Madison I got hit too."

Dope props up the spirits of a large percentage of Skid Row inhabitants, one man guessing that 65 percent of the men use dope in one form or another. Other estimates, however, are much lower.

"Some men," Tim told me, "sell medicinal stuff that they get from the hospitals, or they'll get prescriptions from a county doctor and sell the prescriptions to somebody who really wants the pills. Then the guy who was to use it for a pain killer in his own body goes out and buys a gallon of wine with the money.

"They got what they call 'pushers' on the street. Red Devil is a popular form of dope, something like phenobarbital to quiet your nerves. You take quite a few of them and take wine also and that makes you higher than a kite. A marihuana cigarette is 50 cents a stick or 10 dollars a pack. Those on dope usually start with marihuana, then lose their kick and take heroin. After they shoot the vein, there's no hope."

I asked "Tim" about some of the notorious joints along South State.

"The biggest one on State Street was Boots' Tavern until it was torn down 18 months ago [to make way for the new Jones Commercial High School]. Anything could happen in there. It was patronized by police officers also. Lots of times I was thrown out the back door for drinking a guy's shot while he was watching TV, or something like that. The bartender himself would throw you out. Boots was quite a man. If he'd tell you to leave and you didn't move fast enough, he'd throw you out. He's opened a place on Madison now, a block towards Des Plaines.

"The Show Boat is a notorious one, along with the 666 Club and the 700 Club. They're after-hour places. The 700 Club is a call house—if you want a girl you call the Show Boat and meet them in the 700 Club and go from there. Skid Row men don't often go there; they make a few nickels by spotting customers. It used to be if you wanted to know anything you'd ask a cab driver, but now ask a bum on Skid Row and he'll let you know what's happening because he gets around. You can't get in the 666 Club unless the attendant knows you. You don't get in unless you push the buzzer on his door. If you don't look good to him, he won't let you in."

In this twilight world of Skid Row, festering with disease, crawling with cockroaches and bedbugs, reeking with the sickening smell of cheap wine and beer, writhing with dope, there looms a light of hope, a place where the burdened can find rest—and God. It's just north of the 666 Club on South State—but unlike the Club, the door is always open.

Chapter 2

THE OLD LIGHTHOUSE

FILTHY DIRTY, unshaven, and sick, Ben Engstrom, 55-year-old former electrical foreman at the United States Steel Company Mill, Gary, Indiana, quivered as the white-jacketed doctor checked him over. From Skid Row's twilight world, Ben had been admitted to Cook County Hospital, a sprawling charity institution on Chicago's near West Side. Drink, which had ended his career at the steel mill, now threatened his very existence.

Looking into Ben's bleary eyes, the doctor leveled with his patient. "Engstrom, your only hope is extensive therapy. We'll arrange to admit you to an institution where you can get the best psychiatric care."

For an instant the patient's brain—virtually pickled with alcohol—reeled, and he remembered a scene of three years before. Walking aimlessly down South State Street, just south of the Loop, he had stopped at the busy corner of Harrison and State to hear a tall, handsome, broad-shouldered man making a sidewalk speech.

"Take electricity, for example," the man boomed. "Have you actually seen it? Do you understand it completely? No. Yet you have faith in it. You know that it will give you light at only a flick of a switch. God is like that. You don't see Him, but He's waiting for you to reach out to Him. All you need to do is call on Him, tell Him of your need. Trust Jesus Christ, and it will be like pushing a switch—your life will be flooded with light. You'll be born again and saved from the old life."

Moments later the speaker, Harry Saulnier, superintendent of the nearby Pacific Garden Mission, put a compassionate arm around Ben's drooping shoulder. He urged him to confess his need to God and to reach out and receive salvation and by faith trust God to make his life new.

Just the fact that Saulnier knew something about electricity gave Ben, the former electrical foreman, a feeling of kinship to this big man. Soon he bowed his head at Saulnier's suggestion and tried to please his new friend by saying words to God that were supposed to work a miracle in his life. But nothing happened. Ben returned to his old way of life, wandering Skid Row, begging, borrowing, stealing drinks. Seemingly he would exist here a few more years, then join other unfortunates in "potter's field." Or, if he was lucky, maybe his sister would bury him.

Now, three years later, in March 1945, the face of Harry Saulnier came into focus in the foggy mind of alcoholic Ben. "Please, Doc," the patient blubbered, "I want to try something else first. I know where I can get help, if I can only get there. I'd like to see Harry Saulnier at the Pacific Garden Mission on South State Street."

The doctor gave Ben streetcar fare and wished him well. An hour later, seeking the one man he believed could help him, Ben walked into the Mission, remained for the evening service, then walked to the prayer room to talk and pray with Saulnier. This time, like Pilgrim of old, he knelt in faith at the foot of the cross and lost his burden of sin. After his encounter with the almighty Son of God, Ben walked from the prayer room with hope surging in his bosom.

That night, because there was no room left in the Mission dorm, Ben was sent to a nearby hotel where he slept soundly for the first time in months. The next morning the day seemed brighter, the air purer as Ben rolled from his cot and joined other Skid Row men who had come into the Mission to escape the chill March winds. A Mission attendant gave him clean clothing and invited him to a Bible study for new converts before breakfast.

Though still in a weakened physical condition, Ben had to pinch himself, for he still felt like a new person. And the man who led the Bible study kept emphasizing this very fact: "You have been born again. You have a new life. Christ is now your life. He is in your heart, giving you new desires. You have been born into God's very own family. Listen what John 1:12 says: 'But as many as received him [Christ], to them gave he power to become the sons of God, even to them that believe on his name.' Walk today, and everyday, with your Saviour. He will never let you down."

Later, with four one-dollar bills in his pocket, Ben tested his new spiritual legs in a walk along South State. It had been nearly 24 hours since he had had a drink. The smell of beer from a tavern met his nostrils. His ear caught the sounds of the bar: the clinking of glasses, the babble of men slumped on stools.

Ben Engstrom stood there a minute—maybe two. Then resolutely he turned and walked to his warm new home, the Old Lighthouse.

Though he's had other battles in which drink sought to recapture him, today Ben Engstrom, a silver-haired man bearing the wrinkles of 76 years, is one of thousands of trophies of grace of the modern era of the old Pacific Garden Mission where God has been rescuing men and women from the brink of hell since 1877. Ben himself continues to live at the Old Lighthouse where he has served as building engineer for 21 years. He delights in telling how God, in grace, mercy and mighty power, redeemed him from the gutter and made him a citizen of heaven. I can see him now in a Mission meeting, an air of dignity about him, holding his silvery head high and his shoulders back, telling men of the street the story that never grows old to him.

Miracles as thrilling as that of Ben Engstrom are repeated time and again at 650 State Street, dubbed "A Doorway to Heaven" many years ago. Annually, in past years, as many as 10,000 persons have walked to the prayer rooms of Pacific

Garden Mission and made professions of faith in Jesus Christ. The Mission firmly believes that this is the only hope for a real comeback, based on II Corinthians 5:17, a Bible verse often used as a sermon text at PGM: "If any man be in Christ, he is a new creature: old things are passed away; behold, all things are become new."

Today the Mission, second oldest in the United States, is one of the largest and most efficient institutions of its kind. It was here I sent Doc, the erstwhile physician who helped introduce me to the Skid Row the Mission serves. Housed in four buildings, the Pacific Garden Mission serves not only Skid Row derelicts like Doc and the Ben Engstrom of yesteryear but GI's, destitute families, and up-and-outers who find their way here for spiritual counsel. In addition, the light from the Old Lighthouse beams out across the U.S.—and many parts of the world—through films, books, and an expertly produced dramatic radio series, "Unshackled!" The program featuring true stories of Mission converts, is broadcast over 205 radio stations in the U.S. and 25 foreign countries. Annually hundreds report that the broadcast has brought them into vital contact with Jesus Christ.

For nearly a century Pacific Garden Mission has welcomed an estimated six million persons, and only heaven's records list the great host of those who met the Saviour there. Executives, lawyers, doctors, and scientists have joined cooks, sailors, common panhandlers, and crooks in walking down the aisle as audiences have burst into singing such familiar invitation songs as "Just As I Am" and "Jesus, I Come."

"Everlastingly at it," a slogan coined and made famous by Mel Trotter at the mission he founded in Grand Rapids, Michigan, typifies the Old Lighthouse on South State. When the day staff isn't on duty counseling and winning souls, the night staff is throwing out the lifeline. Figuratively, the door never closes. In summer and winter, in sweltering heat and bitter cold, doormen stand on the sidewalk from 8 A.M. till 10:30 P.M. distributing gospel tracts and inviting passers-by inside. If a GI needs a bunk at 2 A.M., the night man welcomes him and tucks him in. Or if a woman seeking shelter rings the bell of the Women's Division, she is taken in and given care by a member of the staff of that busy wing of the Mission.

From the early days of the Mission, gospel services have been the backbone of the ministry. For many years three services have been held daily—one in the morning, one at noon, the other in the evening. Full houses of some 350 people are not uncommon, especially on Saturday nights when visitors from many churches gather with Skid Row men and women for a two-hour song and testimony service.

Not long ago I looked in on a rousing Saturday evening testimony meeting, pencil and notebook in hand. A group of junior high young people from Wheaton (Ill.) Bible Church provided the special music. With Harry Saulnier leading, the crowded mission hall became a corner of heaven as one after another stood and told what Christ had done for him.

"Make them short. No preaching. Just tell simply what Christ means to you!" Saulnier urged graciously.

But some of the testimonies were long, and a few preached. They were old-timers, full and burdened for those in the audience to share what they had discovered in Christ. Short testimonies from new converts were given timidly. Amens rang out time and again.

A thickset man in the front row told the audience that he had once come to the Mission with his wife. An alcoholic, he had listened to the gospel and returned home under conviction. Later, back at the Mission, he went to the prayer room and was saved and delivered from drink. "I call this the 'House of Miracles!' " he bellowed. "Here Christ delivered me from sin and drink."

A woman of perhaps 60 testified that God had saved her at home 32 years ago as she read the Word. A man with a built-in PA system said he had "trailed the devil for 48 years like the tail of a comet." He had met Christ, and his life had been changed in a split second.

The crowd listened eagerly as a small girl came to the pulpit and recited Psalm 23. Someone told me that her mother had been on the verge of giving up when she visited PGM and found the Lord.

Busloads of church folk, oldsters and young people alike, come from hundreds of miles away, visit the Old Lighthouse regularly and invariably go away fired up over what they see and hear. A church in Albion, Indiana, reported: "We truly were blessed visiting your Mission. Everybody feels the same. Many testimonies at church on Thursday and Sunday nights verified the blessings we received being in your service that evening."

A representative of a Chicago area church was blessed through serving: "One of the teen-age boys I brought received Christ. My assistant led a man to Christ in the counseling room. I talked to one man but don't think he was really under conviction, and a young man we talked with outside the Mission received Christ. Now we've got another group that wants to come this Saturday."

PGM deputation workers carry the fire and spirit of the soul-winning ministry to distant points, challenging church members to win souls and exhorting the unsaved to come to Christ. In one recent year, teams preached to more than 45,000 people and saw 1171 profess Christ as Saviour.

Back at the Old Lighthouse the some 80 staff members—personal workers, secretaries, office workers, doormen, receptionists—together with the superintendent and department directors pray fervently at several daily separate sessions asking God for a great harvest of souls. And because of their prayers, and those of countless thousands elsewhere, God blesses with souls daily.

A policeman brought a man to the Mission at 2:30 one June morning. Though the dormitory was closed and filled with sleeping men, the night man greeted the stranger and took him to the Servicemen's Center for a snack and coffee. He slept in a chair the remainder of the night. Before he left, he was able to say:

"Right here at the Mission the miracle happened. I recovered my fellowship with the Lord Jesus! How good it was to experience His love and guidance again. Now I am living for Him. I know that without Him I would be nothing."

A World War II veteran who had promised God in North Africa, in the heat of battle, that he would live for Him wandered into the Mission not long ago, a pitiful wreck of a man. He had failed to keep his promise when he returned and had resumed a machine shop business. Ultimately, because of drink, he lost the business. Then his wife and three children were killed in an automobile accident. This sent him into a drunken tailspin, and for 18 months he was a Skid Row wanderer. In the Mission he placed his faith in Christ and before he left he announced:

"I know that God has forgiven my sins and saved me, and I am going back home to Wildwood, New Jersey, to the parents that loved me and prayed for me."

"Except for the souls the Lord of the harvest so graciously gives, Pacific Garden Mission would be merely another social service organization," explains Superintendent Saulnier. "But the cooks prepare some 600 meals a day for a purpose. Some 285 beds are made daily for Skid Row men, GI's, and women and children for one primary purpose. The four buildings are kept spic and span with one aim in mind. That precious souls might be won!"

At the Old Lighthouse personal workers look upon every man as a precious soul for whom Christ died, and they desperately want to communicate the gospel to such men. Likewise, women personal workers deal tenderly with homeless mothers and fallen women of the street. Through such dedicated workers the Holy Spirit works to transform those who have lost all hope because of the weight of sin upon them.

At the Old Lighthouse it's all part of the fruitful soul-winning ministry begun in 1877 because God gave two humble, unlikely people a tremendous burden for salvaging human wrecks by courageously beaming the blessed gospel light to them on Skid Row, Chicago!

Chapter 3

TELEGRAM FROM THE ROCKIES

THE DAY DAWNED bright and clear that late summer in 1877 in the small Colorado mining town where Colonel George Clarke, a stocky, balding, middle-aged man, was about to close a real estate deal. Ordinarily he would have been happy, for the deal promised him a substantial profit. Even being temporarily on business in Colorado, away from Chicago and the slums where his wife had been dragging him to visit the poor, should have made the colonel's heart sing.

However, that wasn't the case. As the Colorado day progressed, thunder growled beyond the snowcapped peaks, threatening a storm. But already lightning flashed within the colonel's heart, and each flash revealed the delicate features of his wife—and the haggard outcasts she wanted to help. In a growing way this tiny woman he had married four years earlier was giving her time and energy to visiting and ministering to unfortunates. During the Civil War, in which Clarke had risen to lieutenant colonel with the 13th Illinois Volunteers, she had started a little mission Sunday school at the corner of State and 23rd Streets to reach the poor for God. This wasn't so bad. After all, he himself had been helping. But now Sarah was praying about starting a mission to minister the gospel of Christ to drunkards and other derelicts along the levee—the stretch of South Clark Street from Van Buren to 22nd Street, near the Chicago River.

His real estate deal forgotten, Colonel Clarke talked long with God on his knees as he pondered his problem. "O God, You know I love You, and I want to do what is right and good in Your sight. You know what a mess I make of preaching and how my heart aches for the miserable people dear Sarah wants to reach. Show me, O Lord, what I must do, and give me power to do Your blessed will."

Right here in the Rockies several years earlier Clarke had wrestled with God concerning the salvation of his soul. About to transact a shady land deal, he had remembered the prayers of his saintly mother and broke before the Lord. Confessing his sin and need of forgiveness, he had felt the cleansing stream from the Saviour's Cross and from that time had counted himself a member of God's family.

Now he wanted definite directions from his heavenly Father. Somehow he felt like a runaway boy out here dabbling again in real estate while Sarah continued the work among the people of the levee. Finally, the storm over, George Clarke lifted his head and looked unto the mountains and above to the blue sky. "Yes, Lord, I'll give You my life and will preach the gospel to the people of the levee. I'll trust You to give me the ability."

A short time later the town telegraph operator began tapping out a message. The exact wording of the message Sarah Dunn Clarke got that day in 1877 in Chicago was never recorded, though in substance it read: "Plans changed. God wants me to join you in starting a mission. George." Tears in her eyes and a glow in her heart, Sarah whispered a thank you to God and began to think about the best place for a mission.

The catastrophic Chicago fire in 1871 had sent most churches to the city's outskirts, so a gospel work was desperately needed in the area now infested with gambling halls, saloons, and brothels. But where would God have them begin this counterattack against sin? Sarah Clarke wondered.

The decision would await George's return from Colorado. Meantime she would pray for God's wisdom and leading.

Mrs. Clarke had been in the habit of taking matters to God for a good many years, though it had been in only comparatively recent times that she had felt God's closeness to her and His power throbbing and working in her life.

Born November 13, 1835, in New York's Cayuga County, she grew up in a Christian atmosphere. Attending Sunday school, she was taught to abstain from card playing, dancing, and theater attendance. But not until she was 20 did she really have a personal encounter with God. A friend sensed her need of knowing the Saviour personally, and returning from the Wilkes-Barre Seminary and standing on the platform of the Scranton depot, the friend asked Sarah Dunn to give her heart to God. This prompted her to place her trust in Jesus Christ for her salvation, and a desire was kindled in her heart to please God through her life.

But another encounter with God was to change the course of her life. After teaching school in Elmira, New York, she moved in 1861 to Waterloo, Iowa, and here continued faithfully attending church. But God dealt with her in her home to prepare her for the ministry He would lead her into later in Chicago.

One day Sarah Dunn was putting the finishing touches on an elaborate decoration for the family home. As she paused to admire the work, it seemed that an audible voice spoke to her: "What are you doing to decorate your heavenly home?"

Thoughts of perishing souls marching to a Christless eternity flooded Sarah's mind as she pondered this penetrating question. Time, she reasoned, was a precious gift from God—in reality it was God's time, not hers, since she belonged to Him. "Why should I spend priceless time on earthly adornments when souls need to be won for the Master? Surely this is the way I can adorn my heavenly mansion through all the cycles of eternity."

From this time on, her consuming passion in life was the winning of sinners to Jesus Christ and spending her time in the service of her Master. Even when she moved to Chicago and sought to make fashionable calls to assure her social standing, her conscience wouldn't let her continue. So, wearing simple clothing, she began visiting needy families and ministering to both their spiritual and material needs.

Shortly it dawned on Sarah that this was God's calling in life for her.

In 1869, with the aid of several friends, she opened her mission Sunday school at State and 23rd. During the early days of the school, in a business transaction, she met Colonel George Clarke. Two years after the Chicago fire they were married.

The colonel, like Mrs. Clarke, was a native of New York state, having been born in Ostego county on February 22, 1827. He had studied at Beloit College, Beloit, Wisconsin, and became one of its first graduates. He then became the principal of the Milton Academy. Later he edited a paper called the *Sauk County Standard* and, after studying law, was admitted to the bar in 1853. Finally, his interests turned to real estate and business took him to Colorado, where he had his first encounter with God. His first wife perished in the Chicago fire.

Following his second marriage in 1873, wanting both to please God and the tiny woman who had become his wife, Colonel Clarke assisted in the Sunday school mission. He tried occasionally to preach, and he gradually learned the lesson of giving to the Lord—diverting funds to "the Lord's treasury" once earmarked for Cuban cigars and the entertainment of friends.

But not until he wrestled with the Lord in Colorado the second time did he decide that ministering the Word to the unfortunates of Chicago was to be his task for the remainder of his life.

On September 15, 1877, the Clarkes put the finishing touches on their work in a tiny store at 386 South Clark Street, virtually next door to a notorious place called Hinky Dink's, and spread the word that they would have services that evening. It was the first rescue mission west of Jerry McAuley's Water Street Mission in New York, at that time the nation's only other mission. If the Clarkes were aware of this work, there is no record of it.

"Colonel Clarke's Mission," as it was known in its early days, featured a wheezy organ and the unpolished but fervent preaching of the colonel himself. As he talked to noisy, restless crowds, made up of drunks, dope addicts, harlots, and thieves, tears trickled down the colonel's cheeks. More often than not, he preached on his favorite text, John 3:16: "God so loved the world."

Seating capacity of the Mission was about 40 when the audience crowded together on the backless, wooden benches. A potbellied stove kept out the Chicago chill; kerosene lamps supplied flickering light; and heartwarming Bible quotations graced the walls. Behind the table from which Colonel Clarke preached, a large sign proclaimed, "GOD IS LOVE." A warning on the left wall, "THOU GOD SEEST ME," was contrasted with the invitation on the right wall, "COME UNTO ME, ALL YE THAT LABOUR AND ARE HEAVY LADEN, AND I WILL GIVE YOU REST."

"Saloons on either side, with their banjos and accompanying instruments, were a great combination," penned Mother Clarke in describing the opening of the Mission. "However, we held the fort—Mr. Clarke preached, and I tried to keep crooked men straight.

"But such a coming and going was never seen before. Order—heaven's 'first law'—had never been injected in their minds, and it took the wisdom of Solomon to separate the drunken men and keep that crowd in order."

Despite the confusion, God honored the preaching of His Word, and during the first days four professed Christ as Saviour, three going on to give outward evidence of changed lives. In three years in the tiny Mission on the South Clark Street levee, the old, old story of Jesus and His love and power moved the hearts of hundreds. Night after night, as the colonel pleaded from his table at the front and Mrs. Clarke moved tenderly among the audience, God loosed Satan's chains from harlots, burglars, drunkards, and other patrons of brothels, gambling joints, and opium dens.

Then came the day in 1880 when Colonel Clarke went hunting for larger quarters. His nose for a good deal in real estate, now consecrated to God, led him finally to a building recently vacated by the notorious Pacific Beer Garden, "a place where the vilest and toughest were accustomed to come for cheap beer . . . the most murderous joint west of New York City." Here the Colonel rented a sizable room. The new address was 100 East Van Buren Street (later, in 1909, changed to 67 West Van Buren, when Chicago changed its numbering system). Near the southwest corner of Van Buren and what is now Federal Street, the Mission put out the welcome mat to the countless sinners who patronized the dens of iniquity that made the area a festering sore in Chicago's backyard.

Proclaiming the Mission as "the greatest on earth" and occasionally fishing there for souls himself, Dwight L. Moody, fresh from evangelistic meetings in England, urged the Clarkes to advertise to the world that the old Pacific Beer Garden had been transformed. "Just strike out the word *beer* and add the word *mission,*" he advised.

Thus, "Colonel Clarke's Mission" became the "Pacific Garden Mission," a name destined to become world famous as God was about to add to the list of converts some men who would herald the same glad news of Christ far beyond Chicago's Skid Row.

Chapter 4

COLONEL AND "MOTHER" CLARKE'S CHILDREN

AFTER THE CLARKES LEASED for God the area once occupied by the notorious Pacific Beer Garden, they threw themselves into the work with even greater ardor, resulting in an endless stream of gloriously transformed lives. They never had children of their own but, in a real sense, these were their children. Many of them in later years tenderly called Mrs. Clarke "Mother." The Spirit of the living God was honoring the simple gospel messages preached faithfully night after night by the colonel and others who came to assist in the ministry of fishing for men.

Over the door a sign proclaimed, "HOPE FOR ALL WHO ENTER," and day and night the Clarkes tried desperately to convey this message to drunkards, outcasts, and others who crept in from the surrounding world of barrooms, opium dives, gambling establishments, and red-light houses.

The first of a line of famous converts of Pacific Garden Mission gave Colonel Clarke a hard time the night he came to Christ in 1880. Harry Monroe had just been released by a federal judge in Detroit from a counterfeiting charge. Hitting Chicago, he automatically entered a saloon and ordered a schooner of beer. As he lifted the glass, he suddenly stopped. *If I drink this,* he thought, *I'm right back where I was.*

He shoved the glass back toward the bartender and stalked out. Moments later, passing the Mission, he heard music. Twenty-seven-year-old Harry Monroe pushed open the door, stood there for a moment, then sat down. As the meeting closed, Colonel Clarke approached Monroe and asked him to accept Jesus.

"You stick to your business, and I'll stick to mine," the thickset Monroe fired back.

The big-hearted colonel did stick to his business, for he sensed that the message delivered that evening by D. W. Potter, a prominent Chicago banker, had brought conviction to the heart of the hardened young man. "Young man, do you know that Jesus loves you and so do I?"

Monroe trembled as the Mission superintendent told him how the blood of Jesus could wipe away all of the sin of his soul and how God could give him a wonderful new start.

Moments later a penitent Harry Monroe was talking to the heavenly Father. "I quit booze from this minute on," he blurted. "God be merciful to me, a sinner, and save me for Jesus' sake."

That night the Colonel put Harry up in a cheap room, since in those days the Mission did not have dormitory space. For the first time in 12 years, Harry wrote to his mother back in Massachusetts, sharing with her the glory that filled his bosom.

The next day, Sunday, he gave his first testimony in the Mission. Within a few weeks, after the Colonel discovered his ability to sing, Harry was given charge of the song services and helped make the Mission hall throb with glad gospel songs that became strong competition for the tinny banjo music drifting from the barrooms nearby. Unknown to Harry Monroe at the time, it was God's way of training him for a great ministry as the next superintendent of the Old Lighthouse.

Though they worked long hours and faced times when they weren't sure how they would pay their bills, the Clarkes never let discouragement cross their threshold. In a brief history of the Mission written 37 years after they flung open the doors of the Old Lighthouse, Mother Clarke wrote that the word *discouragement* "was never in our vocabulary." In her cursory style, she penned this illustration:

"In the early history of the Mission . . . a dummy train conveyed us . . . [to] our home [in Morgan Park on Chicago's South Side] . . .

"[We] had been tramping in the rain and slush all day, taking our late train as usual, at the midnight hour, obliged then to walk nearly two miles from the train to our home, in a terrific storm, facing a heavy sleeting hail and rain all the way. Entering the house [we] found his satanic majesty on hand, and with a slight [tap] on the shoulder, and with a modest voice [he] said, 'Does it pay?'

" 'Yes,' I very emphatically replied, 'I'd walk ten miles—or all night—if I could be the means of winning a soul.'

"That insinuation never accosted us again. *Disappointments* have been many. But discouragement *never.*"

Their secret, of course, lay in the fact that their lives were wholly wrapped up in serving God and helping and loving the people to whom He had sent them to minister. It was no 9:00 to 5:00 job and then home for a quiet evening. On his sixty-third birthday Colonel Clarke, in a lengthy poem written to Mrs. Clarke, put it in these terms:

Not oft we've sat around our hearth,
On winter's stormy night,
To look upon the glowing coals,
Of fires burning bright,
But trust we've brought to darken'd hearts,
A little more of light.

In bringing the gospel to the people of the twilight world of their day, the Clarkes practiced sacrifice in the strictest sense of the word. During their society days when Colonel Clarke's business know-how gave them a good income, they had lived on a level expected of well-to-do people. But, with their income reduced considerably as Colonel Clarke gave himself wholly to the work of the Mission, they found it harder and harder to produce ready cash to keep the Lighthouse door open.

At times when finances were at an ebb, Mrs. Clarke wrote, "We had a rich Father and we trusted Him. 'He who marks the sparrow's fall' has always shielded us in times of storm."

Determined not to close the Mission door to any needy person, the Clarkes went to their knees on many occasions. Once God met a financial obligation through a miracle as thrilling and wonderful to the Clarkes as was the miracle of the manna from heaven to the children of Israel. And, indeed, the 19th century miracle was not a great deal unlike the one of Old Testament days. Mrs. Clarke described it in these terms:

"Next morning . . . we beheld our home garden nearly covered with mushrooms (a little in advance of the season) and when they were gathered and prepared for market, sold for a sufficient income to replace the expenditures of the previous night. No mushrooms were ever seen there before. Nor any since."

The mushrooms were sold to the then already famous Palmer House in downtown Chicago. Little did patrons that night know they were eating heavenly food.

God seemed to speak to the Clarkes about "indulgences of former years [that] could be disposed of. So," related the Mission mother, "we placed *all* on the altar—all of our jewelry, of every description, diamonds, and other valued presents (with associations too sacred to mention)—all alike was given to the Lord, for His cause—and for souls."

The Lord blessed this consecration, for soon Colonel Clarke was given opportunity to invest in a mining operation that increased their income so that they had few financial problems for ten years.

But even with this additional security, the Clarkes didn't change. Their bankbook belonged to God. If there were no funds in the Mission account to pay a bill, Mother Clarke immediately wrote a personal check.

Twice a week Colonel Clarke "held the fort" alone as the Mission mother visited jail prisoners or patients in the County

Hospital. God gave many souls as the tiny woman stopped and talked to prisoners and patients as if they were her own sons and daughters.

On a sultry Sunday afternoon, August 7, 1880, Mrs. Clarke greeted the guard cheerily at Cook County Jail. As he opened the heavy barred door for her, he commented, "It's sure a scorcher. Wouldn't have blamed you for taking this afternoon off." Mother Clarke, assuring him that she had to be about her Father's business despite the weather, trotted on to talk to the men behind the bars of the cells.

In cell 79 she saw "one of the most forlorn, discouraged, brokenhearted specimens of humanity eyes ever looked upon." Mrs. Clarke, less than five feet tall and wearing a little pancake hat, looked out of place as she stood there quietly pleading with the prisoner to look to God for cleansing and a new start. Soon the man fell to his knees and sobbed out his story to God, asking His forgiveness and the new life He offered.

"This man developed into a marvelous Christian character," Mrs. Clarke wrote. "Loyalty, love, and devotion seemed to be the dominant Christian graces controlling his life." For 24 years he served the Lord until his death in June 1912.

One of the most colorful children of the Clarkes was a 71-year-old man who became known after his conversion as "Sunshine" Harris. Claiming to be an infidel, he was a drunkard for 50 years. Occasionally he came into the Mission to antagonize the workers. Colonel Clarke often pleaded with him to begin anew with Jesus, but Harris returned to the streets, picking up cigarette butts to satisfy the awful craving for tobacco that he had. Finally, in August 1899, he bought a Testament, and the first words he read were, "Thou fool, this night thy soul shall be required of thee" (Luke 12:20). Angry, he laid the Testament down, but a few nights later he went to the Mission and raised both hands for prayer.

"I was assisted by a Christian lady to the altar; and when I called upon the Lord, He heard my cry. And the load of sin mountain high rolled off," Harris later testified. "I rose to my feet and exclaimed, 'Thanks be to God for His unspeakable gift and for Pacific Garden Mission!' "

He returned to his room that night and thoroughly house-cleaned, discarding bottles of whiskey and beer, pipes, tobacco, and cards and putting in their place an open Bible. For eight years, until his death in 1907, Harris spread sunshine wherever he went, often testifying in the Mission of his life-changing encounter with Christ.

"Jimmy the Rat," an Indiana farm boy, was a trophy of grace that Mrs. Clarke often pointed to as an example of the mighty power of God to unshackle a person from the worst sort of habit. Jimmy at sixteen fell victim to dope and three years later became a prisoner, living a ratlike existence, in an opium den near the Mission. Once he heard a group from the Mission holding a street meeting and singing, "I am so glad that Jesus loves me, Jesus loves even me." He started out of the opium den but was dragged back.

Finally one day, Jimmy was beaten and left unconscious on a pile of lumber. Rain and the fresh air revived Jimmy, and he made his way to the Mission. He started up the aisle, holding up both hands and calling out, "I want somebody to pray for me!"

Mrs. Clarke came quietly from the platform and put her hand on his arm and led him to a front seat. When she knelt, he dropped on his knees beside her. That night Jimmy exchanged his old life for God's eternal life. Later, he returned to Indiana, married, raised a family, and lived a useful life. It was said that each evening he would gather his family together for prayer and always there was the petition, "God bless Pacific Garden Mission!"

The Clarkes were indeed happy together in the Lord's service as they watched their family of spiritual children grow. But in 1892 Mother Clarke was left alone when God called the Colonel from his labors. The Mission mother's heart was saddened but, with Harry Monroe stepping in as superintendent, she worked on. In a tribute to the memory of her husband, she wrote:

I'm coming soon to meet you, dear,
The journey now is almost o'er;
A few more sheaves to gather here,
We'll meet up there to part no more.

But it wasn't really to be soon. For nearly a quarter of a century after that, as long as her health held up, the Mission mother continued faithfully gathering in sheaves. And she was to live to see one of the sheaves she and the Colonel had already brought in (in 1886) become one of the greatest evangelists of all time.

Chapter 5

KID IN THE SAGE-GREEN SUIT

IN THE EARLY 1880's a train from Marshalltown, Iowa, eased into Chicago. Off stepped a country lad with uncut hair wearing a sage-green suit. After inquiring about directions, he legged it to A. G. Spalding's old store at 108 Madison Street. Strangely, though he arrived at 7 A.M., the store wasn't open; the lad himself had always gone to work at the 7 o'clock whistle.

Fingering the dollar he had in his pocket—all the money he had left after buying the green suit—he waited. Finally at 8:00 the store opened, and the young man showed a clerk a telegram he had gotten from Marshalltown's Pop Anson, captain of the National League's Chicago White Stockings (now the Cubs). That was his passport.

"So your name's Billy Sunday?" the clerk mused. "How'd Pop get on to you?"

"His aunt Em's a great baseball fan," Billy explained. "She always came out to see our Marshalltown team play. And she even went to Des Moines and watched us whip 'em 15 to 6 for the state championship. I did a few things in that game. Aunt Em kept telling Cap Anson to give me a try, and here I am."

About 10:00 Dalrymple, the left fielder of the Chicago club and batting champion of the National League, strolled in. Others came. Billy was introduced to them. He felt more and more like a hayseed as he compared himself to these well-groomed professional athletes.

Finally, Cap Anson came in and welcomed Billy warmly. Then with a twinkle in his eye he said, "Billy, they tell me that you can run some. Fred Pfeffer is our crack runner. How about putting on a little race at the ball park this morning?"

"Anything you say, Mr. Anson," Billy squeaked.

Soon they went to the ball park on the lakefront, situated on Michigan Avenue from Randolph Street to Adams Street. Larry Cochrane, one of the pitchers, lent Billy a uniform. It didn't exactly fit. And not owning baseball shoes, Billy chose to run barefoot. So there were chuckles galore as Billy and Pfeffer got set for the race.

"Go!" Cap Anson shouted.

A moment later the players were pounding Billy on the back and good-naturedly jeering Pfeffer. The hayseed kid had won by fifteen feet!

Winning the race opened the hearts of the players to Billy Sunday and made the first step toward a regular job with the Chicago club. As he was leaving the ball park following practice, Cap asked him, "Got any money for a place to stay and eats?"

"Yeah, a dollar."

With an oath, Cap tossed him a 20 dollar gold piece.

At first Billy served as treasurer of the club, but then the day came when he stepped into the batter's box in an actual game. Recounting his early experiences, Sunday wrote:

"I struck out the first four or five times at bat. The ball would pass me and be on its way back to the pitcher before I swung at it. I corrected this defect by using a lighter bat and not gripping it clear to the end. . . . Then, I used to pull away from the ball; instead of stepping straight ahead with my right foot, I stepped away from the plate. The pitcher would keep the ball on the farther side of the plate and I'd miss the old apple. Mike Kelly showed me how to do it, and I soon caught on. One season I batted .356 and was fourteenth in the list."

Even so, Sunday was never a great hitter—adequate, to be sure, averaging about .260. But his defensive ability and blinding speed brought fans to their feet and gray hairs to the heads of opposing managers. He was the first man to circle the bases in 14 seconds. He stole bases with a headfirst slide and stretched singles into two-baggers and two-baggers into triples. One opposing manager ordered his players to throw to the base ahead of the one they would ordinarily throw to if the runner was Billy.

But little did Sunday or anyone else dream that one day he would become even better known in the Lord's service as a world-renowned evangelist. In his early baseball days he was as tough, rough, and profane as the next ball player of that day. But a sudden change came into Sunday's life in 1886 after he had been with the White Stockings three years. He once told about it in these words:

"I walked down State Street in Chicago one Sunday afternoon with some baseball players whose names were world renowned. We entered a saloon and drank and then walked to the corner of State and Van Buren Streets, which was then a vacant lot. Some men and women were in a Gospel Wagon, playing instruments and singing gospel hymns that I heard my mother sing in the log cabin out in Iowa. We sat on the curbstone and listened. A man rose. His name was Harry Monroe, an ex-gambler and counterfeiter.

"Well, we sat on the curb listening to men and women playing on cornets and trombones and singing gospel hymns that many of the churches have blue-penciled as being too crude for these so-called enlightened days. Harry Monroe stepped out and said, 'Don't you men want to hear the story of men who used to be dips [pickpockets], yeggs [safecrackers], burglars, second-story men, drunkards, and have done time in the big house, and who today are sober, honest, have good homes, and are trusted and respected; of women who used to sell their womanhood to whoever would buy, were slaves to dope and drink, and are now married and have children of their own? Come down to the Mission and hear stories of redeemed lives that will stir you no matter whether you have even been inside of a church or have wandered away from God and decency.'

"I turned to the crowd that sat there with me and said, 'Boys, I bid the old life good-bye.' Some laughed, some smiled, some shrugged their shoulders, and some looked with mingled expressions of admiration and disgust. One fellow said, 'All right, Billy, if that's the way you feel about it.'

"I went to the Pacific Garden Mission that evening and liked what I heard. I went back again and again, and one night I went forward and publicly accepted Christ as my Saviour. If the same floor is in that old building, I can show you the knothole in the board upon which I knelt that dark and stormy night. I have followed Jesus from that day to this every second, like the hound on the trail of the fox, and will continue until He leads me through the pearly gate into the presence of God and it [the gate] closes on its jeweled hinges."

For three nights after he met Christ, Billy "never slept a wink," he told his audiences later in great evangelistic campaigns. He was afraid of "the horselaugh the boys would give" when they showed up for practice. He entered the ball park "with fear and trembling," saying to himself, *I am not a thief. I am not a drunkard. Why should I worry?*

The first man to meet him grabbed his hand. It was Mike Kelly, one of the top players in the league. He said, "Billy, I see by the papers what you have done. Religion ain't my long suit, and I haven't been to mass for so long I have forgotten how the priest looks. But I won't knock you, my boy, and if anyone does I will knock them." Then came Pop Anson and others—Clarkson, Flint, Williamson, Gore, Burns, Dalrymple—all with an encouraging word. "I felt as if a millstone had been dropped from my shoulders," Sunday remarked later.

Billy Sunday became an even better baseball player after his encounter with the Saviour. In the very first game as a new Christian he found the pressure on as the White Stockings sought to hold a 3 to 2 lead in the ninth inning. Detroit had two out, a man on second, and a man on third. Charlie Bennett, their catcher, was at bat. He had two strikes and three balls on him. John Clarkson, great White Stockings pitcher, reared back and sought to throw high and close, knowing Bennett's weakness. But his foot slipped, and the ball sailed in low and Charlie hit it on the nose.

Sunday turned at the crack of the bat and started back toward the stands in the right field. As he sought to outrun the ball, he prayed: "O Lord, I'm in an awful hole. If You ever helped me, please do it now, and You haven't much time to make up Your mind."

Seeing that the ball was about to drop into the edge of the crowd, Sunday yelled, "Get out of the way!" He leaped, and the ball hit and stuck in his glove. He tumbled to the turf but jumped up with the ball in hand. Pandemonium broke loose as excited fans threw cushions, pop bottles, and hats into the air. Tom Johnson, later mayor of Cleveland, Ohio, hugged Sunday and shoved a 10-dollar bill into his hand, saying, "Billy, buy yourself a new hat and come to the Palmer House tomorrow, and I will buy you the best suit of clothes in Chicago." Next day he bought Sunday his first tailor-made suit.

After a hilarious welcome in the clubhouse, Billy dressed and was met outside by a dark-brown-eyed, black-haired girl named Helen Thompson. She threw her arms around him and kissed him. "That was OK," Sunday observed. "We were engaged." They were married on September 5, 1888.

Sunday played five years with Chicago and then transferred to Pittsburgh for a year and then to Philadelphia. From the time of his conversion, he became an eager Bible student. As months passed he testified in local churches and invited people to come to Christ. In Philadelphia God's work loomed more important than even his beloved baseball. But to complicate matters, Sunday was offered a new contract for 3,500 dollars, a top figure of those days. He declined it. Later, he explained:

"I had a three-year contract with Philadelphia. I said to God,

'Now if You want me to quit playing ball and go into evangelistic work, then You get me my release.' And so I left it with God to get my release before the 25th day of March and would take that as an evidence that He wanted me to quit.

"On the 17th day of March—St. Patrick's Day, I shall never forget it—I received a letter from Colonel Rogers, president of the Philadelphia club, stating I could have my release."

Billy quit baseball and entered the YMCA as an assistant secretary at $83.33 per month—a far cry from the 500 dollars he would have received as a player. And sometimes his $83.33 was six months overdue, for the "Y" in those days was poor, though fervent in proclaiming the gospel. Billy had a hard time of it at first, sometimes barely having enough to pay his house rent. But this was all according to God's plan. Eventually Billy Sunday became an evangelist who led thousands of souls to Christ until his death at 72 on November 6, 1935.

In the more than 40 years he preached, he never forgot the Old Lighthouse where he responded to the glorious gospel. For many years he served on the Mission's board of trustees. In his great campaigns across the land he told of the great work of God in the mission outpost in Chicago. When in Chicago, he and "Ma" Sunday often dropped into the Mission and gave a word of testimony; and they often participated in anniversary rallies, helping raise money for the annual budget.

As a further encouragement, Sunday remembered his spiritual birthplace with financial gifts. When he closed a ten-week campaign in Chicago, he gave a cash love offering of 42,000 dollars, the net income after campaign expenses. That gift paid two-thirds of the cost of moving the Mission in January 1923 to its present address on South State Street.

But years before the Mission moved from Van Buren Street, while Sunday was still in baseball, a new era was beginning in the little soul-winning station.

Chapter 6

THE REIGN OF HARRY MONROE

WITH THE PASSING of Colonel Clarke in 1892, round-faced, thickset Harry Monroe, a man's man as well as God's man, stepped into the driver's seat at the Mission, though Mrs. Clarke remained very much in the picture as the Mission mother.

The glorious procession of transformed men continued as the excounterfeiter pressed home the claims of Christ. Harry's own story was known far and wide. Billy Sunday told it time and again in his meetings across the land, as did Mel Trotter, who came to Christ under Monroe in 1897.* And it was not unusual that some of the details of Harry's story spread through the twilight world of the levee, sending hoboes and other riffraff shuffling into the Mission one by one to get a look at the new leader of the rescue station. When they didn't come to the Mission, he took the gospel to them, having introduced the idea of the Gospel Wagon. From the horse-drawn wagon, workers preached, gave testimonies, and sang the gospel to people on the street. These outdoor services were the forerunners of the famous street meetings of later years.

Some of those who visited the Mission were small-time hoodlums who learned to respect Monroe and occasionally confided in him. If one would hint at plans for pulling a job, Harry pleaded with him not to carry out his crime but to come to Christ and begin laying up treasures in heaven.

From the standpoint of homiletics, Monroe would have flunked at the outset in a contest to name Chicago's most pol-

*See chapter 7.

ished preacher, for he was simply not a great preacher. He had little formal Bible training, yet he stuck to sound doctrine. Mainly, of course, he proclaimed that Jesus could unshackle the worst of sinners, and every message was intended to move them to the Saviour. Harry shook sinners over the fires of hell and then sought to lead them right to Calvary.

Billy Sunday and Mel Trotter were, of course, the outstanding converts of Monroe's day, but there were countless others who also turned from idols and began to worship the true and living God under his influence. Many went into some form of full-time gospel work, including Lew Speegle, Jacob Dudley, George Preston, John Troy, and Martin O'Connor.

Ed Card also came to Christ during the reign of Harry Monroe, and his life was marvelously transformed. Only in recent years have full details come to light, thanks to the patient research of Jack Odell, writer-director of PGM's radio program, "Unshackled!" Mission records had indicated that Card met Christ during the Monroe years and went on to become superintendent of the Sunshine Mission in St. Louis, Missouri. Odell discovered that Card actually had never made much of his story. When pressed for details, about all he would say was, "The old days? Well, I'll tell you. I was a great drunkard and a great sinner."

Ed was born in Nova Scotia in 1853. As a young man, he came to Chicago where he landed a job as a railway express messenger. He became a good employee in the eyes of his employer and earned a promotion to agent. It must have been about then that he married. In time there were two children. Their early impressions of their daddy, however, were spoiled by the fact that by this time Ed had become a hard drinker. As usually happens, there was a period during which he was able to juggle his drinking and his job. His wife did her best to cover up for him when he disappeared, but there was a limit to how long that could continue.

Then finally it happened. The boss came to his home and

Ed wasn't there. His wife made the announcement when Ed returned:

"You're fired, Ed. They don't want you there anymore. Your boss brought your last paycheck."

As the words sunk in, Ed muttered, "Nobody wants Ed Card. But, yes, I know somebody who wants me." He beckoned to one of his daughters. "Come here, Pettie."

The small girl backed away and cowered behind her mother's long skirt. "Mama! I'm afraid of Daddy."

Ed dejectedly stumbled out of the house to find another drink. He didn't come back—not that night nor for a good many nights. In time, as he became more and more disreputable-looking, bartenders drove him out almost as fast as the weather drove him in. And, in this condition, Ed Card hit Skid Row.

The night he stumbled into Pacific Garden Mission, Ed heard the voice of Harry Monroe preaching of the unshackling power of Jesus Christ. But his brain reeled, and he fell to the floor. Monroe called, "Somebody help that man!"

Mother Clarke helped revive him. When some of the liquor had left Ed's brain, she talked to him about placing his trust in Christ to free him from sin and all that had dragged him to the gutter. Finally he put his whole case in the hands of the almighty Saviour.

Paul wrote, "If any man be in Christ, he is a new creature" (II Cor. 5:17). Ed Card became walking evidence of the truth of that statement. Probably the first real proof occurred when Ed went back to his wife and children. They discovered that they had a *new* daddy.

Later, after helping start Sunshine Mission in St. Louis, Ed Card became superintendent, serving the mission from April 1903 till his death 30 years later on February 20, 1933. A kindly man with a white mustache and known as "Daddy" Card, he often said: "I would rather kneel beside a poor helpless man than have all the gold in St. Louis. To win a soul for Jesus Christ is for me the greatest joy I know."

Thus Card carried on in the tradition of Harry Monroe, who was preaching the night he came to Christ. Monroe himself was a master at soul-winning, both in dealing personally with individuals and pointing them to the Lamb of God and in drawing the net in meetings. It was Monroe who taught Billy Sunday his first lessons in giving the invitation and in talking man-to-man with a sinner regarding the steps of salvation.

Annually in his last years at the Mission, Harry reported to Sunday and Mel Trotter of God's continued blessings at the Old Lighthouse when the Great Triumvirate—as Carl Henry termed them in his book, *A Doorway to Heaven*—came together at a retreat for mission workers at Winona Lake, Indiana. By this time Sunday had made his home at Winona. Ma Sunday would cook a country dinner for these three great converts of the Mission, and they would talk over old times as they ate chicken, mashed potatoes, green beans, tomatoes, hot biscuits, and all the trimmings.

In the year 1912 tragedy struck, causing Mission trustees to look for a new superintendent. Monroe had labored nearly 32 years in the Old Lighthouse from the year of his conversion. He spent 20 of those years as its leader. On the verge of a nervous breakdown, probably brought on by overwork, Harry walked one night off a moving train and suffered injuries that took him away from the Mission except for occasional visits. Mel Trotter stepped in to hold things together, for Mother Clarke was now 77 and had been severely injured in an accident in a revolving door of a State Street department store.

By 1915, Monroe felt well enough to accompany Mel Trotter on a nationwide tour, but in December he became so ill that he was hospitalized. In July 1916 he died in his home in Morgan Park. Monroe was buried in Mount Greenwood Cemetery, not far from the grave of the man whom he succeeded, Colonel Clarke.

Mother Clarke lived for another two years, during which time she was a complete invalid, unable to converse with anyone. She had been nursed by Anna Andrews, who left her bedside only one day in six years. The nurse dropped dead in January 1918 and two weeks later, never recovering from the shock, Mother Clarke joined her beloved Colonel and Harry Monroe.

The Mission mother's estate, most of it resulting from Colonel Clarke's earlier business investments, came to about 100,000 dollars. She left it all to Pacific Garden Mission. This was a blessing, for active supporters of the work numbered only seventy-five. Harry Monroe had remembered the Old Lighthouse too, willing 1000 dollars to be charged against his real estate. However, it was discovered that he had not left any real estate and had little personal property. The Mission trustees therefore passed a motion waiving any claims the Mission might have against his estate. And no one was sorry at all, for it was no surprise that Harry Monroe had so few earthly treasures. He had spent well over a quarter of a century doing nothing but winning souls. The fact is, he had loved his job so much and considered it so important in a right sense that he had once said, "I'd rather be superintendent of Pacific Garden Mission than president of the United States!"

Among converts of the Mission, probably only one man surpassed Harry Monroe as a mission leader—his old friend Mel Trotter, the drink-mad hobo who came to Christ under Monroe's ministry.

Chapter 7

BAREFOOT WALK ON SUICIDE ROAD

AN ICY WIND off Lake Michigan stabbed through his thin clothes as Mel Trotter, the hobo, dropped off a boxcar in Chicago in January 1897. Uppermost in his mind was a problem: how to get money for a drink to ease his mad thirst. Despite the freezing temperature, he sold his shoes and bought a drink. Then lonely, desperate he considered his next move as in his stocking feet he stumbled along ice-covered streets hour after hour. Nobody seemed to notice him.

Trotter had been in Chicago on other occasions; he knew Skid Row only too well. This dark, twisted, devil-ridden section of town swallowed him up without a notice, and nobody cared how often he drifted in and out of town riding the rods.

To Trotter, no one aside from his wife, Lottie, seemed to care about him at all. One miserable, wet night another unpaying passenger had pushed him off a moving freight train. As he lay in the mud, bleeding and drunk, he had stopped caring.

This had been a climax to a series of blows in Trotter's existence. To begin with he had made unwise choices in his early years.

As Mel grew up in Freeport, Illinois, his dad, William Trotter, had been a bartender and an alcoholic. His mother, Emily, thoroughly believed in prayer, and she taught him a prayer when he was a child that was to dog him all his life: "Now I lay me down to sleep, I pray the Lord my soul to keep."

When Mel was 17, he became a school dropout and began

drifting. Finally he became a barber, but the taste for liquor he had learned from his father began to control him. First, he found himself getting skinned in poker games and then losing customers. After all, nobody wants his neck shaved by a barber with the morning-after shakes!

But Mel braced up time after time. During one of his braced-up times, he met and married a wonderful girl, Lottie. Little did she know that his first love was alcohol.

But it didn't take her long to find it out. He stumbled into the house one day, and innocent little Lottie thought he was sick! Then things added up, "Mel, you—you're drunk!" And then she said painfully, "Have you ever been like this before?"

He had to admit the truth. But instead of leaving him, or even becoming angry, Lottie whispered, "Mel, I love you, and I'll help you all I can." She didn't mention prayer that night, but Mel began to sense that she wasn't taking this blow alone. Lottie belonged to the same God to whom his mother prayed.

That was only the first shock for Lottie. Not long afterward Mel lost his barbering job because of his drinking. But Lottie was so understanding that he made her a promise, a big promise. "Lottie, I'm never gonna touch another drink as long as I live. Honest!"

Lottie was encouraged, and then she shared a secret with Mel, something to help him keep his promise: "Honey, we're going to have a baby!"

Mel walked with a firmer step and held his head higher in the days that followed. Soon he got a job as an insurance salesman, and for weeks he did well. Then gambling habits took over. He gambled to fatten his earnings so he'd have plenty for the new baby. But he lost and then gambled to make up the deficit. The vicious circle got tighter and tighter until the day after his son was born when he lost the insurance job too!

Into this black abyss flickered a ray of light, of hope, in the person of a kindly friend. Trying to cheer Mel, he said, "You've tried like I've never seen a man try to give up this drinking habit. You've tried all the cures; I know that. But I think I've got a plan that'll really do the trick for you."

Then he told Mel about a vacant farmhouse he owned, 11 miles from the nearest town and saloon. He wanted the Trotters to live there away from the temptation of liquor.

"I honestly hate liquor now," Mel responded. "I'll take you up on your offer."

The Trotters moved to the little farm. For three glorious months they were like honeymooners—with the little boy. During that time Mel didn't touch the bottle once. But what Lottie didn't know was that, for the last two months, a craving for drink was gnawing right through Mel's will power.

"You ta-take the baby inside, Honey," he told Lottie after a happy buggy ride one winter night. "I'll put the horse away, and I'll be right in."

But as the door closed, he wheeled the horse and buggy around and lashed the horse into a mad dash for town. Mel licked his lips, hardly able to wait to walk into the town saloon to order his first drink since he had moved to the farm.

After a few drinks, he was the same old wisecracking, devil-may-care Mel. "Hey, fellows, drinks are on me. The bartender can have my horse and buggy. Let's drink 'im dry!"

Next morning an alcohol-soaked Mel staggered the 11 miles home, the 11 miles that was supposed to separate him and drink forever!

Wet-eyed and unsmiling, Lottie helped him in as tenderly as ever. Just her look and touch broke Mel up, and once again he swore off drinking and promised her he'd never do this to her again.

With the horse and buggy guzzled away in that one lost night, Mel, Lottie, and the boy had to move back to the city. Mel could hardly farm without a horse, and there was no money for another one. The new place was hardly a home—just a cold, bare room off a hallway.

One day Mel came back to the room, cursing himself for

having made himself out a wretched liar once again, this time by a ten-day drunk. As he opened the door, he paled. Lottie was just placing their son on the old iron bed, and he immediately knew something was wrong. Then he heard Lottie pray: "Father, God, I've had my thoughts on my baby more than on You. Now, I want to turn to You. You are all I have left."

The little son was dead!

Mel rushed outdoors in a frenzy and hardly knew what he was doing until he returned home the next afternoon. Lottie was still there, this time with a little white casket. She thought this bitter blow would bring Mel to his senses. "Mel, Honey, surely now you'll give up drink for good."

Red-eyed, Mel choked out, "I promise."

Two hours after his son's funeral he came home again—blind drunk! Lottie turned as if she were leaving, but instead she dropped to her knees and prayed with her hand holding Mel's: "Lord, I'm Your child. From this day I'm going to serve only You and others. You have my baby with you now. I still have my husband, and I love him very much. By Your grace I shall pray that he will someday belong to You as I do. And I believe he will."

Lottie's faith that Mel would find God never wavered. Perhaps she had been praying for him that night when he had been shoved from the moving freight, for as he lay in the mud that little prayer his mother taught him seeped through his brain and lips, "Now I lay me down to sleep, I pray the Lord my soul to keep."

Perhaps she was praying for him as he wandered Chicago's Skid Row that cold January day in 1897. His feet were beyond feeling as he hobbled along Chicago's icy streets. Tears trickled from his eyes, partly because of the cold, partly because of the voice that kept taunting him. "Trotter, you're hopeless. You're a no-good bum. The world would be better off without you. Keep walking east. Let the murky waters of Lake Michigan get you out of your misery."

Stumbling along on Van Buren toward the lake, another drink guzzled to give him courage, Mel turned wildly as a curly haired man seized his arm. With a cheerful word, he led him through a door into a warm building and propped him up on two wooden chairs. For a time Mel didn't know he was in the Pacific Garden Mission, nor that his sympathetic escort was Tom Mackay, an ex-drunkard and cardsharp who had been converted from his misery and sin to Christ only a few weeks earlier.

Mel stirred and glanced toward the front of the room where a man was praying. "O God, we ask You right now, move in that poor boy's heart and mind and save him!" Somehow Mel knew that the man was praying for him.

He fell asleep; and when he awoke, he heard that same voice, the voice of Mission Superintendent Harry Monroe, telling about his conversion from counterfeiting. One sentence in particular struck Mel: "I was just 27 years old when I happened into the Pacific Garden Mission—just 27 years old."

Mel was just 27 years old too, and it began to dawn on him that he was in a mission—not in Lake Michigan.

Harry Monroe kept talking, and a warmth crept into Mel's heart. Though he never quite knew what turned the tide in his heart, he was soon staggering down the aisle, hoping someone could do something for him. He cried out to God that night for forgiveness, and God heard his sincere cry—for a sense of forgiveness flooded his soul.

From that night the thirst for alcohol left him, and God gave him complete victory. He learned that Jesus had said, "If any man thirst, let him come unto me, and drink" (John 7:37). Mel did that, and Jesus took away the other evil thirst. Lottie's prayers were answered!

The Pacific Garden Mission became the brightest spot in Chicago to Mel Trotter. It was natural for him to go into the same kind of work. In order to rescue other lost souls like his had been, he helped to found sixty other rescue missions around the country. Billy Sunday often called on Mel, at the conclusion of the great Sunday campaigns, to "come and help the brethren" get started with a rescue mission. From 1912 to 1918 Trotter served as general superintendent or overseer of Pacific Garden Mission, though he necessarily had to spend most of his time at the thriving mission he founded in Grand Rapids, Michigan. During this period the Chicago mission was actively led by able acting superintendents, including Bob Ingersoll, who served from 1916 to 1918.

As the years went by and Trotter preached the gospel across the country, people got to calling him the happiest man in the world and "the man who raves about Jesus." When the theologians wanted to ordain him into the ministry, they tossed up some pretty tough questions for a boy who didn't even finish high school. But the clincher was a breeze that even a doctor of theology couldn't trip him up on:

"How do you know you were made a new man in Christ?"

Mel wasn't joking when he replied: "Gentlemen, that's easy. I was there when it happened!"

On his spiritual birthday anniversary, Mel always arranged a great testimony meeting at his Grand Rapids mission. His own testimony was always the highlight of the program. In January 1940 it appeared that he would be too ill to observe his forty-third spiritual anniversary in the customary manner. He had become ill on a tour to the British Isles and had been hospitalized. But he asked God for a bit of extra strength and came to the meeting, speaking a few words to the large audience. It was his last public appearance at his mission.

On September 11, 1940, Mel Trotter died at the age of 72 at his home in Macatawa Park, near Grand Rapids. Today thousands still remember Mel as their spiritual father and others thank God for him and the sixty rescue stations God used him to plant in cities across America. At Pacific Garden Mission he will never be forgotten. Not only is he one of the greatest converts of the Old Lighthouse but when the going was rugged in the years of World War I, Mel kept the light burning brightly until God brought another husband-wife team on the scene as keepers.

Chapter 8

PA AND MA TO SKID ROW

THE STORY Charles E. Crawford was telling especially impressed the Mission pianist, Ma Taylor, that night back in the 1920's. Crawford, who worked at the American Bible Society, was giving his testimony in a Mission meeting:

"My heart sank the time I was told by my district manager that I would have to be bonded. For I knew that in the light of my record before conversion, no bonding company would accept the risk." Heartbroken, Crawford had stolen away to the shipping room to pray. Then, his face beaming, he testified that later the district manager got a report from the Bible Society's governing board. "They voted to waive the rule and I didn't have to be bonded. In spite of the fact that my record was black as midnight before I came to Christ, the board recognized that Calvary covers it all," he boomed out to the Mission audience. "I not only was to continue my work without being bonded but my salary was increased!"

Out of his testimony that night came these words from the pen of Ma Taylor:

> Calvary covers it all,
> My past with its sin and stain.
> My guilt and despair,
> Jesus took on Him there,
> And Calvary covers it all.

Within a short time Ma Taylor had completed "Calvary Covers It All," and it quickly became a song sung across America and around the world. Almost sixty gospel songs flowed from the pen of Ma Taylor, but none better summarizes the message she and Pa Taylor proclaimed the eighteen years they served at the Mission than "Calvary Covers It All."

The Taylors were keepers of the Old Lighthouse from 1918, through the Roaring Twenties, and on till 1936. Pa's foghorn voice stopped many a derelict dead in his tracks and turned him into the open door of the Mission. As Pa preached the gospel and told how to find forgiveness of sin through Christ, Ma prayed for the outcasts of society who filled the Mission. And then as the invitation was given, she was at the piano playing and praying that the prayer room would be filled. Quite often it was.

It was Pa Taylor's preaching and Ma Taylor's praying that God used to transform Walter "Happy Mac" MacDonald, who went on to become a famous evangelist, preaching across America and Canada for nearly thirty years until his death in 1963. He came to Christ under most unusual circumstances. A vaudeville comedian, MacDonald was finding it harder and harder to keep his audiences laughing as whiskey threatened his very career. Accepting the invitation of Miss Alberta Schultz, a new Christian, to attend a service at Pacific Garden Mission, MacDonald was captivated by what he heard. When he wasn't busy with an engagement as entertainer, he dropped into Mission meetings for more of the powerful preaching of Walter Taylor, the rousing singing, and the testimonies.

One night the comedian, so much under the influence of alcohol that his body trembled, sat listening once again to a forceful message. MacDonald sobered noticeably as the preacher's crooked index finger seemed to point again and again at him. Then words that Taylor quoted from Psalm 2 completely unnerved the vaudeville funny man: "He that sitteth in the heavens shall laugh" (Ps. 2:4). Then followed a penetrating laugh from the preacher as he interpreted how God's laughter might sound.

This haunted MacDonald until he returned to the Mission the

next night, May 29, 1925, failing for the first time to fill his engagement as an entertainer. At the moment he was scheduled to be entertaining, he was instead on his knees confessing to God his sin and need of the Saviour.

Turning his back on the entertainment field, MacDonald assisted the Taylors in their work at the Mission for two years, singing and leading song services. As he grew in grace and knowledge of Christ, he came to love his spiritual parents in a greater way. At times it seemed that Walter Taylor, an able preacher who knew the Bible well, was too hard on him as he sought to ground the new convert in the Word. "You're not worth your salt unless you read the Bible and pray," the superintendent told him. But such training paid off, and MacDonald often thanked God for the schooling he got under the Taylors. It was he who first called them "Ma" and "Pa."

MacDonald not only got excellent tutoring from Pa Taylor in preaching and introducing individuals to Christ but around the Mission he put the teaching to work in practical experience. On one occasion he dealt with one of his old drinking buddies, Doc, the gravel-voiced barker for a burlesque house on South State. Reconstructed, the story unfolded in this way:

"Well, if it ain't the little Reverend Happy Mac," Doc greeted sardonically one day as MacDonald was walking down the street. "Happy, say it's a lie! Say it ain't true that them Mission heads got my old pal."

"No, Doc, it isn't a lie. I've become a Christian. I'm through with the old life."

Things climaxed later when eight of his old drinking friends, including Doc, met MacDonald on the street. They lined up, four on each side, and he had to walk between. MacDonald spoke, and they responded with, "One, two, three—*ptoo*!" They spit on his new tan suit and shoes. Unlike the Happy of old, he responded pleasantly, "Your aim is excellent, Doc. Caught my new trouser leg and my shoe."

"That all you got to say?" Doc glared.

"Not quite, Doc. There's this: When you get to know Jesus Christ the way I've just this minute discovered I know Him, you'll be able to unclench your fists. You'll let a guy spit on you, and it'll be all right!"

MacDonald didn't see Doc again for three weeks. One night from the Mission platform he noticed him sitting in the audience on the front row! As the invitation was given that evening, Happy Mac hopped down from the platform and slipped into a seat beside Doc.

"Doc, what did you come for tonight?"

"You're not mad at me, Happy?"

"The Lord won't let me get mad anymore, Doc."

"Happy, you been a Christian long enough to know how to lead a guy to Jesus?"

"Yes, Doc." Joy surged in MacDonald's heart.

"Then I'm your customer."

Old Doc showed MacDonald a letter that had resulted in his coming to the Mission. His aged mother was dying, and he was about to go to her bedside. And to prepare, he had first to become a Christian. "I promised my mother I'd do it before she died. She's waited 54 years for me to do it. But now that you've led me to Jesus, I'm gonna beat it home," Doc revealed. "Pray, Happy, that I'll get there in time to tell her all about it."

Two weeks later Doc was back in Chicago. He'd had three hours with his mother, and his news had brought great joy to her heart.

Doc continued on the street—but now helping the Taylors as MacDonald had been doing. His job was to invite people to come into the Old Lighthouse to find Christ. But one day a couple of weeks after he started, Doc dropped dead on the sidewalk. He joined his old mother with the Saviour.

Pa and Ma Taylor had been handpicked for the job of keepers of the Lighthouse by Mel Trotter—and God. Great things had been happening at the Mission, and Trotter, anxious to devote full time to his Grand Rapids mission, wired the Taylors. Their background made them a perfect team.

Pa Taylor had, in the years when the Clarkes were nursing the Mission along in its infancy, been successful in business. Then a year before Mel Trotter was converted, Walter Grand Taylor, 30, grief-stricken over the death of his first wife, came to Christ in his room. The date was February 21, 1896. His wife had been a Christian, and he also wanted to be ready to meet God.

Spiritually alive and full of zeal, Taylor left the business world and went into YMCA work. Soon he enrolled in Moody Bible Institute where practical work assignments took him to Pacific Garden Mission. Here he met Mel Trotter, Harry Monroe, Mother Clarke, and others. His first convert was U. S. Abell, later a widely known Christian cartoonist, who came to the Mission in 1897.

Wedding bells sounded for Walter Taylor in 1898 as Dr. R. A. Torrey officiated. His bride was Ethelwyn "Bobbie" Robinson, whom he met in a Christian boarding house when she volunteered to play the piano while he sang a solo.

The newlyweds began praying that God would direct them into His chosen work for them. After Walter graduated from Moody Bible Institute in 1900, they served briefly in the Parkhurst Church House, New York, and then went to Colorado for a year as home missionaries among railroad men and miners. Here he began feeling like a runaway Jonah, for God had been speaking to him about doing mission work. He shuddered as he remembered an incident when he had been assisting in services at Pacific Garden Mission:

A dapper dresser, with wavy, golden hair, Taylor compassionately put his arm around the shoulders of down-and-outers while praying with them. Once Mel Trotter came up and quietly lifted Taylor's arm away. Walter didn't think much about it at the time. But one night, after the meeting, he mentioned to Mel that he had a problem:

"Tell me, Mel, do you ever find yourself itching at the end

of a meeting? I feel as though something were crawling around inside my shirt and biting me."

Trotter smiled and straightened out young Taylor quickly: "Now you know why I keep lifting your arm off these fellows' shoulders. Lice."

Nevertheless, Taylor said yes to God concerning mission work, and he accepted a call to become superintendent of the Old Brewery Mission in Montreal. Here he grew a moustache and spent 16 years in a fruitful ministry, winning people from all walks of life—up-and-outers as well as the downtrodden, and women and children in a summer fresh air camp.

In 1918 the wire came from Mel Trotter while the Taylors were in a soul-winning ministry at Camp Sheridan; the Lighthouse in Chicago needed a keeper. Walter arrived September 3, 1918, and Mrs. Taylor came 12 days later.

A colorful character who later thanked God for the open door of the Old Lighthouse during the Taylor era was George Delos Snow—pool player, poker player, card shark, and professional cheater extraordinary. Good-looking and a great actor, he worked for the house and could deal cards from the bottom and make it appear they came from the top of the deck. He always had an ace in the hole—until the night of February 11, 1919, when he got so fed up with his rotten life that he came to the Mission. Under the ministry of T. B. Davis, who was preaching that night, he came to Christ and exchanged his old life for a new one as white as his name.

For many years he testified in churches, missions, and in the noonday meeting conducted by the Old Lighthouse at State and Harrison. In his characteristic way, he'd begin his testimony, "Well, here stands five feet five inches of Snow." Then he would go on:

"I tell you the devil had me tight, and I wasn't trying to get away either. Say, you've heard these wise guys get up and tell folks how to get rid of their bad habits. All you got to do is to sign a pledge, or join something or other, or just exert your will power, and you can get by all right. They make me sick! Fat chance a fellow has of exerting will power when the devil has got him hog-tied. But you see I had something in my favor. I had a mother who never let up praying for her boy. You'd think she'da got discouraged and quit, for her prayers didn't seem to be answered. But she didn't.

"Mr. Devil told me it was too late for me to change, even if I wanted to. He'd bring to mind all the miserable, wasted years of my past life. But, oh boy, I heard something different when I got to the Mission. I heard of a Jesus Christ who saves men from their sins, cleans 'em up and starts 'em all over again. Gives them a new life and peace instead of a heartache. And, friends, I tried it—or rather I tried Him—and it worked! I went to see my mother right away afterwards. When I met her I said, 'Ma, I went down to Pacific Garden Mission last night and got saved.' And she said, 'Oh, thank God! I can die happy now.' And later she did too, and she's up there now waiting for me."

Another trophy of grace during the Taylor years was Scotty Lawrence. This songwriter was so talented he once took a bet that in twenty minutes he could write a song that would become a national hit, and he proceeded to do it in half the time. Drink and dope dragged him down to Skid Row, but one night in 1921 he opened his heart to Christ as Ma Taylor and two other women knelt beside him and prayed him into the Kingdom.

Cleaned up both on the inside and outside, Scotty went to New York, later married, and spent years in children's work and writing glad gospel songs. The first stanza of his very first song summarized his testimony:

> One day in sin I was told of a love
> Coming from One who is reigning above,
> Gladly I listened, 'twas music to me,
> To know, tho' a sinner, that I could be free.

It was during the Taylor years, in 1922, that a trustee Louis A. Crittenton sat successively with an adding machine on two

Chicago street corners, counting pedestrians passing the Mission at 67 West Van Buren and those passing State and Polk Streets. His tabulation bore out what many had believed all along—fishing was better on State Street than on Van Buren, for the hobo jungle was shifting. Actually the tape revealed the fishing should be 17 times better on State Street than on Van Buren.

State Street had been dubbed "Murderer's Row" because of the number of people killed there year after year. For many blocks south of the el tracks Satan peddled his wares in the most brazen manner. Along the Row some 5000 men flopped nightly in the cheap hotels. The Mission trustees believed God was leading them into this stronghold of Satan, and the most promising building was at 650 South State. Formerly it had housed the notorious White House, a den of drink and sex. The trustees voted to buy the building and later paid 67,000 dollars for it—42,000 dollars from Billy Sunday's Chicago campaign offering and the balance from Mother Clarke's estate.

The first meeting at this site was held on Wednesday, January 31, 1923. And it was here that Pa and Ma Taylor served for 13 more years. The Taylors retired to Florida, where Pa died on October 23, 1947, and where Ma died January 20, 1951. T. Donald Gately succeeded Pa Taylor and headed the work for four years.

During this time God was preparing a young electrical mechanic to take over in 1940 and to begin turning up the wattage of the Old Lighthouse to cause it to shine in dark places around the world as never before.

Chapter 9

GOD'S ELECTRICIAN

HARRY GEORGE SAULNIER has been associated with the Mission for a longer period than anyone else except Mother Clarke. In April 1965 the Mission staff surprised him with a testimonial party honoring him for 25 years of service as superintendent. He officially took over as keeper of the Old Lighthouse on March 1, 1940. For ten years prior to that he had assisted in services, and for six years he had served on the board of trustees.

Perhaps it was because Saulnier served on the board that he was almost overlooked as a candidate for the position of superintendent, though he and another trustee, Caspar Henning, had once tried to start a rescue mission on Chicago's North Side. Upon the resignation of Donald Gately, the board of godly businessmen overseeing the operation of the ministry thought long and hard concerning whom they could get as Lighthouse keeper. They compiled a list of 40 men, but Saulnier's name did not appear. Though the board prayed much that God would lead them in choosing a successor, weeks passed without agreement.

Finally, with Gately scheduled to leave at the end of February, the board felt that a decision definitely had to be made at their February meeting. How would God make His will known? Unable to attend the meeting, attorney Paul Fischer sent a short list of suggestions in order of preference. At the top of his list stood the name of fellow-board-member Harry Saulnier. All eyes turned on Harry as the list was read, and he sat there stunned. Until now his name had not even been whispered as a possible suggestion. Quickly, the board made a unanimous decision and gave Saulnier a week's time to make his decision.

Harry discussed the new turn of events with his wife, Gene, that night, and for a week they prayed about it. It would take a definite step of faith for him to leave the security of a good-paying job he had held for 18 years as electrical mechanic at Commonwealth Edison Company, the firm supplying power for Chicagoland. And the prospects of taking over the great responsibility of running the famous old rescue mission made the decision even more complicated. Somehow God would have to speak.

On Friday night, with time running out, Harry and Gene arose from their knees after a period of prayer. "Harry, I think the Lord wants you to say yes," Gene volunteered.

"Gene, I feel that way too," he responded thoughtfully.

Moments later Cap Henning, Harry's long-time friend and board secretary, answered his phone. "OK, Cap, I'm coming," Harry said joyfully.

At Commonwealth Edison, officials, hearing Saulnier's story, suggested that he take a six months' leave of absence and decide then if he definitely wanted to leave the company. Thus, six months later in his small office in the rear of the Mission Saulnier got a call from the Edison Company: "Six months are up. Ready to come back?" The going was by no means easy by this time, but nevertheless Harry Saulnier was having the time of his life making the light shine brighter at the Old Lighthouse. So he said a grateful "No thanks," hung up the phone, and rolled his sleeves higher. Nevertheless, just in case he should change his mind, the Edison Company extended the leave for three more months. But Harry was never to return.

In those days, as well as now, there was plenty of work to do. Somehow it seemed the ministry was resting on its laurels and not moving ahead.

In the early months, God gave Saulnier specific ideas for growth and outreach, but he realized he would have to work gradually. Humanly speaking, he couldn't immediately make drastic changes; for when he first came there was only $1.56 in the bank, and the Mission had few faithful supporters. But in those early days Saulnier began to win friends as well as souls, and he personally began to make the Mission a more efficient operation and a more inviting place for the men of the street.

Every individual has his own tastes, and a soul-winning electrician would be expected to differ in approach from his predecessors, regardless of their success. One of Saulnier's first moves was to redecorate the red, white, and blue when he arrived in March 1940. Though the blue ceiling stood for heaven, the red portion of the walls for the blood of Christ, and the white portion of the walls for the righteousness of God in Christ Jesus, the combination failed to impress Saulnier. Not that he didn't believe in the symbolism, but Skid Row men could hardly be reached through such subtle means. So, an inviting, easy-on-the-eyes beige went onto the walls and the ceiling. Except for the neatly lettered Bible texts, the men would get the gospel from the pulpit not the walls.

Next Saulnier, electrician that he was, prayed that God would help him improve the lighting system. One day he got a call from his old firm, Commonwealth Edison. They were replacing fixtures in the downtown office. Could he use some? So it was that he was up on a ladder one Saturday praying as he worked, "Lord, You've just got to help me. Send somebody, please."

About noon Arthur Burnett, of Waukegan, Illinois, walked in and looked up. "Whatcha doin'? Puttin' up new fixtures?"

"Sure. You don't happen to be an electrician, do you?"

"Yep, I just happen to be—need some help?"

Harry climbed down from the ladder, washed up, and took his newfound helper to lunch. Then they returned, and soon the Mission auditorium shone with new light.

As the months passed, Harry Saulnier desperately yearned and prayed for more space for the Mission, then housed in a single three-story building, 25′×100′. To take it out of its hole-in-the-wall category, adjoining buildings would have to be added. Most desirable of the next door buildings was the four-story Loyal Hotel, a run-down flophouse. But for years the owners only laughed at the Mission efforts to buy the hotel. They indicated that if they ever sold the property, it would be for a parking lot.

Finally, in the early months of 1941, the two buildings to the north became available, and the Mission offered 30,000 dollars. "Yet," declares Saulnier today, "we didn't have 30 cents, much less 30,000 dollars. But God began to work and by November the buildings were ours. God met our needs through gifts and a sizable loan from Christian friends."

These buildings were used for the Servicemen's Center and Women's Division, new ministries launched in Saulnier's early years.

But the matter of acquiring the Loyal Hotel continued as a burden on the hearts of the superintendent and the trustees. This added space would allow the Mission to house many more Skid Row men and thereby increase the soul-winning efficiency.

In 1955, after many contacts back and forth, the Mission got a yes from the hotel owners, provided a price tag of approximately 180,000 dollars would be agreeable. On July 7, 1955, earnest money was put down, and by November 7, 120 days later, the entire amount had been paid. God had answered fervent prayer through both small and substantial gifts. One of the miracle gifts was from a woman in Arizona who wrote and asked if the need still existed. A special delivery letter to the woman from Saulnier resulted in a 1000-dollar gift, coming a week before the final payment was due.

A few days after the signing of the final papers a crew of Mission workers, with Saulnier leading the way, moved into the old flophouse to begin the huge conversion task. Vermin-infested little cubicles, with chicken wire stretched over the tops, were torn down. Here men had flopped for 75 cents a night, the fee actually being more per cubic foot for a "room" than for most rooms at the Hilton, two blocks away on Michigan Avenue. On the first floor, the remains of a smelly, cheap tavern had to be torn out. All in all, tons of rubbish, including a rusty .32 caliber revolver found in a wall which had no doubt figured in many crimes, were carted from the old hotel during renovation.

And here, over a period of four years, God faithfully supplied funds—some 450,000 dollars—for remodeling and transforming the old building into a functional Mission unit. Today the Mission chapel occupies the tavern and hotel lobby area. The chapel is quite unlike the traditional rescue mission auditorium, being bright and cheerful, and with some 300 comfortable, modern contour chairs. The platform is attractively bordered with potted artificial flowers that are changed with the seasons: for example, spring would feature forsythia with its yellow, bell-like blossoms, and pink snapdragons. Neatly lettered Scripture texts in yellow letters on a brown background proclaim the message of salvation on the dark beige walls of the softly lighted chapel. A Hammond organ and two Baldwin pianos, one of them donated by Billy Sunday, are near the platform. The auditorium could be a church sanctuary except for the bullpen at the rear, a segregated area where drunks and others who would likely disturb a service are seated. Keeping watch over these men, who often sleep through services, are pictures of some of the heroes of faith in PGM annals—the Clarkes, Billy Sunday, Mel Trotter, Harry Monroe, and Pa Taylor.

Upstairs, where men once flopped on filthy cots, are three dormitories for Skid Row men, each identical with 75 sturdy army-type beds and toilet facilities, including 12 white porcelain showers for each floor. On the fourth floor are beds for some of the staff.

Except for new men, derelicts who look to the Mission for aid know the rules. For example, men who want lunch must arrive in time for the noon gospel service, and those who want overnight lodging must come to the evening service at 8:00.

In an increasing way under Harry Saulnier the procedure in handling men has been orderly and smooth. Except for regulations governing the flow of from 150 to 200 men at a time, utter chaos would result. After the evening service men are given tickets indicating the floor where they will sleep. Each man is frisked by a worker in order that all weapons and bottles of alcoholic beverages may be separated from their owners. In the dormitory each man checks in with his Social Security card and is given a clothes hanger with a number. He strips and hangs his clothing on the hanger, which is hung for the night in a delousing unit. Next the man showers and is given a nightshirt. His number tag directs him to the bed he is to occupy.

Next morning at 5:30 the men are awakened. The early hour is primarily for those who must report for jobs in the slave market. Those needing clothing visit the clothing room and are given clothing donated to the Mission by Christian friends. Breakfast is served at 6:30.

Through the years Saulnier has insisted on wholesome food for those served by the Mission, and today Gus Hollis and his crew of fifteen men meet those demands. The meals aren't lavish, but the food is appetizing and nourishing, plenty to hold body and soul together.

During the course of a day the kitchen crew prepares 30 gallons of cereal, 60 gallons of soup, and 30 gallons of coffee, in addition to more substantial meals for the rehabilitation staff.

Interestingly, the kitchen and dining hall, where 375 men can be served at one time, is kept spotlessly clean. After the Skid Row men vacate the area, the staff moves in. To avoid the confusion of men stumbling over chairs, Skid Row men stand to eat. Chairs are moved in for the staff and guests of the Women's and Children's Division. On Saturday nights visitors, sometimes as many as 100, are served dinner in the dining hall.

Thanksgiving, Christmas, and New Year's Day are days when

the kitchen crew serves up the biggest meals for Skid Row men. In some years as many as 800 men have been fed on these holidays. Annually, for Thanksgiving and Christmas, a poultry farm contributes a total of 2400 pounds of turkeys, and the meals served would rival those on most American tables.

During the year a number of other firms help keep the mission larder filled, cutting down considerably on expense for food. Occasionally leftover food is sent from a North Side hospital. Bread, sweet rolls, and hard rolls are regularly picked up from two bakeries and chain food stores. Large quantities of canned soups come with the compliments of a soup company.

Christians outside the Chicago area also help the Mission feed Skid Row men and women, as well as the families who come to the Old Lighthouse for aid. For example, C. W. Aeppler, of Oconomowoc, Wisconsin, who for many years was in the honey business, has since 1954 sent as many as 300 pounds of honey a month. He even furnishes honey dispensers with his own label etched on the glass in two colors with a Scripture verse included.

Big, burly Carl Dreesman, a tractor dealer from Iowa, regularly sends certain food supplies to the Mission. Saved from a life of sin and drink through the witness of Paul Hutchens (widely known writer of Christian fiction books), Dreesman made his first contribution to the Mission through Hutchens when he heard the author was coming to PGM to speak. Dreesman became so impressed with the ministry of the Mission to alcoholics and others that he then began to send the food supplies to the Mission. He also started a program among farmers in the area to collect good, usable men's, women's, and children's clothing. These he boxed and shipped regularly to the Mission through the efforts of another Christian, Cornelius Pals, a trucker, who for many years arranged and paid for each shipment. Today Dreesman, who flies his own plane, is a regular visitor, coming in for Christian fellowship at a place he learned to love before he actually saw it.

In the early days when he began to turn up the wattage of

the Old Lighthouse, Harry Saulnier had only a couple of assistants. Over the years God has sent both full-time and volunteer workers. Today the Mission has a full-time staff of some 80 men and women. Many of these regularly burn the midnight oil to get their jobs done.

The clean-up crew, under Bob Vehue, is the second largest rank-and-file unit, numbering approximately 6 to 10 men at any given time. All are men who have made professions of faith in Christ and who are being rehabilitated as they work and study the Word while living for a time at the Mission.

There are countless volunteer workers, some of whom come to the Mission regularly several times a week to assist in personal work or help with some other phase of the work.

Since 1936 teams from some 25 Chicagoland churches have conducted gospel meetings each evening in the Mission, a ministry which not only is important in the program of the Old Lighthouse but also gives men and women practical and rewarding experience in soul-winning. Most are laymen ministering the gospel through song, testimony, and preaching, as well as in man-to-man counseling in the prayer room. They are people like lanky Cliff Clark, of suburban Wheaton, who on a volunteer basis directs the work of organizing rescue mission teams at Wheaton Bible Church. A retired Pennsylvania Railroad employee, Clark makes no claim of being a preacher—but he has learned to plead earnestly for souls and to handle the Word effectively. Equally important, he shows a burden for the souls of Skid Row men. I've seen him stand up straight and tall, his shoulders back and his head up, as in prayer meeting at the church he has asked prayer for the Skid Row ministry conducted by him and his men.

Even though a different church group is in charge from evening to evening, Harry Saulnier usually appears to give the audience a friendly greeting and announcements, and often he conducts the invitation. Over the years thousands have responded to his earnest, clear-cut invitation to come to the Saviour.

Often he leaves the platform and moves among the audience speaking and pleading with men, sometimes going to the rear of the chapel to invite a man to the prayer room.

Believing there is a right and wrong way for visiting groups to deal with soul-winning activities in the Mission, Saulnier personally outlined a plan that is posted and brought to the attention of teams:

1. Group and friends meet in the prayer room at 7:30 P.M. for prayer.

2. Personal workers must kneel down with open Bible. Don't do personal work without a Bible.

3. Afterwards, bring man or woman to the person in charge of prayer room.

For the person in charge of the prayer room, rules state:

1. See that there are plenty of Gospels of John and inquiry cards.

2. Line chairs in twos.

3. See that everyone kneels when dealing with an individual —with an open Bible.

4. Question converts after they have been dealt with.

5. Be sure they have the assurance of salvation.

6. Give them a Gospel of John and have them sign on page 6.

7. Get complete information including permanent address of parent or other relatives (for follow-up).

8. Invite them to our Bible class.

One of the most important and fruitful phases of the many faceted Mission program today is the follow-up program worked out by Saulnier. As men who have made professions move on, letters go out to encourage them. Attempts are made to put them in touch with a Bible-preaching church. In addition, efforts are made to enroll all new converts in the six-lesson course on the Gospel of John, a series that has brought assurance of salvation to hundreds and caused others to place their trust in Jesus Christ for the first time. Thousands have signed up and have taken the course as a result of reading about it in the Mission's monthly paper, the *Pacific Garden Mission News.*

Under Saulnier, the anniversary rally, held usually in November though the anniversary date is September 15, has become a significant event on the evangelical calendar in Chicagoland. Some 2,000 persons generally come to the rally, held the past 18 years in the Conrad Hilton Hotel, two blocks away from the Mission on Michigan Avenue, compliments of the hotel management. Until her death in 1957, Ma Sunday, Billy's widow, was a colorful participant. Many souls are saved each year and Christians go home fired up to serve the Lord more earnestly as they hear testimonies of transformed Skid Row drifters and others.

Thus, the influence of Harry Saulnier, under the direction of the Holy Spirit, has made a world of difference in the operation and outreach of the Old Lighthouse on South State Street. Today the entire ministry is a model of efficiency, reaching the heart by means of ministering to physical needs. Saulnier takes no credit himself. He puts it this way in utmost seriousness: "Why, it's *all* a miracle of God. Even the very doorknobs are of Him!"

Chapter 10

SAULNIER, THE MAN

TOWERING FOUR STORIES above the sidewalk on the Loyal Hotel wing of the Mission, the imposing 35-foot Pa Taylor memorial sign silently proclaims to passers-by and others for several blocks to the north, south, and east: "CHRIST DIED FOR OUR SINS" and "JESUS SAVES." This sign also identifies the Mission. Cost of upkeep alone is about 78 dollars a month: 48 dollars for maintenance and about 30 dollars for electricity. A man and his mother years ago convenanted to keep the sign burning. By night especially, with its red neon letters, the sign attracts the eye. People have come to the Mission from nearby hotels after seeing the sign. Soon after the sign was erected in late 1947, the message, "JESUS SAVES," stopped an ex-newspaper reporter from suicide and he came into the Mission and found hope in Jesus Christ.

In a remarkable way the Pa Taylor sign, a visible symbol of the new Pacific Garden Mission, typifies the man whose idea it was to raise the 3500 dollars necessary to erect it. Harry Saulnier, whose second-floor office is almost within reach of the sign, stands 6 feet 3 inches, and day and night is given 100 percent to beaming forth "the glorious gospel," as he often terms it. Not only is he burdened for the souls of the unredeemed who come to the Mission and others touched through the many facets of the Old Lighthouse ministry but wherever he goes he spreads the good news by handing out gospel calendars and tracts. "No Christian is well dressed unless he has gospel tracts with him," Saulnier says. Often, under the guidance of the Holy Spirit, he will graciously explain the way of salvation to someone—on a train or plane, in a restaurant, or on the street. The place makes no difference.

On many occasions I have walked with Harry to the Dearborn Street Station, two blocks from the Mission, for dinner in the Fred Harvey Restaurant. On the way there and back it's difficult to carry on a conversation with him, for suddenly he has dropped back or turned aside. "Here's good news," I've heard him say time and again or, "A calendar for your wallet, sir!" Always, there's a friendly, warm ring to his voice and a smile to go with each piece of literature. His manly, neat appearance and the touch of white-haired dignity about him undoubtedly are used of the Spirit in these contacts.

The witnessing experiences of Harry Saulnier would fill a book. But the following serve to illustrate the fact that he is "incessantly at it," as one former, close associate put it:

Larry Foss, who was employed at the Mission for a time, says he got his baptism in tract distribution work in a Chicago train station. He was accompanying Saulnier on a deputation trip, and they arrived at the station 15 minutes early. (Hearing this, Harry's daughter Nancy exclaimed, "How could that be!") With crowds swarming on all sides, Harry took off his hat, and Larry removed his as Saulnier offered a word of prayer aloud, asking God to bless and use the tracts he held in his hand. Then Harry proceeded to divide a stack of tracts with Larry and directed Larry to begin passing them out in one area of the station while he distributed them elsewhere.

On deputation tour in Alberta, Canada, Saulnier took time out to go for a ride up a ski lift at Banff. On his way up he handed out tracts to people coming down on the ski lift a long reach away. Later, when he got to the bottom, he noticed a man reading one of the tracts, and again, typically, Saulnier, in his big, friendly way, hurried to him and said, "Hey, what do you think of it?" This opened the door for a time of man-to-man witnessing.

There have been times when Saulnier has run into trouble

with his holy boldness. On the way to Saudi Arabia by plane from Egypt, he passed out tracts as naturally as he had always done back in the U.S. At the Jedda airport he was suddenly grabbed by a couple of Muslim customs agents, and for a time "I thought I was on my way to being hanged," he chuckles. He was released, but they confiscated all his literature. Once on a train in Canada, he had given tracts to everyone in one coach and was starting on another coach. The conductor, of another religion, ordered him to stop. But Saulnier rejoiced that he had gotten as far as he did.

Visible fruit resulted from a train ride through Pennsylvania—and in this case it was the conductor himself, though Saulnier wasn't aware of it until a month later. He tells the story in these words:

"While on my way to Baltimore to speak at a mission anniversary meeting, I was passing out tracts and speaking to people here and there on the train, which was about 17 cars long. I left my open Bible on a table by my seat, with a copy of the tract 'God's Way of Salvation' nearby. At Altoona a new Pullman conductor got on. Passing through my car, he noticed the green and white cover of the tract, and he picked it up.

"I had no contact with him on the train, but a month later he came to the Mission and attended a testimony meeting I led. Dressed in his conductor's uniform he stood and gave his testimony. He said he picked up a tract, 'God's Way of Salvation,' on his train a month ago, and it brought conviction to his heart. 'Before I got to the end of my run I had read the booklet through five times,' he said, 'and before we pulled into the station at Washington, D.C., I got on my knees and accepted Christ.'

"After the meeting I said, 'Let me see that booklet.' Sure enough, stamped on the back cover was 'Pacific Garden Mission.' "

In his early years Harry Saulnier was shy. Until he was 23, he was not prepared to be a witness. Born of French parents in New York City on August 19, 1902, he struggled for years trying to be religious. He could not comprehend the way of salvation though he went to Sunday school and church and even attended a Christian and Missionary Alliance boys' camp when he was eight. Night after night, in his teens, Harry stopped for an outdoor gospel meeting in Fordham Square to hear testimonies. The group distributed gospel portions, and Harry carefully gathered the New Testament library of twenty-seven books.

In his earlier years as part owner of a sign company, it appeared that Harry was destined to help light Broadway in New York rather than to beam the gospel light on South State, Chicago. But he later sold out his interests and moved with his family to Chicago in 1922 where he went to work for the Commonwealth Edison Company.

Actually, for several years Harry had passed as a Christian, having joined Edgewater Presbyterian Church soon after coming to Chicago and becoming active in Christian Endeavor. But approaching his twenty-third birthday, he questioned his relationship to God. At the Edison Company a friend Vic Cory had an abiding peace that Harry didn't have, and he kept telling Harry that he needed to "get right with God through faith in Jesus Christ."

On his twenty-third birthday, August 19, 1925, Harry begged off from work and attended a special service at North Shore Church where Cory was a member. Here, under the preaching of John Roach Stratton, then pastor of New York's Calvary Baptist Church, he came under deep conviction of sin. He returned to two evening services, but strangely, Stratton gave no invitation. Upon returning home the second night, Harry went to his room, and, without preparing for bed, knelt and began praying. "O God, I need You," was the theme of his prayer. He told God all of his troubles and confessed that he needed God to run his life. As dawn began to break, he awoke from sleep, still on his knees, with the sunlight of God's grace filling his soul for the first time. God had heard him, and he had been born again!

As he dressed for work, Harry sensed that a victory had been won. At noon he read from the New Testament he had regularly carried as a result of his interest in Christian Endeavor, the North Shore division of which he had recently become president.

"That noon it was a brand-new Book to me," Saulnier remembers. "Oh, I can still recall that first flash and first indication that something had changed, that I was different, making the Book itself different to me."

What happened after that is ably told by his longtime friend, Dr. Victor E. Cory, founder and chairman of the board of Scripture Press Publications, Inc., Wheaton, and a member of the board of trustees of the Mission:

"From the time of his conversion, Harry began to dig out the great spiritual truths of the Word. He attended Moody Bible Institute Evening School.

"He became a flaming leader for Christ in Christian Endeavor, serving as president of CE in Chicago. Here he got his start in open-air gospel meetings, a ministry that he loves to this day. Today, when he attends conventions of both the Gideons and Christian Business Men's Committee, men look to him to head up street meetings. His foghorn voice can be heard 'a mile,' and God has used Harry's voice and winsome way to bring countless men to the foot of the Cross in open-air meetings.

"In 1928 Harry had married my sister-in-law, Gene Beryl Tucker, and I remember that he was in jail the night after his eldest daughter, Nancy, was born—all because a policeman on the beat ran him in for conducting a street meeting! Harry spent half the night in that 'dungeon' until the captain, when informed who he was, released him.

"Harry showed himself an able leader in his years in Christian Endeavor, being the spearhead of a movement that opened up Soldier Field in 1933 for a series of great Easter sunrise services. A crowd of some 15,000 poured into the huge stadium, and the way Harry and his committee handled the first service won the respect of Soldier Field officials. As a result, the services were conducted annually by Harry and his team until 1943, when he became too busy with the Mission.

"We praise God for the day he brought Harry to head up the Mission. He came as an energetic man with a mop of black hair. Today he's as energetic as ever for the Lord, though with a mop of white hair. To me Harry Saulnier is one of the wisest of God's servants, based on the verse in Proverbs: 'He that winneth souls is wise.' "

Since his Christian Endeavor days, Saulnier has enjoyed street-meeting work as much as the average layman might enjoy a round of golf. For many years he led meetings a half block from the Mission at State and Harrison where he first met Ben Engstrom. Street meetings are no game with him. They are serious business. Some years ago at a night street meeting at Kenmore and Lawrence, on Chicago's North Side, he felt constrained to cup his hands and yell at the top of his voice, "Anybody else want to be saved? If you do, stick your head out of your window, or otherwise let us know." He paused and looked about through the darkness but saw no movement. Suddenly a man stepped from a parked car. The group holding the service had no idea that anyone was even in the car, but the man said he had been listening and wanted to be saved. Saulnier says that this taught him a lesson: "You can never tell when someone might be listening to the gospel at a street meeting. Never give up; never leave a stone unturned."

At annual gatherings of the Gideons, the Christian Business Men's Committee, and the International Union of Gospel Missions, Saulnier—when he is present, as he often is—invariably leads the street meetings. In Savannah, Georgia, a handsome young couple were saved at a Saulnier-led street meeting. During a Gideon convention a fellow Gideon sidled up to Saulnier and pressed a 10 dollar bill into his hand. "Harry, use it as God would have you. You'll never know what you've meant to me." Saulnier looked at him amazed because he had no idea he had had any influence on the man whatever. The man explained that he had been in a number of street meetings which Saulnier had led, and this experience had helped to bring him out of his religious shell to the point that he himself was willing now to participate in outdoor meetings and to witness boldly for the Lord.

In Mission meetings themselves Saulnier shows himself master of every situation, it seems. He pleads tenderly and urgently for the lost to come to the Saviour and seems always to know the newcomers in the audience from the old-timers. In testimony meetings, a regular Saturday night event in the Old Lighthouse, the Lighthouse keeper is in his glory, encouraging new converts, as well as seasoned veterans, to share what Christ has done for them. One dear man became extremely emotional one evening, walking up and down an aisle shouting about what God had done for him. As he finished and sat down, all eyes turned upon Saulnier, who was leaning very patiently upon the pulpit. Unruffled, he smiled and roared, "Amen! Well, it's certainly better to shout than doubt."

Though his close friends generally concede that Saulnier's homiletics leave much to be desired, his tenacious allegiance to the fundamentals of the Word and manner of speaking have caused at least one person to compare him with the late William R. Newell, a widely known preacher, Bible teacher, and author of yesteryear. And, indeed, Saulnier in his years of growing up in the faith admired Newell and followed his teaching closely. Even to this day he promotes Newell's verse-by-verse study books in Romans, Hebrews, and Revelation. In 1952 Saulnier visited Xenia, Ohio, and Earl Eavey, head of a grocery chain, heard him speak, and later wrote the famed Bible teacher about Saulnier's resemblance to him:

"When William R. Newell goes Home, he 'still speaketh.' One of his dear friends and students, one Harry Saulnier, has been with us for the past two days. He spoke by proxy for

W. R. Newell five times in Xenia, and he certainly is the above named gentleman over and over and over again. He told the people exactly the things you would have told them, in the same tone of voice. When speaking of our identification with Christ, he yelled out, 'You are DEAD to sin. You died with Him on the Cross. You are ENLIFED with Him.' Really, Mr. Newell, it was uncanny the resemblance between Harry Saulnier and yourself in the pulpit. He looks like you, he talks like you, he acts like you, he hollers like you."

As busy as he is, Saulnier is never too busy to pray. If he is hurrying to a deputation meeting, or even just going to the drug store, he prays before starting his car, asking God to protect and guide. At a CBMC convention in Montreal in 1963, according to Charles F. Steinhofer, of Hackensack, New Jersey, Saulnier witnessed to a cabdriver. Then halfway up the steps of a restaurant into which he and the Steinhofers were hurrying, he turned and said, "Let's pray for that cabbie." And while people were waiting behind them, he prayed aloud briefly for the soul of the cabdriver.

Each day Saulnier is in close touch with God about Mission problems, and under his leadership the staff gathers every Tuesday morning for an extended prayer session in addition to the regular prayer schedule of three times a day and more. One problem he and the staff prayed long and hard about regarded the possibility of the city's taking over part of the Mission for erection of the new Jones Commercial High School. For a time it appeared that hard work of the past would be suddenly nullified. But prayer was answered, asserts Saulnier, as the Mission was left intact and the school bought property adjacent to the Old Lighthouse. It's no wonder that one of his favorite booklets, which he often has offered to Mission friends through the *PGM News,* is E. M. Bounds' *Power Through Prayer.*

Man of God that he is, Saulnier nonetheless has his rough edges. Some he probably isn't aware of; others he deeply recognizes. Sometimes, because he is naturally a high-pitched personality, he appears impatient with those with whom he works as the pressure builds up. Once an admirer wrote him that he had the face of an angel as she heard him preach in her church. An employee chuckled as the letter lay on his desk, for at that moment he was "acting like a bear." He could delegate work more than he does, some of his close associates agree, but Saulnier, dog for work that he is, often would rather do it himself than possibly have someone muff the job. Some things he insists on doing because he feels "it is the superintendent's job"—for instance, signing receipts for all gifts. At the bottom of each he writes "Hallelujah!" and a Scripture reference. Some have dubbed him "Hallelujah Harry" because of his fondness for this term of praise.

I asked Ben Engstrom, at the Mission for 21 years, to give his candid opinion of Saulnier. "Harry has the biggest sort of heart," Ben began. "Sometimes he talks big and tough, but he's the first to step in and put a compassionate arm around a man in need. Maybe one of the men will get disgusted with a Skid Row man and tell him he's been around too much. Harry, stumbling into such a situation, will, with good reasons, bring the man back in and urge the men to be patient. 'After all, the Lord is patient with us,' he says. 'Where would we be if that wasn't the case?' This is real God-given patience and love."

Because of his knowledge of rescue mission work, Saulnier has often been called on by others for counsel. The Rev. Truman Thompson, superintendent of the Denver Rescue Mission, says, " 'Iron sharpeneth iron; so a man sharpeneth the countenance of his friend.' I have sought the counsel of this man of God many times. He is warm and sympathetic, but is firm in his convictions. My heart has been encouraged and my ministry enriched through the times of fellowship I have had with him."

In early 1965 Saulnier was called to Anchorage, Alaska, by Grant Speicher and members of the local Christian Business Men's Committee to help them in launching a rescue mission ministry. In recent years one of the best-known missions, drifting into mere social work through visionless leadership at the board level, got back into the soul-winning business as Saulnier was asked to come with his doctor's kit.

At PGM Saulnier looks to a godly board of businessmen to oversee the Mission program, some of them the same men who elected him to the superintendency in 1940. "Without dedicated godly laymen at the top guiding a rescue mission, it's so easy for a good work to crumble," Harry asserts. Working with him on the board of trustees are: Roy Baumann, Caspar F. Henning, J. Paul Bennett, M.D., Russell G. Johnson, Richard B. Stanley, Carl H. Johnson, Paul C. Benson, Clayton F. Brown, Victor E. Cory, John C. Ewing, Herbert C. Hansen, Charles B. Jensen, Philip A. Lind, Lorne H. Renner, and H. G. Swanson, Sr. For many years a trustee and close adviser was Freelin A. Carlton, manager of the huge State Street Sears store, who some years ago moved to Arizona. He and Frank E. Sandberg, a retired businessman living in Florida, are trustees emeritus of the Mission.

Saulnier's own family stand solidly behind him in his ministry at the Old Lighthouse. His wife, Gene, works closely with the Women's Auxiliary and conducts deputation meetings from time to time. She also does personal work at the Mission. For some years the Saulniers' eldest child, tall, sturdy David, from the same mold as his father, helped lead singing at the Mission and worked as film secretary. He now plays and sings in a gospel quartet that ministers regularly in churches and missions, known as "The Westerners." Nancy is vice-president in a brokerage office in the Chicago Board of Trade Building and often visits the Mission. Carol, the youngest member of the family, is a "homebody."

Lance B. Latham, Saulnier's pastor, thanks God for Harry's faithfulness as a member and Sunday school teacher at the North Side Gospel Center. "I can see very easily how a person in his position could latch on to some rich church where he would get a lot of help for the Mission, but I believe Harry, ever true to the Lord, prefers to go where he has fellowship with the Lord and loves the message and our trying to stay to God's ways of doing the work of the Lord," says Latham. "I just feel that I am doing just about nothing when I stand alongside of him and see the wonderful vision and work God has given him. I just noticed last Sunday when he was so faithfully taking one of our older men home after the service, seeing a person sitting on a bench across the street, he took time out and talked to him about the Lord. I am sure he is not after the big things; he is after the hearts of men."

Dr. Walter L. Wilson, the "beloved physician" from Kansas City, Missouri, summed up Harry Saulnier with this comment: "My precious Brother Saulnier is a walking advertisement for our Lord Jesus and a constant example of the presence and power of the Holy Spirit."

Chapter 11

GOOD-BYE, SKID ROW!

SKID ROW as a state of existence is as old as man, beginning with the skid in the Garden. Happily, by love and grace, God made a way back for Adam and Eve, clothing them in coats of skin and promising a Redeemer. However, rejecting the way of faith, their son Cain walked Skid Row "a fugitive and vagabond in the earth" (Gen. 4:14). Later, even godly Noah fell victim to wine and spent at least an evening on Skid Row. Weak-faithed Lot lived for years on the Row, and the last glimpse of him after he fled Sodom before its destruction reveals him in a drunken, immoral state. There were, of course, many others in Old Testament times who partially or fully lived a Skid Row existence.

In New Testament times, in the country of the Gadarenes, a man with an unclean spirit dwelt among the tombs—Skid Row, first-century style. No man could tame him. Then Jesus came. By His power, the man was transformed in an instant! People came out to see what had happened. They simply could not believe their eyes, for now the madman of the tombs was "sitting, and clothed, and in his right mind" (Mark 5:15).

Jesus compassionately loved the Skid Row people of His day, and wherever He went He ministered to them. He dealt tenderly with the sin-stained woman at the well. Significantly, the first person to whom He appeared following His resurrection was none other than Mary Magdalene, out of whom He had cast seven devils!

It is this same divine power—Christ's matchless power to transform man at his worst—that for nearly a century has made the Pacific Garden Mission so much more than a mere social service agency. For over the years men and women, suddenly free of harrassing demons and binding cords of sin, have in great numbers gone from the Old Lighthouse each year whole and in their right minds and back to a useful place in society. In addition to the many who have heard the call of God into special Christian service, countless others have gone home to parents, wives, husbands, children, and sweethearts. They have rolled up their sleeves and returned to work to support their families and have become reliable workers and respected citizens of their communities and churches.

That isn't to say that none has ever slipped. Some have slipped as badly as Noah. Then there are always those whose faith is weak or even nonexistent, floundering souls like Lot who escaped Skid Row city but who when last heard of had fallen again to a miserable state. A case in point is "Bill," who came to Pacific Garden Mission to grow spiritual legs after he had testified to "a wonderful transformation in my life" while in prison. He talked of continuing his studies at Moody Bible Institute, but he never got around to it. Later he drifted away, became a carnival worker, a junk picker, and a hard drinker. One day he was found shot to death in the snow outside his home, a dilapidated shack near a junkyard outside of Western Springs, Illinois.

Evidently in Bill's case the gospel seed had fallen among thorns. Such heartaches go with any soul-winning effort, but happily there are many who represent good ground, who keep the Word and bring forth fruit.

A man from Sacramento, California, returned home a few years ago after being lifted by Christ from Skid Row. A little later he wrote the Mission: "I called my wife. We met and had a good talk, and God was there also. We worked everything out, except what I was going to do about a job. But God had that figured out, too, because Saturday morning I got a job on a ranch with a good salary. Within a month or two, we can get our debts straightened out. So we are praising God and walking with Him, and we are praying for His guidance in our lives."

Though Elmer Medek was never a down-and-outer, drink and self ruled his life. But all changed June 25, 1960, the night he came with his wife to the Mission upon the invitation of a friend.

In the Mission meeting, Medek, hearing the gospel, saw his sins from God's viewpoint, and that night he and his wife both received Christ. How much of a difference did it make in Elmer's life? Three days before I wrote this chapter, Bob Schultz, branch manager for a large lumber company in the Chicago area, told me of hearing Elmer Medek's story on PGM's "Unshackled!" radio series. He had worked with an Elmer Medek thirty years before, and he wondered if he was the same man whose story had been told over the airwaves. Knowing Harry Saulnier, he phoned him and obtained Medek's phone number.

"Are you the same Elmer Medek I worked with in Villa Park?" Schultz asked, after identifying himself.

"Yep, that's me."

A revealing conversation followed, and Schultz has since seen Medek on a number of occasions.

"Why, I remember him as one of the most selfish persons I've ever known—a completely despicable character, the kind of guy few people could stand," Schultz commented. "Now he's entirely changed. Often Medek gives his testimony at the Mission on Saturday night meetings. Has a good job—is assistant purchasing agent for an electrical firm in Chicago."

Believe it or not, Carl Graden took his first step toward Skid Row when he was but eight years of age. "No son of mine is going to grow up without being able to hold his liquor like a man!" his father boasted, and he gave Carl a man-sized drink.

Years later, living in Rockford, Illinois, Carl Graden depended so much on liquor that even his dad's horrible, violent death from alcoholic poisoning failed to shake the bottle loose from Carl's hand. Then, after a complete nervous breakdown, Carl's mother was dead too, heartbroken over the way alcohol had ruined her family.

During these days, oddly enough, Carl Graden contributed to his church, and went regularly to Sunday morning services—when he wasn't too hung over. His minister tried to turn him from his drinking but with no success. One thing, however, stuck with Graden: a story about a drunk who walked into the Pacific Garden Mission.

Ultimately, Graden hit Skid Row, Chicago. On the night of January 11, 1944, when he was 43, Graden blacked out in the snow. When he came to, he walked into the Mission to get help. That night Graden trusted the Saviour and the miracle of redemption took place inside. The fetters and chains that had shackled him were broken.

Carl Graden later left Chicago and married. His wife, Ruth, became a Christian after she saw the change Christ had made in Carl. Until his death in 1964, in a traffic accident, he was a barber in Seattle, Washington, and active in a church in Bothell, Washington.

George Mohr always claimed it was the prayers of his little German mother that ultimately brought him to the Mission and gave him a new start in life. She died when George was a boy and he began a lonely existence. Unfortunately in his late teen years he began depending on liquor like his mother had depended on praying. In the years that followed he married and had five children. His wife, Sally, remained patient with him as he drifted through one job to another, from one drunk to another.

Ultimately, Mohr left his family and became an alcohol-soaked derelict. In an empty boxcar or sleeping on the ground in some Skid Row alley he'd hear his mother praying for him and cry. Once he fell asleep with his legs across a rail on a siding. Next morning an empty coach had rolled in and stopped six inches from his legs! God must have been remembering the prayers of his little German mother.

Soon after that Mohr went to work in a government camp in Muskegon, Michigan, and for the first time in eight years he wrote home to the family. A few days later he got a letter from his daughter, Ruth. He had been on an all-night binge, but then, as if a cold knife had been jabbed into his brain, he sobered up. For black as death before his eyes were words like these: "My heart is too heavy to write much. Mother died suddenly yesterday evening. She was drawing water at the kitchen sink. . . ."

Not long after that, beaten and whipped, Mohr landed in Chicago in 1940 and staggered into the Pacific Garden Mission. A sign in the window said, "Mother's prayers follow you." In the Mission prayer room that night, George knelt with Harry Saulnier. "I know you're drunk, George, but God can get to you," Saulnier said gently, as if he was talking to a child. "When you say the word, He can get through!"

God did get through and a mother's prayers were answered. Eleven years later, in the *Pacific Garden Mission News,* George testified:

"Now, I'm filled and satisfied and happy, no longer drifting or hunting anymore. The Pacific Garden Mission gave me medical care for a solid year, and now I'm living!" Mohr, who lived in Cleveland, died a few years ago in his eighties.

Leonard Pollari, born of Finnish parents, earned the title of "black sheep" as he let liquor run his life and run him right out of the Army. In 1947 he hit Skid Row, Chicago, and one night wandered into the Mission, where the smile and testimony of a Jewish man and then the smile and testimony of a sailor impressed him. Later he ran into an old buddy who also had a smile—and a testimony too. He invited Pollari back to the Mission, and there he made a profession of faith in Christ. But, neglecting Christian fellowship, Pollari slipped back to drinking. Then he returned to the Old Lighthouse and renewed fellowship with Christ and His people. For a year he lived the life then slipped again. Later, back at the Mission, Pollari talked with Harry Saulnier, and he suggested that Pollari truly make Christ the center of his life and soak up more of God's Word. Today, after working in Chicago for several years, Lenny Pollari is still a man with a smile and a testimony, employed as a repairman in Lewistown, Illinois. He is married, has two children, and is active in a local church.

A man who will long be remembered at the Old Lighthouse is Howard La Bounty, a pitiful human wreck who was towed into the Mission one June afternoon in the early 1950's by his sister, Mabel Pulaski, who had compassionately searched for him on Skid Row after his mother and then his father had died heartbroken over his condition. La Bounty, a truck driver for 31 years before succumbing to drink, came into the Mission like a whipped, dirty stray dog. He had been sleeping in boxcars, under trees, in alleys. Haakon Evans, then assistant superintendent, who tenderly took charge, recalls La Bounty vividly:

"In my years in mission work, I have never seen another person in Howard La Bounty's condition. His thick gray hair was long and matted and his tattered clothing was slick with grease and filth. His eyes were blank and he could barely mumble."

Someone put La Bounty under a shower and scrubbed him, then shaved him, washed and cut his hair and gave him clean clothes. Then he was given food and taken to the evening service. That night he became a new creature in Christ. He became a wonderfully transformed person as the love of God motivated his life in the years that followed. One time, as he assisted in the work at the Mission, he was viciously bitten on a finger by a crazed derelict. For many weeks he was hospitalized. Later, back on the job La Bounty had a decision to make. Haakon Evans told him that the man who had attacked him was upstairs in the Mission. "Would it bother you if we let the man come down here to the dining hall where you are working?"

"Why, bring him on down and we'll feed him, Mr. Evans. God forgave me. Why shouldn't I forgive that man?" La Bounty said in the sweet way that typified him after he became a Christian.

La Bounty helped at the Mission for several years, then took a job elsewhere, continuing to walk with Christ. He died three years ago.

Hundreds of other stories of men helped by the Skid Row division of the Mission could be told. Each would be as amazing as the next, as much a miracle as the marvelous transformation of the wild man of the tombs in the land of the Gadarenes. For, after all, the same Saviour touched them all.

Chapter 12

CALLED TO SERVE

AMONG THE CLEAR INDICATIONS that God's hand of blessing has rested in power on the historic Old Lighthouse year after year is the fact that hosts of its converts have gone into some phase of full-time Christian service. And this is amazing when you consider that most of these people got a miserable start in life and were once the worst sort of sinners.

Today some of the key people who help keep the light of the Old Lighthouse itself gleaming brightly are men who themselves experienced the miracle of a transformed life in the Mission.

By the time he was 14, Arnold Vander Meulen had been in criminal court twice and was an alcoholic. By the time he was 16, he had been in and out of jail several places over the U.S., and at that age became the youngest boy ever sentenced to the Southern Michigan Prison. His mother practically broke down when the sentence was pronounced. But she and his father, both praying Christians, held on to God for Arnold's salvation.

Arnold tells the remainder of his story in these words:

"I served three years, got out, and once again bummed around the country, drinking, taking dope, fighting. Then came Pearl Harbor and the draft. But even in uniform I refused to have any relation with God. Twice I deserted. When arrested, I slugged my guard and escaped.

"Now I was a fugitive for sure. Sometimes as I went from state to state I heard from the folks back home in Grand Rapids, Michigan, and always it was the same thing: 'God can save you from the uttermost to the uttermost, Arnold. We love you, Son. You're all wrapped up in prayer.'

"I shrugged off every reminder of my sin and of God until on New Year's Eve 1947 I took a cheap peek at my life and felt sick. I was in a dive on South State Street in Chicago. It was nearly 11:00—only one more hour of 1947 left. And somehow for the first time in my life I was scared! I wished I could run home and cry on Mom's shoulder. But I couldn't; so I began walking, hoping the cold night air would help. Soon I was looking up into the big sign in front of Pacific Garden Mission: 'JESUS SAVES.' I had laughed at those words on missions over the country, but now they gripped me.

"The Mission doorman invited me in, and I sat down in the back, sobbing. I hunted through my pockets until I found the prayer Dad left me last time he had visited me in jail. From a crumpled piece of paper, I read: 'God be merciful to me a sinner, and save me now, for Jesus' sake!'

"And with that, as I turned my back on sin and my face to the Son of God, I became a new creature and new desires took the place of the old ones. No one had said a word to me. Prayers had done it all!

"Some time later, still at the Mission, I was wondering what to do about my past crimes. To give myself up would mean years in prison. But God knew about my weakness and took the whole matter into His own hands! For a man came up to me and said:

" 'F.B.I. You're under arrest.'

"In Superior Court in Grand Rapids I was arraigned on a charge of forgery and got two to fourteen years in the Southern Michigan Prison, to which I had been sentenced when I was sixteen.

"In prison I was invited to teach a Bible class. Over the months it grew from a handful to some 600 members. Another miracle took place as the Army, hearing of my new life, dropped charges for desertion and made me eligible to collect enough bonus money to pay for my bad checks: $153.50, the amount I owed to the penny!

"Then came that day nineteen months after my imprisonment when the warden announced: " 'Arnold, the parole board says you can leave us. This time we hate to see you go. But God bless you. I know He will.' "

God's blessings on Arnold Vander Meulen are evidenced by the fact he has been used to found rescue missions in Grand Rapids, his hometown; Bristol, Virginia; and Battle Creek, Michigan. He returned to Pacific Garden Mission in 1960 to direct its deputation ministry. In a recent year his teams have preached in 400 services to approximately 65,000 people, resulting in some 900 professions of faith in Christ. Vander Meulen himself is often engaged to preach. He is on the road across the U.S. and Canada representing the Mission about 40 weeks a year, preaching and giving his testimony in prisons, service club meetings, church gatherings, and on radio and TV.

In the late '40's in Peoria, Illinois, a tavern owner opened his place one morning only to find that thieves had broken in during the night. Suddenly he saw that one was still there in a drunken stupor from beverages he had guzzled. The owner began to beat the man, Augustus Hollis, shellacking him from wall to wall. Later in the county jail, bruised and groggy, Hollis tried to take his life by hanging himself with his belt.

The suicide attempt resulted in his being sent to the state hospital for the criminally insane for two years. Then, when Hollis was released, he drew two to four years in the state prison for the burglary charge.

In 1961 Gus slouched over a wine bottle in Boots' Tavern, then two doors from Pacific Garden Mission. By now he was fast on his way toward becoming a Skid Row fixture, though in past years he had been paid well as a pantryman in a private club. Suddenly in his foggy state he heard snatches of words from a song, "No one ever cared for me like Jesus." The song was coming from the loudspeaker of the Mission and was being sung by Ruth Smiley.

Gus stumbled into the Mission. A personal worker came to him with a warm word of greeting and asked him to go to the prayer room for counseling and prayer.

"No," Gus mumbled, "not now—I've got two bottles of wine in my pocket, and where I go the bottles go." Pulling away, Gus said he would talk some other time.

Gus tells the remainder of the story:

"I returned the next day and the gentleman showed me from the Bible where I was wrong and how Christ could change my life to be a useful one. I professed the Lord, but for the first months I stumbled and slipped away.

"Then, in desperation, I came back to the Mission and talked with someone else. I told him what had happened.

" 'Gus,' he explained, 'you must give your *all* to the Lord. You can't carry the load yourself. You tried and failed. Each morning pray, asking the Lord to carry you through the day. He says, "Ask, and it shall be given you. Knock, and it shall be opened unto you." '

"I followed his advice, and the Lord began giving me complete victory over the sin that had dragged me down. He has kept me from drink. I have my trust in Him, because I no longer trust myself."

Today barrel-chested Gus Hollis, using the talent he developed while serving in the Merchant Marine in the early 1940's, serves the Lord full time at the Old Lighthouse as chief cook, heading up a kitchen crew of 15. He is responsible for meals served to Skid Row men and others helped by the Mission, as well as meals for the staff.

Chief custodian and head of the work crew at the Old Lighthouse is a lean, lanky young man with dark hair and dark eyes. His name: Robert Vehue. To see him today you would never dream that on at least three occasions Bob cheated death in situations brought on by alcoholism.

Once, in Latin America, he went on a drinking binge and ended up swallowing a dozen sleeping pills. A friend rushed him to a hospital where he was nursed back to health.

Later, back in the States, in a drunken condition he made a smart remark to a gang of young men. They chased him until they cornered him and beat him to within an inch of his life.

Under treatment for the wounds suffered in the attack, Bob began going through horrible suffering as the result of sudden withdrawal of liquor. He was headed for delirium tremens.

It seemed that the whole world was against him. Voices taunted him. Suddenly one night Bob grabbed a glass water carafe from his bed table, smashed it, and plunged the jagged glass deep into his throat.

Bob began to run and found himself standing on a roof, rain pouring down and blood covering him. And there, glowing in the dark, it seemed that he saw the grinning, staring face of Satan!

Out of the hospital later, he went on his last drunk. When it was over he was penniless and homeless. A policeman directed him to Pacific Garden Mission where the Holy Spirit moved in his heart and brought him into a personal relationship with Jesus Christ. The desire for drink has vanished and peace rules Bob's heart as he directs the work of keeping the Old Lighthouse bright and clean.

Undoubtedly one of the most refreshing personalities serving the Lord at the Mission is none other than the ex-steel mill foreman saved from a life of alcoholism in 1945 through the preaching and personal work of Harry Saulnier—curly-haired, aged Ben Engstrom. Serving as building engineer, he cares for electrical equipment and keeps radiators hot when temperatures sag during wintry months. Ben has had the joy of sharing his story with thousands, in magazines, on the radio, and in meetings both at the mission, in Chicagoland churches, and elsewhere as he has traveled with PGM deputation teams.

Among those who have been saved and fired up at the Mission to go elsewhere to serve is Jack Martin. As a youth, he struck out on his own, the victim of a broken home. At 14, he worked with a carnival, doubling as a cook and washer and doing the bally for the "world-famous" glassblower. When he was 15, Jack found that a few good stiff drinks kept him from getting tired from the two jobs and made him more a part of the rollicking carnival crew.

As the years passed, Jack drank steadily and ultimately became enmeshed in gambling. As troubles weighed upon him, he turned to marihuana.

In 1947, by this time unable to sit still five minutes without a cigarette or a drink, he landed in Chicago. One day, being stabbed by stomach pains and tired of killing time looking at movies, Jack strolled past the corner of Harrison and State. Suddenly he stopped. A crowd was watching a big man doing a coin trick. But when he began talking about the most wonderful Gift in the world, Jack realized the man was a preacher. Yet he stayed and listened, and even raised his hand for prayer when the big man said he'd pray for those who had a need. Jack wanted prayer—for his stomachache.

After the street service the big man approached Jack. "My name's Pete Tanis—I'm from the Pacific Garden Mission. Now that I've prayed *for* you, I want to pray *with* you."

Later, living temporarily at the Mission on Tanis' invitation, Jack Martin pretended that he was a Christian, helping out in the kitchen and attending gospel services and Bible classes. Then one day as Edward Ockert, former athletic coach at Moody Bible Institute, taught the Converts' Bible Class, Jack opened his heart to the Saviour and became a new creation.

At the Mission Jack met Jo Young, a former model who had come to Christ in a Youth for Christ rally, and some months later they were married. With a God-given desire to be used to win others to Christ, they served for a time at the famous Keswick Colony of Mercy in New Jersey, helping bring the gospel to alcoholics. Later Jack became superintendent of the

City Rescue Mission in Peoria, Illinois. In 1963, Jack and Jo, with their three sons and their daughter, moved to Spokane, Washington, where Jack today directs the Union Gospel Mission.

John Fink in more ways than one followed in the footsteps of Jack Martin. By the time he was 14, he had learned to drink and was earning his own money doing a mechanical man act on the famous Boardwalk in Atlantic City, New Jersey. When he was 16, he considered suicide because drink had gotten a viselike grip on him.

John tried the Navy, but drunkenness and undisciplined conduct resulted in his discharge. Leaving Great Lakes Naval Training Station north of Chicago, he came to Chicago and began a tour of honky-tonks and saloons. He was fairly drunk when he drifted out of a tattoo parlor and stood on the sidewalk, wondering what to do next. Up the street a red neon sign blazed out the message, "JESUS SAVES—PACIFIC GARDEN MISSION."

That night John Fink came to heckle, but instead he got under conviction as he heard the gospel. One Scripture verse stuck with him: "Believe on the Lord Jesus Christ, and thou shalt be saved" (Acts 16:31). That night, a Gideon Bible in his hand, he knelt beside his bed in his hotel room and put his trust in Christ. Delivered from sin and the curse of alcohol, John Fink served for a time as a counselor in the Old Lighthouse and in 1964 went to Atlantic City where he founded and became the first superintendent of the newly formed Atlantic City Rescue Mission.

Over the years scores of other PGM converts have gone into some phase of mission work, either as helpers or superintendents. In 1884 "Curly" Tom Mackay, son of a saloonkeeper and he himself a panhandler and alcoholic, came to Christ in the Mission and later became head of Los Angeles' Helping Hand Mission and a great open-air preacher on the West Coast. He was probably the first PGM convert to head another mission, though

Harry Monroe and Mel Trotter were the most famous mission workers among those saved at PGM.

Percy E. Diehl learned to drink as a boy in Traverse City, Mich., and had one foot in hell the night he came to the Mission in the 1930's. Today he and his wife, Albina, assist in the work at the Olive Branch Mission on Madison Street, Chicago.

Clyde Parker, a Missouri boy who became a gambler and boozer, swung on crutches into the Mission on April 22, 1956. Today he helps win souls in the Bible Rescue Mission on Madison Street in Chicago.

In addition to mission workers, the Old Lighthouse has produced a host of preachers, evangelists, chaplains, and missionaries. Besides Billy Sunday, among the old-timers are such men as Robert Atchison, a tramp who found Christ in 1893 in the Mission and went out as a missionary to the Orient and became known as the "Mueller of Japan" and the "Mikado." George Preston was another. His mother's prayers reached from Northern Ireland to Chicago in 1910 and George responded to the invitation of Harry Monroe to receive Christ. A gifted singer who sang on the operatic and theatrical stage, Preston later became an evangelist, preaching and singing the gospel until his death in 1941.

Others include Billy Driver, the Scot who laid down his carpenter's tools to serve as an evangelist till his death in 1927; Lew Speegle, the street fakir, who became a lay evangelist in Wisconsin; Martin O'Connor, the liquor-loving plumber who, by God's power, threw away the bottle to become a missionary evangelist in northern Wisconsin; John Troy, son of a famous European physician who found himself penniless and friendless in Chicago, then received Christ at the Mission in 1908 and went out as a much-traveled evangelist; Elias Auger, a drifter who found an anchor in Christ in 1899 and for more than thirty years was a Baptist minister and chaplain; Elmer Wagler, who trusted Christ in 1921 and overcame a stuttering tongue to preach the gospel and become head of the Southern

Highland Evangel; Royal L. Leeson, a Skid Row resident saved in 1924 who went to Latin America as a missionary; and George Quilty, who once thought that anyone who wasn't a Jew was a Christian until he encountered Christ in the Mission in 1921 and became a lay preacher as he continued his work at Western Electric Company.

Countless people already trusting Christ for salvation have been fired up at the Mission and have gone out in fruitful service. Holland Oates, saved from a life of drunkenness shortly after the death of his infant daughter, was a "settled" Christian when he visited the Old Lighthouse soon after World War I, a row of cigars displayed in his coat pocket. A personal worker talked to him about giving himself wholly to God, and this was a step toward Oates' becoming an itinerant preacher among the farmers of Wisconsin until his death in 1939. Another who came to the place of complete surrender at the Mission is John R. Rice, today a famed evangelist. The night he came to the Mission in May 1921 he saw sinners, almost hopeless in their despair, find forgiveness and peace. That night he promised God that "if He could help me save sinners, He could have me to preach to sinners. Thus," Dr. Rice says, "I became a preacher of the gospel of Christ."

October 8, 1931, found Arthur E. Petznick, who had left home at 20, sitting in a pool room on the corner of State and Harrison in Chicago. When policemen came in the front door, Petznick ducked out a side door into a cold drizzle. Friendless and penniless, he faced another night on a park bench. As he was passing the Old Lighthouse, the doorman handed him a tract and invited him inside. Petznick tells the rest:

"The first thing that greeted my eyes was a sign on the wall which asked: 'HOW LONG SINCE YOU WROTE TO MOTHER?' In five years I had not so much as sent her a card. I relived my childhood days and saw how I had dishonored and disgraced my mother. Oh, I was miserable. Then I heard Dad Taylor preach the gospel as I never heard it before. The invitation was given. I raised my hand and a personal worker came and took me into the prayer room. There I cried to God from the depth of a broken heart, and God heard me. And His dear Son came to abide in me."

Arthur Petznick soon entered Moody Bible Institute, graduated, and became a pastor. For many years he has pastored the Bible Baptist Church in Phoenix, Arizona.

Time and space fail in the telling of others. For many books could be written of the long parade of those who met the Saviour at Pacific Garden Mission, rose from ruined lives, and in the power of their new Lord went forth to unfurl the gospel banner in Satan's strongholds throughout the world.

Chapter 13

A HAVEN FOR WOMEN

POLICE, while engaged in a routine investigation of a stabbing in an apartment building on Chicago's West Side, discover a Puerto Rican family living in unimaginable filth and destitution. Garbage litters the living room and the baby, naked except for a heavy coat swathed around him, lies on a stained mattress. The sole furnishings of the room are two incredibly dirty mattresses and a chair. Four other children appear sickly and neglected. The mother is mentally retarded, the father in prison serving 199 years for murder. The family needs help—*now.*

A dejected woman, looking middle-aged rather than just 35, walks unsteadily down a street south of Chicago's Loop area. Once a respected office worker but now a victim of drink and dope, she needs a real friend in the worst sort of way.

A 26-year-old wife of a sailor traveling from California to Great Lakes Naval Training Station arrives in Chicago where a man snatches her purse containing her money, bus tickets, and baggage check. Frightened and alone, she too needs a loving hand extended to her.

Actual cases, all of these represent problems faced around the clock 12 months a year in big, bustling Chicago. In the heartrending situation involving the Puerto Rican family, police brought the mother and her five children to Pacific Garden Mission's Women's and Children's Division where they were given care and some days later turned over to grandparents. As for the 35-year-old alcoholic and dope addict, she was welcomed, and a supervisor lovingly cared for her and tucked her into a clean bed for her first restful night's sleep in weeks. The sailor's wife was given overnight lodging, her baggage was obtained, and next day she was sent on to her husband.

But best of all, in each of these cases, the women were counseled directly from God's Word and, with the exception of the Puerto Rican mother, who was mentally retarded, each responded to God's love and eagerly opened her heart to Jesus Christ before leaving the Mission.

This, briefly, is the 24-hour, seven-day-a-week job of the Women's and Children's Division of the Old Lighthouse, one of the few shelters in Chicago where women and children are welcomed into a homey atmosphere and at the same time are told of the One who once said, "Come unto me, all ye that labour and are heavy laden, and I will give you rest" (Matt. 11:28). Annually as many as 6400, including individual women and mothers and children, are guests of the Mission. Night after night the Division's ten beds are occupied and often children must sleep on couches and on mattresses on the floor.* Since many individuals and families stay at the Mission over a period of several days—some for several weeks—there is much exposure to spiritual counseling, resulting in a high percentage of professions of faith in the Saviour. In one recent year 109 decisions for Christ were recorded.

The vision for the women's work of PGM was given by God to Mrs. Susan Wymer, a godly soul winner who today, even in the twilight years of life, continues her weekly visits to Dwight Reformatory for Women in Dwight, Illinois, to point delinquent girls to a new life in Jesus Christ. One day in 1941 Mrs. Wymer, with a friend, called on Harry Saulnier and jolted him with, "Mr. Saulnier, we've been thinking about getting a women's work started here. We need a division of the work where women of the street can come and be dealt with.

*As this was written, the Women's and Children's Division was being enlarged so that 50 beds could be added. Plans were also being made to house waifs and other children not accompanied by at least one parent or guardian.

There are so many girls wandering the streets who need the Saviour."

Pieces fell together in jigsaw-puzzle fashion as Saulnier thought about it. For a long time he had been bothered by the lack of adequate means of dealing with women needing spiritual counseling.

"Mrs. Wymer, we don't have any money right now for this kind of work, but go ahead. Do what you can. We'll trust the Lord for this just like we trust Him for everything else. Amen?" Saulnier didn't know it then, but he had just made one of the major decisions that would take Pacific Garden Mission one step closer to becoming a model big-city soul-winning station.

At first the ministry consisted mainly of counseling. But as God began supplying extra funds, the staff prepared and furnished the second floor, and later the third floor, of one of the two additional buildings the Mission had obtained in November 1941. By late 1943 a sign was hung out welcoming needy women and offering overnight accommodations. Here was a relatively new approach to rescue mission work—one destined to pay off in great dividends in souls won to Christ.

Miss Grace Vander Ploeg, a Chicagoan working as a missionary in Paterson, New Jersey, came to head up the new division. In her nine years with the Mission, she became acquainted with the girls of the burlesque shows and taverns on South State. Some of them would wind up in Women's Court and appeal to her to get them out again.

Eventually Miss Vander Ploeg was spending almost as much time in court as at the Mission, so in 1950 she left, believing that God wanted her to work full-time at the Court. Later she married Wilfred A. Willett. She continues in this ministry to this very day.

In Norfolk, Virginia, in 1946 God was beginning to shape another vessel for service in the Women's Division. Yeoman 2/c Elaine Chobanoff, an Elyria, Ohio, girl serving in the WAVES, met Christ through a Navigators representative.

In 1950 Elaine Chobanoff, by this time a graduate of Moody Bible Institute, was a Thursday evening volunteer worker at the Mission. During her MBI days she had become acquainted with rescue mission work, and God led her back to PGM to take Mrs. Willett's post.

Currently assisting Miss Chobanoff is Mrs. Hildred Stout, 52, a pleasant-faced widow from Pennsylvania who became interested in the work of PGM when she saw *Out of the Night,* the first PGM film, at a Bible conference more than 12 years ago. She told the Lord then that if He should someday take her husband she would like to work with women at Pacific Garden Mission. Ten years ago her husband died, but there was a long training period—helping in a nursing home for eight years—before she came to the Mission in 1964.

One Saturday morning I dropped into the Women's Division and talked with Mrs. Stout, who was then on duty. (Currently, she has night duty and Miss Chobanoff, day supervision.)

Among the women being cared for then was a 70-year-old pensioner who had checked in at 2:00 that morning.

In the living room Mrs. Stout introduced me to "Mary," a chubby, baby-faced girl of about 19 whom I took to be of Mexican descent. Her boyfriend had been arrested the night before, and police had brought her to the Mission.

Mrs. Stout ushered me to the third floor to a comfortably furnished parlor just off the kitchen of the Women's Division, and we sat and talked of recent cases. Some days before, in the same room, I had chatted with Miss Chobanoff. Both supervisors agreed that mentally unbalanced women outnumber even alcoholics among those who have found their way to the Mission during the past six years. Statistics reveal that there are some 8½ million people with serious mental difficulties in the U.S., and some experts estimate that the total may be much higher, perhaps 15 to 20 percent of the population.

Among the mentally afflicted, "Edith," an 18-year-old Negro girl, stands out in Mrs. Stout's memory. "She is a beautiful girl,"

Mrs. Stout declared. "I told Elaine, 'Believe me, she could go a long way with her appearance.' But she was so mixed up. When anybody would get in a conversation, she'd think they were talking about her. She would go into a tantrum. She would throw her hands up in the air and scream and cry and call me. Also, she apparently suffers from claustrophobia. She felt closed in and complained that the beds were too close together. One night I finally moved her out into the hall, so she could be near my bedroom and could call me if she needed me.

"One night Edith told me that she was going to go to work at 9:00 as a waitress. I picked out a nice uniform for her and patted her on the shoulder as she left. 'Edith, you look real sweet. Be a good girl now.' But after two or three nights I began to get suspicious. She was going to work at different hours, and I was getting up at 2 and 3 o'clock in the morning to let her in. Surely a restaurant wouldn't have those hours.

"Finally, I brought her up here and I counseled with her. She said she accepted the Lord. For about two days it seemed that she might be working the 6:00 to 12:00 shift, but then the hours changed again. I had another talk with her. Edith, I don't believe you're really working.'

"She put her head down, and I said, 'Have you been?'

" 'No,' she said. 'I have a friend on the North Side, and I've been staying with him.'

"Before Edith left us after several weeks, I learned from an outside source that she had had a baby before coming here, something she had withheld from us. She was startled when I mentioned that I knew about this phase of her life. I still pray for Edith, though we haven't seen her for some time."

At this point Mrs. Stout went into an adjoining room to answer a phone. I caught snatches of the conversation at our end, and the delight in Mrs. Stout's voice indicated this was one of her girls. Somehow I was not surprised when Mrs. Stout returned a moment later, smiling, and announced, "Why, that was the girl we were just talking about—Edith. She's in a mental hospital. Wants to come back and pick up some books and things she left."

Thus, Edith's story was still being written. There would be at least one more contact with her. If only somehow she would come to Jesus Christ and be unshackled.

Another type of girl who finds love and understanding at the Mission is the unmarried expectant mother—like the mentally ill, a serious problem on the national scene. Miss Chobanoff helps put these girls in touch with welfare authorities who work out details for their care. The Mission often provides maternity clothing; and before each girl leaves, she is given a layette.

The spiritual counsel and Christian love shown these frightened, frustrated girls make deep impressions. Several babies have been named for the two supervisors. One Negro girl, wanting to honor Mrs. Stout, however was troubled. "Mrs. Stout, what is your middle name?" she asked forthrightly.

"I don't have any," she replied.

"Oh, you don't."

"No, but why do you ask?"

"Oh, I wanted to name my baby after you if it's a girl, but I don't believe I like Hildred too well."

Even so, before the expectant mother went on to be hospitalized elsewhere to await her baby, she had come to like the name. Mrs. Stout never heard whether the baby was a boy or girl, but if it was a girl there's undoubtedly one additional Hildred in the world because a girl in need was taken in at the Mission.

Among alcoholics who have been helped is "Anne" whose pastor phoned the Mission from a nearby state. Anne, a 42-year-old woman from the community, needed aid desperately to break a drinking habit that had plagued her home for 18 years. Her husband had just said that he was giving up on her and would find someone to care for their little girl.

"We will be looking for her," Miss Chobanoff told the pastor.

The church people put Anne on a bus, and a few hours later

she was being put to bed in the Women's Division. She had the shakes and Mrs. Stout gave her hot coffee and aspirin. It took half a dozen more cups of coffee at intervals to get through the night.

Next morning Miss Chobanoff counseled with Anne and read to her from the Bible. That night, her mind clearer, the woman attended the service in the Mission chapel and made a profession of faith in Christ. During the next five weeks both Miss Chobanoff and Mrs. Stout helped her get established in the Word. When she appeared strong enough to return home, the Mission supervisor surprised her with a wardrobe of clothes and put her on a bus, committing her to the Lord. A letter several days later indicated that a victory had truly been won: "What surprises me," she said, "is that I can walk uptown and I can pass those taverns. I don't even want to go in!"

Later, though, when her husband got tired of a "religious, goody-good" wife, Anne slipped back to drink. But she quickly packed up again and headed back for Chicago and the Mission where she knew she would receive help and grow still stronger. As this is being written, Anne is still at the Mission.

Homeless families—some with fathers out of work, others out on the street because fathers have left home—regularly come or are sent to the Mission. One day in 1961 police deposited a mother and her five children in the Mission. Marie Harrington and her brood were living in a car, having been put in the street for failure to pay rent. The thrilling events that transpired in the days and weeks following are summarized in a letter Mrs. Harrington wrote in 1964:

"I was against staying in a mission, but was I in for surprises! Even though the Women's Division was cramped and it seemed as if children were crawling out of the woodwork, my five kids and I were made to feel at home.

"Bit by bit my antagonism was melted by the concerned workers who were always ready to take time with my troubles. And little by little the love of Christ began drawing me. It impressed me that everyone sang a hymn before we sat down to eat. One night when someone baby-sat for me, I attended the evening service, and at the invitation went forward and accepted the Lord Jesus Christ as my Saviour.

"The three weeks I stayed at the Mission changed the course of my life. The Lord Jesus promised to make everything new, and He has. Four of my children [the fifth is a toddler] have received Christ, and my husband returned home and also invited the Lord into his heart. I appreciate the counseling I still get from the Women's Division."

Women shackled by both alcohol and narcotics stumble up the stairway to the Women's Division as a place of last resort for help. "Helen" couldn't stumble up the stairway, however—she had to be helped. For during a lost weekend making a round of taverns on West Madison Street, she met with an accident and was taken to Cook County Hospital, her leg broken. The social service department of the hospital later referred her to the Mission.

"That was OK with me," she later said. "I was sick from the lack of narcotics. Besides, I wanted to see what kind of racket they had. What impressed me, though, was that everyone was so happy and laughing. I thought, 'If I could only feel like they look!'

"I went to a meeting that night. I thought they didn't know what they were talking about, having never been hustlers, drunks, or junkies. Next morning I didn't leave and nobody asked me to. I worked, helping with the dishes, all the time seeing peace and happiness around me. That's what I wanted.

"At the meeting that night when they asked if I wanted the Lord to forgive me, I still said no. Saturday I got new clothes and that night at the meeting I burst into tears. I wanted so terribly to be decent—to have peace.

"Elaine took me to the prayer room where we talked for hours. I told her that if I had to stop drinking, life would be impossible. She said that the Lord would help me stop. Suddenly I felt strong and got down on my knees and asked the Lord to save me from my sins. I said, 'Lord, You've heard what You have to work with. If there is anything here You can use, I am Yours.'

"I felt like I was scrubbed inside when I got off my knees. The wonder of it all, even after all these years. It was January 11 that I was converted. January 11 is my birthday."

One of the most unusual cases ever to come to the Women's Division was Mary Howell, sent by a social worker when a judge released her from Women's Court in Chicago. She learned to drink in New York City, then after going to Kansas City began to hop from job to job as well as tavern to tavern. Later, living in a little room over a saloon in St. Louis, she fell victim to delirium tremens. A voice seemed to say: "Mary, get down and pray." She got on her knees beside her bed. But then the voice directed to get on the other side. She got on the other side, and now the voice was directing her to change sides again. Around and around the room she went, until she looked out the window and thought she saw her boyfriend, Frank, hanging from a telephone pole.

Finally, Mary called the police and ended up in a psychopathic hospital. Some time later she made her way to Chicago. It was the year 1930 and the Skid Row population was larger than ever because of the Depression. Here began a pattern of living death that went on almost unchanged for 27 years! Again and again Mary Howell was in and out of Women's Court and Women's Prison at the Bridewell. Later, it was the standard thing to take her to the County Psychopathic Hospital and finally to the State Hospital, either at Kankakee or Manteno.

When Mary arrived at the Mission in 1957, things happened swiftly. She tells it in these words:

"I got a bath and clean clothes, and Elaine Chobanoff prayed with me following the evening service. I confessed Jesus Christ as my personal Lord and Saviour, even though my mind was still confused. During the night, Elaine read Scripture to me.

I had ugly thoughts: It seemed that Elaine was planning to kill me. Yet, somehow, as she read the Bible almost the night through, the words began to make sense to me. I can't be sure what she read but sometime during the night she probably read this verse from John 4 which has become so true in my life, 'Whosoever drinketh of the water that I shall give him shall never thirst.' I'm so glad that I drank of the water that Christ gives."

Today, if you should visit Pacific Garden Mission on a Saturday night and attend the testimony service, the soloist just might be a small, dainty woman of about 60—Mary Howell. Because of her love for the Old Lighthouse and her desire to communicate the gospel to others, she sings with all her heart. You wouldn't rank her with the better voices of our day, but if you knew her story, you'd think her singing as sweet as that of a nightingale. Is it any wonder that Mary Howell and thousands of other women thank God for the day they came to the Women's Division, a haven in a big city?

Chapter 14

WELCOME, GI!

IN THE SUMMER of 1942 the U.S. and its allies were finding the going extremely rough. German submarines and bombers sank 22 of 33 ships, including 15 American ones, in a convoy in July. In the Pacific the U.S. and Japanese navies swung wildly at each other, the U.S. gaining an advantage in winning the Battle of Midway in June but reeling back when the Japanese invaded Guadalcanal in August. Young men in growing numbers were being inducted into the armed forces to strengthen the American military program.

That same summer, in Oklahoma City, Oklahoma, for special meetings, Harry Saulnier spotted a war-related news item that quickened his pulse:

"The U.S. Army will take over the Stevens Hotel, the world's largest, and the Congress Hotel on August 1 to house members of the air forces. . . . The Stevens Hotel, which has 3000 rooms, is expected to house between 9,000 and 10,000 men. The Congress has 900 rooms and will accommodate about 5,000 men."

Laying aside the newspaper, Saulnier exclaimed, "This is it!" Anyone who happened to hear him may have wondered what he meant but not the Lord. God knew all about what had been going on in the mind of the big Frenchman who in his two years at the helm of the Pacific Garden Mission had already shown that he could not be content with the status quo. For months the streets of downtown Chicago had been dotted in increasing numbers by young men and women in khaki and blue. Ever since the Lord had given the Mission two additional buildings, it was a growing desire on the part of Saulnier and the staff to minister to this transient, spiritually needy crop of war-bound Americans. A few blocks away the USO Center swarmed with GI's; PGM would, by God's grace and the aid of His people, open a *Christian* Servicemen's Center! With the Army-commandeered hotels only two blocks away, the challenge was more colossal than ever.

Saulnier rushed back to Chicago to set machinery in action.

On November 29, Claudus M. McDaniel, director of the Center, opened the doors and welcomed the first GI's. Here they could unwind while playing ping-pong or shuffleboard in the recreation room, or they could write home or just relax while reading wholesome books and the latest Christian magazines in the library at one end of the chapel. Always available, as today, were refreshments in the Canteen with its Western motif. But best of all, friendly, fatherly personal workers were there to show the GI's how to enlist in the Lord's army.

In the first two months nearly 5000 soldiers, sailors, marines, and coastguardsmen, including women in the various branches, crossed the threshold of the new Center. And in many homes across the land Christian parents rejoiced as unsaved sons and daughters placed their trust in Jesus Christ in answer to prayer. All told, some 100 GI's professed Christ in the first two months, and many others were restored to fellowship with God. Two hundred and fifty New Testaments, supplied by the Gideons, the Chicago Bible Society, and the Moody Bible Institute Colportage, were distributed, along with 20,000 pieces of gospel literature given to GI's on the street and in nearby train depots, as well as in the Center.

The guest register at the Center looked like a worldwide directory of American army and navy bases. Men from Hawaii, Australia, New Zealand, and Canada signed the book. GI's in increasing numbers found their way to the Center from Chicago area stations like the Stevens and Congress Hotels, Navy Pier, and Great Lakes Naval Training Station. Because of the spiritual tone of the Center and the fact that war is a serious matter,

GI's unhesitatingly opened up and talked to counselors about problems.

Among the godly counselors in those early days of the Center were C. E. Bulander, head of the personal work corps, Mrs. Bulander, Edward Ockert, C. E. Davis, and John Baergen. Many Christian laymen and students from Christian schools in Chicagoland came to assist, along with faithful groups of women from area churches (as today) who prepared refreshments in the Canteen from 9:00 A.M. to midnight. In homes and churches hundreds were backing the ministry with fervent prayer.

On December 15, 1942, two weeks after the official opening of the Center, joy filled the hearts of the PGM staff as the final payment of the 30,000 dollar mortgage was made on the buildings housing the Center. Retiring the mortgage reduced the Mission endowment fund to a small amount. Established by gifts from Mother Clarke, Billy Sunday, and others, the fund was used to help pay for the Mission building as well as the buildings housing the Center.

By the spring of 1943, with the Allies sending the war into high gear, GI's in greater numbers were finding salvation. The report was: " 'The fields are already white unto harvest.' Opportunities are limitless for personal soul-winning. The boys are eager to hear the Word. Face to face with danger and death, they are concerned about their souls."

In the month of March 398 decisions were recorded, and the number soared to more than 800 in April and 764 in May. Among these was a Canadian in Scottish Highland kilts who knelt in the Canteen kitchen and received Christ. Another was an Indian boy just graduated from a Chicago training school. After accepting Christ he handed the personal worker an unopened whiskey bottle, signifying his clean break with Satan and the world.

A sailor named Milo was typical of many of the GI's stationed at Chicagoland installations. He told his story in these terms:

"I got my first liberty on a Saturday night. Chicago was a

new town to me. My buddies had been sent to another school, so I was alone in a strange city. A gang of fellows from Navy Pier took me with them and we headed for the Loop. I felt like celebrating—it was a long time between liberties. I ended in a bar on South State. I knew that liquor was the devil's instrument, but I couldn't stop using it, although it didn't satisfy.

"I went walking down South State, wondering how to spend the rest of the evening. At the Servicemen's Center the doorman invited me in. The folks in there had something I wanted. I was convicted that night, but I wasn't ready to trade sin for salvation. However, the Lord never let me rest until I surrendered. Sunday I went with the gang again, but there was no joy for me. I started back to the Pier early. God guided my steps to the Center. I went in tired of my load of sin and longing for peace of heart. Christ cleansed my heart that night, and as the burden of sin rolled away unspeakable peace came into my life. I returned to the base a saved and happy man. I had done nothing. Jesus Christ paid it all on Calvary!"

Interestingly, Carl, a friend of Milo's, also found his way to the Center and came to Christ, unknown to Milo.

When he came to the Stevens Hotel, Carl found a real stamping ground on nearby South State. Everything he naturally looked for he found there—places to drink and gamble. Winning—or losing—a week's army pay in an evening was nothing to Carl. After a drinking party one night, he was walking down the street with a girl he had picked up. In front of the Servicemen's Center the doorman invited them in. Carl completed his story:

"We were drinking coffee in the Canteen—we needed it badly—when Mr. Davis approached our table and led the conversation to things of the Lord. John 3:16 reached my heart, but the gospel only served to harden the girl with me. As soon as I decided for the Lord, she said, 'You're too religious.' And that was that. The poor girl is still roaming State Street looking for servicemen. In February—about two weeks after I was saved—I ran into my old drinking partner, Milo. The first thing he said was 'I'm saved now!'

" 'So am I,' I said, 'Praise the Lord!' "

Carl summed up the fellowship at the Center with this comment: "Since I have been living with the Lord Jesus Christ as my Saviour, I can say with the other boys at the Center that every day is sweeter than the day before. Christian fellowship at the Center is precious, and I have made many real friends."

As news of the busy Servicemen's Center spread to Christians, gifts increased to keep the door wide open. Sunday School classes, young people's societies, and Daily Vacation Bible Schools sent in money. One gift came from a Sunday school class started by Chaplain T. H. Makin, who had visited PGM while on duty at Great Lakes. Another gift was mailed from Camp Roberts, California, with this note from Chicago area resident Pvt. Lloyd Cory: "They had a table tennis tournament, hampered by drunks bumping into the table and the contestants, and I won. They gave me $5 for my efforts. I'm turning it over to be used as God directs for the Center. I wish they had something like that near here. Thank God that He's still in the soul-saving business."

Some of the gifts were used to increase the efficiency of the Center, as a completely equipped dormitory with some 50 cots were added in the spring of 1944. Until then some GI's slept on sofas in the Center, and others, with insufficient money to rent a hotel room, were staying all night in nightclubs and theaters or walking the streets. In the first year, 6500 GI's spent the night in the new dormitory, and more than 800 of these made professions of faith in Christ.

As the Allies gained momentum in both theaters of operation in late 1944, thousands of GI's, including women in uniform who found a welcome overnight in the Women's Division, had visited the Center and hundreds had made professions of faith in the Saviour. Follow-up letters went out to all of them, and cards and letters were mailed to the homes of GI's who signed the register. Naturally, hearts were warmed in homes almost around the world wherever Allied servicemen lived.

Typical of some of the thank-you letters from Christian parents was this one from a Michigan mother: "I didn't know until I had read what you wrote that my son had accepted Christ as his Saviour. I wrote him at once and told him how I rejoiced on knowing about it and that it was the most wonderful gift a mother could possibly have for Christmas. He went into service when he was eighteen, two years ago this February. He expects to be going overseas anytime now. It means everything to me to know he has Jesus with him."

A Tennessee woman wrote of her joy upon hearing from her husband that he had come to Christ in the Center. "He wrote me all about it," she stated, "and said you all had made him happier than he had been since he left home, and he knew now he didn't have a thing to worry about."

A letter from Mrs. David E. Schiesser, of Weehawken, New Jersey, brought both sad and glad news. Her oldest son, Edward, found Christ at the Old Lighthouse and was promoted to heaven three years later. Going through his personal effects, the grief-stricken mother found a gospel tract that he had picked up at PGM. Then it was that she understood the change that had come into his life. Until then Mrs. Schiesser had been speculating into matters of religion and had embraced the Old Testament centered teachings of Seventh-Day Adventism. She wrote: "Edward was only twenty years old June 30, 1943, when he went home to heaven. I know he is waiting on the other shore for me, his mother, who found the tract he got in Chicago in 1940 and thereby was able to shake off the grave clothes of Moses' time and to emerge into the light of the true 'Sabbath,' the Lord Jesus Christ, in whom I find my rest, praise His precious name."

By the time the war ended in 1945, the Servicemen's Center had in nearly three years welcomed more than 450,000 GI's, and personal workers had recorded some 16,000 decisions for

Christ. With the formal closing of the USO Center in 1946, the PGM Center remained wide open, offering servicemen food, overnight accommodations, and recreation—and, best of all, the gospel.* It proved a wise decision, for in peacetime years there has been a continuous stream of men in uniform visiting the Center. In the first five years after the war an annual average of 50,000 men signed in and 5500 professed Christ. During the 1950's, 26,000 servicemen came each year and professions of faith averaged 4500. In the 1960's, the annual averages have been 17,000 visitors and 4000 professions. (Percentages of men making professions of faith have been higher in peacetime simply because personal workers are able to counsel more thoroughly with more men when the Canteen is not crowded.) All told, the Center has hosted over a million GI's and has recorded 108,000 decisions for Christ.

The Korean War, bringing a sharp increase in the draft, swelled the numbers visiting the Center. Some years ago a Japanese major professed Christ during a stay, and more recently a young Ethiopian flier training at Chanute Air Force Base, Illinois, responded to the gospel.

During the war years and in the months immediately following personal workers saw the effects of war upon the minds and bodies of some of the fellows. In 1946 a discharged sailor suddenly became white and broke into sobs as a worker dealt with him. "They kept on coming, coming, coming!" the young man exclaimed. "We couldn't do a thing, for our guns were washed overboard. So they just kept driving at us. There was screaming, and blood ran over the deck, as they kept on coming. Finally, we had orders to leave the ship and leave our wounded buddies behind—many of whom were dying."

The worker tried to calm this ex-sailor as he relived his experience in the battle of Okinawa. Upon hearing of Christ's

*The USO Center was reopened on a smaller scale Christmas 1950. The only other Chicago center is Victory Center, operated by the Christian Business Men's Committee of Chicago. The PGM unit is the only fully equipped Center with a dormitory and open around the clock.

never-failing sufficiency, the fellow opened wide his heart's door and received the Saviour. When he left the Center, he left in God's perfect peace.

The cases of Careaga and Leirmo, GI buddies who came to the Center in 1948, caused much rejoicing among the Mission staff. Sgt. Rudy Careaga came to the Center with a tale of woe. He had come to Chicago to have a good time. Then there was a girl, liquor, and knockout drops—and his money disappeared. A personal worker, Charles Lee Hayes, listened to Careaga's story and offered his sympathy, then proceeded to help Careaga see that his problem had resulted from the sin that ruled his life. Under the mighty power of the Holy Spirit, his heart was melted and a desire to be saved manifested itself. Before he left the Center, he actually was glad he had been robbed, for through the experience he found the Lord Jesus Christ as his personal Saviour.

But that was not the end of contact with Careaga. Next day he returned with another soldier, S. Sgt. Thomas Leirmo, who also had been sampling Satan's dainties in South State Street establishments. Personal worker Hayes dealt with Leirmo about his soul but got the brush off. Next day he spent part of the day taking the two GI's swimming, after buying a pair of swimming trunks for Leirmo. Afterward, the two GI's went on their way to take temporary jobs in a Chicago restaurant until their furloughs were up. Hayes' heart ached for Thomas Leirmo as he prayed for him. He had such a need for Christ, yet the little talk Hayes had had with him seemed to have had no effect.

Then one day about three weeks later, Leirmo dropped into the Canteen to see Hayes. "Hey there," he said, his face beaming. "Remember me? I want to pay back what I owe you for the swimming trunks." Hayes pulled himself up to full height and looked him square in the eye. "Sarge, I'm not interested in the money—I gave you the trunks. I'm interested in knowing how you stand with the Lord."

Leirmo beamed and told a story that thrilled Hayes. "I'm

all right with the Lord. I finally came to the conclusion that there was something lacking in my life. I believed that the Christians at the Servicemen's Center had this 'something.' Then I realized my need for Christ. So one evening, not long after you talked with me, I knelt down in my hotel room and accepted Christ as my Saviour. Until then I had always believed that religion was a theory that no one could prove, but now I know better. No one but the Lord Jesus Christ will ever realize how much my life has been changed. Although I am still in the Army with duties to perform, the inner change—the awakening of my long lost soul—is my cause for rejoicing."

A Richmond, Virginia, boy David Y. Apt visited the Center in 1950 and made a profession of faith in Christ before he shipped out for duty in the Korean War. A few months later his mother, Mrs. David Apt, wrote: "He was sent over to Japan and on to Korea, where he was killed November 21. The letter you sent here to him has been more precious to me than anything I have! After going on to Japan he wrote . . . he was reading his Bible every chance he had. He was killed in action instantly."

Dean Ford, a sailor who came to the Old Lighthouse in 1954, has often thanked God for the strategic placement of the Center. As a 15-year-old he had come into a personal relationship with Jesus Christ but began drifting in the Navy. One day on pass from Great Lakes, he reluctantly joined other sailors in a tour of South State Street's burlesque houses, tattoo parlors, and saloons. Dean didn't like what he saw—until he looked up and saw the big PGM sign, "JESUS SAVES." The doorman invited Dean and his friends in, but only Dean went inside. The others scoffed and left. In the Canteen the young sailor came back to Christ, broken before God and confessing his condition. That night he stayed overnight in the dormitory, rejoicing that he was back in the fold.

In the months that followed, Dean Ford was a regular visitor at the Old Lighthouse. He made many friends. When he was ready to be transferred, he talked one evening with a little man who has now gone to be with the Lord. It was Dan Kearney, onetime Irish song-and-dance man and drunkard who had come out of a mental institution to receive Christ at the Mission and become a new man in Him.

"There are two kinds of tracts in these packages, Dean," he said, giving him the bundles. "There's a lot of meat to both of them. I hope you'll use them often."

Dean told Dan he had no idea where he would use them. But Dean passed them out to other GI's and ordered more and more. Later, he married. Today he and his wife, Wilma, serve the Lord as missionaries under the West Indies Mission in the jungles of Surinam, South America.

Over the years, many GI's and ex-servicemen have returned to the Old Lighthouse with a word of thanks for the spiritual counseling they got, another indication that the ministry bears lasting fruit.

Bob Kelly of Cleveland, Ohio, dropped in one day in 1950 to say thanks to Coach Ed Ockert for pointing him to the Lamb of God three years before. "At the time I didn't understand what was happening, but now I realize I was being born again," he testified. "It has been my privilege to bring a few others to Christ also."

Ockert, incidentally, proved himself one of the Center's most able and colorful personal workers in the 20 years he served. Joining the staff in 1944 when he quit athletic coaching at 70 years of age, he worked tirelessly. Boys were drawn to him as a man. Almost till his death on March 20, 1964, at 89 he bounced about, playing table tennis and shuffleboard with visiting servicemen. But always he sat down with the fellows, Bible in hand, and with a gnarled finger showed them verses relating to salvation. In 1957 Ockert revealed to a close friend that up to June of that year he had been used of God to lead 16,620 boys to Christ. This number, of course, was greatly increased during the next seven years until his death. He won his last soul to Christ at the Center on February 28, 1964, became ill soon afterward, and never was able to return to his job.

Today other faithful personal workers greet and work with the men in uniform in the same tradition of Ockert. Gus Magnuson, an elderly Swede, has been on the staff since 1955. Other workers include Peter Potkonjak, a retired leather worker from Marshall Field's who began working in the Center in 1943; John Nordstrom, former telephone company employee who has been winning GI's since 1950; and John Tichy, ex-missionary to Alaska who has served at the Mission since 1955.

Thus, today the door remains wide open to the man in uniform. Since the military buildup in 1965 in connection with the Viet Nam conflict, the Center is buzzing with increased activity. The message for the GI, however, is the same as in the early days of the Center: "Ye must be born again" (John 3:7).

Chapter 15

FILMING THE PGM STORY

"DEAD!" The house detective examined the dead woman's body for evidences of murder or suicide and then summoned the coroner.

"Yes, it looks like murder, Tom." That was all. Evelyn's death was the climax of a brief but horrible existence consisting of a continual round of brothels, police courts, dope dens, and street walking.

Born in a small Western town, of good parents, the girl had had the normal childhood allotted to every red-blooded American. There were days of horseback riding, games, and playing dolls. And then high school.

"Mother, I've a job at Pop Johnson's soda fountain!" Evelyn, breathless with excitement, announced one evening as she tossed her books on the sofa. "I get 75 cents an hour, and work five days a week." Thrilled at the new independence of making some money of her own, she worked hard for three months. In those prewar days, a schoolgirl could buy a lot of things from her earnings of 75 cents an hour.

One afternoon a stranger entered the ice cream store and ordered a Coke. He watched the girl as she filled her orders, and a satisfied smile lurked in his eyes.

"How old are you, miss?"

"Sixteen, sir, my last birthday."

"You're too beautiful to be stuck to this job. I can help you make big money. Hundreds of dollars a week. Easy. Interested?" He waited, allowing the suggestion of wealth and luxury to take its effect. It was so simple. It always was.

That was the beginning. First prostitution. Then drugs to stifle the conscience. Next, the police court. But one day she heard the voice of Him who said, "I am the light of the world: he that followeth me shall not walk in darkness, but shall have the light of life." And at the Pacific Garden Mission another Samaritan woman found Christ as her Saviour.

And this is why she died. When the man who first enticed her came back into her life, she could give but one answer. "I'm not my own. I'm bought with a price—the blood of Jesus Christ. I can no longer have anything to do with you!"

And so he killed her. Murder? Yes, but a better word is *martyrdom!*

This story, from the May 1945 *Pacific Garden Mission News,* set the creative gears of the mind of Superintendent Saulnier into action once again. For years he had been talking to various ones about putting the PGM story on film to show God's hand in action through the outreach of the Mission. Such a film, Saulnier reasoned, could, if expertly done, arouse slumbering church people to the need for harvesting souls right in their own backyards and at the same time be an evangelistic tool to be used by the Holy Spirit to convict the unsaved and bring them to Christ. The story of Evelyn could easily become part of that film.

In 1948 a new filming company, Cavalcade Productions, operated by Christian men, invaded the Mission with cameras and other motion-picture equipment. By this time Evelyn's story had been combined with other stories in a script that touched on several phases of the Mission ministry. And for many weeks parts of the Mission and places along Skid Row became a film set. In those days the unexpected was the expected.

For example, Loiell Hyler, assistant superintendent and one of the Mission's soul winners of that day, made a forced landing on the seat of his baggy trousers on the sidewalk in front of a South State Street tavern from which he had been ungraciously shoved by a burly tavern employee.

At first glance someone may have concluded that Hyler had backslidden and was a candidate for Mission aid. But in hitting Skid Row with the seat of his pants, Hyler was very much still working for the Lord; for a Cavalcade cameraman that day was carefully recording the incident. Hyler was cast as Bill Jennings, a business executive whom alcohol had ruined. In a later scene in the film Jennings would visit the Mission and drink of the Water of Life and find freedom from his habit and a wonderful new life walking with Jesus Christ.

The film, *Out of the Night,* had its premier showing on the evening of October 15, 1948, in Chicago's Moody Memorial Church. Since that day there have been well over 4000 individual showings of this 30-minute film before an estimated 700,000 viewers. In addition, the film has been shown on several TV stations, increasing the number of viewers into the millions.

Encouraged by the response to *Out of the Night,* Saulnier and the PGM Board authorized another film, *The Street.* It was released to churches, prison missionaries, and others in March 1953. Also a documentary in sound and color, *The Street* dramatizes the story of a young man in a small town who drifts into crime and flees to Skid Row. Here he hides out, visiting taverns until his money is gone. He sleeps in alleys, and frostbite sends him to the PGM Clinic. Here a godly doctor leads him to Christ. Harry Saulnier counsels him and advises him to retrace his crooked way and surrender himself for his crimes. The superintendent accompanies him to his hometown where an understanding judge places him on probation in Saulnier's custody.

The Street, like the first film, has been used widely. Through more than 3000 showings, more than 520,000 have seen this 35-minute glimpse into the Mission ministry.

The Mission has circulated 181 copies of *Out of the Night* and 86 copies of *The Street,* and more than 70 copies of both films have been purchased by outside agencies for evangelistic purposes.

Most showings have been in Sunday evening or midweek services in churches, but some of the most fruitful showings have been in jails, prisons, and military camps and installations.

In addition to the two movies, the Mission in 1960 produced *The Cross Roads,* a color slide and filmstrip closeup look at the Mission in action. This production is available on a freewill offering basis, whereas the motion pictures are normally rented.

No attempt has been made at the Mission to record the results seen from these films, but the harvests have been substantial. Where there haven't been actual conversions, the Holy Spirit has shown young people the pitfalls of sin and stirred many lethargic church members to prayer and action concerning ministering the gospel to Skid Row people not only in Chicago but in their own cities.

Results of the film ministry are reflected in the letters of those who have used the films:

The chaplain of a state training school for boys reported that he showed *The Street* to 150 inmates, and fifteen boys raised their hands to indicate that they were making decisions for Christ.

A Minnesota pastor reported that a businessman about 30 years of age, a father of four children, had come to Christ through a showing of *The Street.*

A report from Idaho indicated that "the Spirit was pleased to move twenty-eight young people . . . to make first-time decisions for Jesus Christ" after they viewed *The Street.*

A West Virginia man showed *Out of the Night* in five churches and in a jail and wrote that "we had two converts at the jail and seventy-nine dedications to the Lord as a result of seeing the picture."

In South Carolina a church used *Out of the Night* to encourage young people to abstain from the use of alcoholic beverages, and some 150 responded to a pledge of abstinence.

Countless pastors and others have reported that church people have for the first time become burdened for the souls of those leading a Skid Row existence.

Now and then there is written into the record of the Old Lighthouse a dramatic account of someone who has come to the Saviour through one of the films. The George Guttrich story is a case in point. His story climaxes in a way that clearly shows the value of the film ministry.

Guttrich grew up on a farm in the sand country of Jasper County, Indiana. Following high school and business school, he married and settled in Chicago. Here the country boy began to live (or so he thought) as he worked directly with the vice-president in charge of a distillery his firm operated as a sideline. Guttrich carried the keys to the sample liquor cabinet of the firm, drinking all he wanted at no cost to him. Part of his job was to entertain prospective customers.

Fortunately, George Guttrich held his own with liquor, finding that black coffee would fix him for a productive working day. But nonetheless he had the habit; and when the company sold the distillery, he began buying his own liquor—a bottle a week—usually for Saturday nights.

Thus, sometimes he had a throbbing head when he sent his son, Gordie, on Sunday mornings to meet an elderly neighbor, a Mrs. Cornett who took him to Sunday school in a little church across the alley.

Faithful Mrs. Cornett invited the Guttriches, who considered themselves average Chicagoans, to the little church, but they went only on special occasions. For example, George Guttrich sat in the little church one Easter feeling like an outsider. He couldn't sing with conviction the songs these godly people sang so lustily. Neither could he smile the way a man named Walter Mishler did when he shook George's hand that morning.

He compared his sour-looking face with Mishler's. Here he was, so tense and full of fear that he wasn't even driving his car except when he had to. *I need what these warm, contented people have,* Guttrich reasoned. *But what do they have? And how do I get it?*

One night in the summer of 1948 nine-year-old Gordie came home from church and walked straight into Dad's room.

"I just gave my life to Jesus Christ, Daddy."

"This really pulled at my heart, and all through the fall months I felt that pull," recalls Guttrich. "I began attending the little church. And one night, on Gordie's invitation, I went to see what he termed 'a swell movie' called *Out of the Night.* As the picture went on, I noticed a little ten-year-old girl wipe away a tear. I only half saw the picture, but in it I felt more than understood the transforming power of Jesus Christ! When it was over, in the silence of my own empty soul, I knelt with the ten-year-old girl at the altar and asked Jesus Christ to cleanse my heart. When I got up, I could not only smile like Walter Mishler, but I went right home and took my wife, Edith, for a ride in the car! The fear neurosis was gone along with my old life. And it's never come back."

George Guttrich's exciting walk with Jesus Christ resulted in his wife's stepping fully into God's kingdom. Thus, as Guttrich himself said in an "Unshackled!" story, "We no longer qualified as an average Chicago family. Unfortunately, God doesn't have any place in the *average* home of today as He now has in ours."

Norma Lawecki of Toledo, Ohio, was the "girl with a heart of stone," according to Mission records, until she saw *Out of the Night.* With an unhappy childhood, part of it spent in a children's home, she became especially rebellious after her mother found Christ as her Saviour and urged Norma to go to church with her. Two times Norma went to the altar and *said* that she wanted Christ, but her life remained unchanged.

Finally she quit church, despite her mom's pleas to go with her, and for about 15 years tried to find satisfaction in pleasure. A physical breakdown in 1950 hospitalized her on two occasions. By this time she lived away from home, a girl as thin as a sapling and a constant smoker. Occasionally Mother would call and beg her to go to church with her, and Norma would play the same record: "No. And how many times do I have to say it? I work all week and Sunday is the only time I have to work at home!"

But then one day Mother called and bubbled: "It's a motion picture. I want you to see at the church. It starts at 7:30."

"I can't make it by then," Norma replied.

"By 8?"

"Well, OK, but it'll probably be half over."

"I'll pray that Harry Saulnier is late getting here from Chicago!" Norma's mother chuckled.

Because of bad driving conditions, so he announced, Saulnier didn't arrive with the film until 8:00. Thus, Norma was there in good time. As the film was shown, she sat as if in a trance. At the close of the picture, she fell to her knees and wept. A woman prayed with her and talked to her about Jesus Christ. Norma told her she had already tried twice to be a Christian, but that didn't stop the personal worker. And soon Norma began to see her trouble: "You mean if I mean business with Christ this time, He'll receive me?"

In her "Unshackled!" story, Norma Lawecki said:

"I found out as I reached out for Him in faith. I became His and He poured out His love on me, washing away all the hate and evil thoughts that had once controlled my mind. Soon He told me to stop leaning on cigarettes, to depend on Him and His grace. And somehow, until I obeyed Him, He didn't have me. Though there have been times when I've disappointed Him, God has done everything He could for me. I didn't have anything before I knew Him. Now I have a home—not a fancy one, but it's ours. He gave me real friends that pray for me—not the fair-weather kind. I can't describe the depression and darkness I knew before I was saved. I didn't want to live but was afraid to die. God has taken all that away. Truly, He made Ezekiel 11:19 come true in my life: 'I will take the stony heart out of their flesh, and will give them an heart of flesh.' "

Is it any wonder, with stories such as these, that the staff of the Old Lighthouse rejoice in the fact that the Mission heeded God's call in 1948 to communicate the life-changing gospel through reels of movie film?

Chapter 16

DRAMA ON THE AIRWAVES

NEVER CONTENT to minister the gospel only to those who wander into the Old Lighthouse, Harry Saulnier in the early years of his tenure talked to the Lord on many occasions about a radio outreach. As the staff grew, he talked with them about the advantages of a Mission broadcast and got many to pray with him. Somehow, sometime, he told associates, God was going to show how the Mission could share by radio the gospel and the way it can change lives.

In the early months of 1945 it appeared that his prayer was being answered. Saulnier sold radio station WAIT, Chicago, on giving the Mission an early-morning 15-minute program. On many occasions he worked at the Mission till the early morning hours, then rushed home for a few hours sleep before arising at 5:30 A.M. to come back into the Loop to be in the radio studio by 7:30. The program, called "Doorway to Heaven," went on at 7:45. Saulnier earnestly presented the gospel and related stories of changed lives at the Mission. Converts themselves often came to tell personally of the transformation Christ had wrought in their lives. Things were going well until three months later when WAIT changed its policy and dropped all religious broadcasting.

Similar programs followed on stations WGES on Chicago's West Side and WMBI, the Moody Bible Institute station. As fine as they were, the programs were only local, and always Saulnier had the feeling that God had greater things ahead for the Mission in the field of radio.

One day in the late 1940's, a conversation with an advertising man sent Saulnier's mind racing in another direction. "Why not dramatize stories of Mission converts like other stories you often hear on the radio?" the ad man suggested. "Make the stories live. Tremendous things have happened in the lives of many of the converts. Dramatize their life stories and you'll appeal to all sorts of people. Perhaps a big company would be willing to sponsor such a program."

Saulnier liked the idea, but he felt it would be impractical to tie in with a sponsor. God's people would underwrite and pay for the broadcast, assuring the Mission of complete control of program content.

The board of trustees voted to move ahead, and Saulnier hired John Gillies, experienced radioman formerly with WMBI, to prepare a 15-minute pilot program. This was presented at the Mission in July 1950. Gillies got a green light to proceed with a half hour script on Billy Sunday, to begin a regular weekly series. John Camp, radio advertising executive, took over the account and arranged for a weekly broadcast at 11 P.M. on Saturdays on powerful, clear-channel WGN. Now the Mission would reach into homes for hundreds of miles across mid-America.

Many names were suggested for the new program, but Saulnier, a man not easily pleased with titles, remained unmoved by them all. On a visit to WGN, Camp mentioned the problem of finding a suitable name. An ex-navy man, sensing the need for a short, descriptive title, suddenly remembered his days aboard ship. "In beginning a radio call, we'd begin by saying shackled and end with unshackled. How about 'Unshackled' for a title?"

Hearing the name, Harry Saulnier straightened and his face brightened, as a man suddenly awakening from a trance. "That's it! It's different and yet it suggests just what we want the program itself to say: that Christ can break the fetters of sin and set the sinner free!"

With John Gillies directing and Lucille Becker at the organ

to provide mood music between scenes, "Unshackled!" got under way officially on September 23, 1950, as a cast of radio dramatists, scripts in hand, gathered in a WGN studio to recreate the life and conversion of Billy Sunday.

Though the program got off to a good start, John Gillies soon resigned. Meantime God had been working in the life of a young woman well known in secular radio circles:

At 33 years of age, Eugenia Price headed up a successful radio production office that turned out scripts for such popular shows as "In Care of Aggie Horn," "Joyce Jordan, M.D.," and "First Nighter." But now, after 10 years in the big time, she was wondering what success had really gotten her. Here she was with the things that money would buy, but she was bored. Finally she called up a childhood chum Ellen Riley, the girl who had played the piano in young people's. Ellen had made Jesus Christ the center of her life and was now serving Him in full-time work in New York City. Ellen spent a week's vacation with Genie and shared Christ with her. But Genie held out until late September 1949, when she flew to New York and decided to have it out with Ellen.

There, in a hotel room on October 2, after a long spiritual struggle, Genie Price caught hold of Ellen's arm and whispered, "OK, honey, you're right. I want all of Him." In that dramatic moment Genie opened her heart and invited Christ to take over.

A year later God had put her in touch with Pacific Garden Mission. And on the first Saturday night in October 1950 Genie Price, who had grown rapidly in the Christian life, was using her radio talents for God, directing "Unshackled!" as it invaded homes and automobiles of late-night listeners in Chicago and suburbs and out across the rolling farmlands of the great Midwest.

While professional radio people were hailing the program as a religious broadcast with distinct quality, the Holy Spirit was moving upon hearts of listeners. As the weeks passed, the mail volume grew. Some letters had contributions in them—

vital to the continuation of the broadcast. But most gratifying were those who indicated that they had heard God's voice. One man brought back to the Lord through "Unshackled!" sang with the converts' chorus during the 73rd PGM anniversary rally a few weeks after the broadcast was begun.

By early 1952 Harry Saulnier could see God's hand working out the details to beam the program to a wider area. In addition to a more choice hour on WGN—7:30 P.M.—a dozen other radio stations were airing the program each week, including WHAI, Greenfield, Massachussetts; WFHG, Bristol, Virginia; WREX, Duluth, Minnesota; and KUOA, Siloam Springs, Arkansas. In later years, Saulnier has seen the network grow to some 230 stations in U.S. and 12 foreign countries on six continents—North America, South America, Africa, Australia, Asia, and Europe. One of the latest stations to begin airing "Unshackled!" is the Trans World Radio outlet at Monte Carlo, Monaco, beaming the gospel to Great Britain and countries of Western Europe. All told, an estimated 10,000,000 people hear "Unshackled!" each week.

In most cases, local stations give time to the Mission as a public service, and the Mission in turn sends the tapes out free of charge. Eleven U.S. broadcasts are sponsored by Christian businessmen, churches, and other groups.

Since 1957, in Chicago radio circles, "Unshackled!" has been treated a lot like some of the drifters whose stories have been told on the broadcast. Whereas WGN welcomed the program in 1950 and recognized it as a popular feature among listeners in years afterward, a policy change in late 1956 kicked "Unshackled!" off the air, and the program landed on WLS in January 1957. In May 1960 WLS changed ownership, and again the Mission broadcast got the cold shoulder as the station decided to do religious broadcasting only on Sundays. Next stop was WCFL, but this too was short-lived as policy changes showed "Unshackled!" the door. Currently, the only Chicago outlet is WMBI-FM on Saturday evenings at 7:00.

All told, the annual budget for "Unshackled!" is 45,000 dollars including actual production and the office expense at the Mission itself. Because the program seldom stresses a need for funds, contributions often fail to meet expenses. As a result more than once the board has talked of the possibility of cutting back on the radio ministry, but because of the fruits of the work such suggestions are always tabled.

From the start, it became clear that the broadcast was reaching alcoholics behind closed doors in city, suburbia, small towns, and farm homes—doors that were perhaps otherwise closed to the gospel.

Probably Bill Morrison is the outstanding example of a listener unshackled from alcoholism. After hearing "Unshackled!" broadcasts begun in March 1953 by the Christian Business Men's Committee of Orillia, Ontario, Canada, on radio station CFOR, Morrison called in a godly pastor and sought help in coming to the Saviour. In early January 1959 Bill read an article in *The Montreal Star* that bothered him. He wrote a letter to the paper giving his story:

> Sir:
>
> Last week there appeared in your paper an article entitled "No Cure for Alcoholism" reporting on statements by Dr. David A. Stewart from Toronto.
>
> I would like to differ with Dr. Stewart, as I myself have found the cure. An alcoholic for forty-one years, having consumed rubbing alcohol, shaving lotion, canned heat, and shoe polish for over a period of twenty years, and having fallen prey to drug addiction for five years, I one Sunday evening heard a radio program from the Pacific Garden Mission entitled "Unshackled!" True-to-life stories were dramatized of people whose lives had been reclaimed from alcoholism and drug addiction, and the fact occurred to me that what God had done for others, He could do for me. I accepted Jesus Christ, and surrendered my life to Him. From that day on, and for six years now, I have had absolutely no desire for

alcohol or drugs, and the Lord has marvelously undertaken financially and in all other ways, for the needs of myself and my family.

The verse in II Corinthians 5:17, in the Bible, states: "Therefore, if any man be in Christ, he is a new creature: old things are passed away, behold all things are become new." This verse has been proven in my life. I am now on the staff of a rescue mission in this city, and living for the One who has so dramatically changed my life.

BILL MORRISON

Many "Unshackled!" listeners probably are not aware of the fact that Jack Odell, the writer-director of the program since the mid 1950's was himself once an alcoholic and is an indirect convert of the Mission radio ministry. After Air Force duty during World War II, Jack returned to Chicago radio circles, becoming program director of WCFL. But unable to resist whiskey, which had been dogging his career since he moved into radio in the middle 1930's, he lost his job in 1949 and found himself driving a cab.

Finally, his old-time school friend Ward Oury badgered him to meet another radio personality. "Maybe Genie Price, whose radio stories are of real people who found victory over the drink habit, will have some advice for you regarding your problem," Oury suggested.

Jack Odell stalled as long as he could, but one night, at the end of his resources, he consented to meet Miss Price. With understanding, she dealt with him. "You're looking for something, aren't you, Jack?"

"Yeah, I guess I am—a way out."

"There is a way, Jack, through Jesus Christ. He is the Way, and He has a brand new life for you too. It's a gift and you can't have it unless you'll reach out of your own free will and take it. But *when* you take this gift, you'll be free. Can you understand that?"

Jack did understand, and that night as he drove home he

stopped his car, confessed his need, and invited Jesus Christ to be his personal Saviour.

In the months afterward Jack found himself hauling country kids recovering from their first sprees over to Pacific Garden Mission for straightening out. But all the time Jack himself was still struggling with the drink problem, trying to get complete victory. One night in May 1953 Miss Price suggested that Jack attend a Mission service. That night, sitting on the platform facing the Skid Row audience, Jack Odell knew God was dealing with him about the bottle. A few minutes later he got up and gave his testimony, and inside, as he spoke, he sensed that at last his thirst was completely quenched with Living Water.

Soon afterward, Jack Odell took over "Unshackled!" as Genie Price moved on to a program of her own, speaking engagements, and book writing. Like Miss Price, Odell has from the start shown untiring devotion to the program, acutely aware of the far-reaching ministry. He personally interviews story subjects, tracks down leads for colorful dramatizations, and writes scores of letters over the months to obtain authentic information for stories. "Jack's ability is uncanny," says Russ Reed, who has long been associated with Odell and the program as a dramatist. "You have to be with and know Jack to appreciate him. He can do an interview and then turn out a polished script from a few scribbled notes. He has a real grasp of the needs of the program."

Odell may be seen in action on Saturdays from 2:30 to 5:30 P.M. in Boulevard Recording Studio, 632 North Dearborn, in Chicago, as he directs the "Unshackled!" cast in dramatizing stories of Mission converts and others.* Each week up to 100 people, including church groups from distant points, watch the production of the program. After the production of the program many travel two miles south across the business district for a

*Plans call for an early move of the production of "Unshackled!" to the Mission itself.

tour of the Mission, a tasty dinner, and then the Saturday evening testimony meeting.

Odell himself serves as announcer for "Unshackled!" as well as script writer and director. From three to six radio artists take parts in a story. And here Christians working the program find opportunity to share Christ with unbelieving artists who appear from time to time. At first, Harry Saulnier hesitated concerning the use of non-Christians. But union regulations required the use of union artists, making it necessary, if the program was to be a quality presentation, to use available talent. As a production was under way one Saturday some years ago, Jack Lester, doing the lead, came over and sat down at the artist's table. "That story is *me*!" he blurted, obviously broken. In the warm spiritual fellowship of Jack Odell, Russ Reed, Harry Elders, and others, Lester crossed over the line and blossomed out as a real believer, and today is going on with the Lord in radio work on the West Coast.

Curiously, some of the conversion stories resulting from "Unshackled!" have themselves been dramatized on the program. Ed and Mary Whitford are today on the foreign field as missionaries because God finally reached Ed through "Unshackled!" Their story was told about six years ago on the program.

Mary had come to Christ one Sunday after Ed had walked out of a church service, taking her with him. She had prayed earnestly for his salvation until one night Ed listened to an "Unshackled!" story. He doesn't remember whose story was told; he only remembers a woman in the story asking, "What are you waiting for? Will there ever be a better time to accept Christ?"

In a moment Mary whispered, "Ed, what are *you* waiting for?"

They were too busy praying to hear the rest of the program. Ed was a new creature with a new-found peace of heart and mind. Inside of a year he felt definitely called to the ministry. He enrolled at Bethel College in St. Paul, Minnesota, and served for a couple of years as pastor of a small church in Wisconsin before leaving for foreign missionary service with Mary.

Glen D. Becker of St. Joseph, Michigan, didn't live to hear his story on "Unshackled!" His granddaughter, Jeanette Becker, wrote the Mission after hearing the story of Ben Engstrom dramatized. Her grandfather was dying of cancer, and she desperately wanted to point him to the Saviour. A booklet, "God's Way of Salvation," was sent to her, and a few days later she reported joyously that "my grandfather just received the Lord . . . and now he's working on Grandmother. In two weeks he's a better Christian than I was in a year." Six weeks later Glen Becker went to be with the Lord.

More and more reports come to the Mission that entire families gather about their radios to hear "Unshackled!" Some report spiritual results. One day in Mendota, Illinois, a young mother sobbed out her heart to God in words like these: "I don't understand what the Bible is all about, but if those people on 'Unshackled!' can get new lives, You must have one for me too. Dear God, forgive me for being mean and cross. Art needs a new wife. The babies need a new mother. Save me or change me—or whatever it is You do for me—right now. In Jesus Christ's name." That was how Mrs. Betty Lou Barker joined her husband, Art, in the Christian walk. Today, with their eight children, they regularly attend a Bible preaching church and make it a habit to listen to "Unshackled!"

A report on "Unshackled!" would not be complete without mention of Joe Carlson, the ex-policeman who spent two years in prison for vote fraud. Out of prison, he served for several years as a watchman and then moved to a better job in a chemical testing laboratory. He retired in 1951 and looked back on a pointless, meaningless life. His mind turned to God, and a fragment from the Bible began flickering through his mind: "Seek ye first the kingdom of God, and his righteousness; and all these things shall be added unto you" (Matt. 6:33). But how did one find the Kingdom of God? Joe Carlson had heard "Unshackled!" several times, so he decided to come to the Mission to find the answer to his question. And so it was that Harry Saulnier pointed Joe Carlson, at the age of 75, to the Saviour. Until his death, he often gave his testimony in Mission meetings.

One of the most unusual instances of a man coming to Christ because of "Unshackled!" was that of a man listed in Mission records as J. P—. Curiously enough, he himself did not hear the broadcast. J. P—'s wife was killed in an automobile accident, sending him into an emotional tailspin. For weeks he went on a drown-my-troubles drinking spree and ended up wandering the streets of Chicago for three days and three nights. He deliberated whether he should commit suicide or seek the help of the police in recovering three suitcases and a radio which had been stolen from him by two men who had dropped him off in Chicago.

At a Chicago police station the desk sergeant was listening to "Unshackled!" when the haggard, penniless J. P— entered. Hearing his story, the sergeant consoled, "Buddy, we'll call somebody at the Pacific Garden Mission. I'm sure they'll be able to put you up. Not much we can do about the stolen items but we'll be on the look out."

After a good night's rest at the Mission and a morning shave, J. P—, an industrial engineer and a veteran of World War II as well as of the Korean War, found Jesus Christ as Jack Parkes, then assistant superintendent, counseled him. Because friends of the Mission were faithful in providing good used clothing, the Mission was able to provide J. P— with the necessary clothes. A job was obtained for him in a Chicago hotel.

With "Unshackled!" now beamed to large audiences on six continents, mail averages several hundred pieces a week. Some of the letters bring encouraging news that the original dream of Harry Saulnier and the board members is being fulfilled as the Holy Spirit is tugging at hearts of people in many lands as a result of the broadcast. A Filipino heard "Unshackled!" on station DZAS, Manila. "I have been a liquor addict for ten years," he wrote, "but not since November 1963 when I accidentally listened to the program 'Unshackled!' . . . I totally promise not to drink any single drop of wine, through our Lord Jesus Christ sake [sic]." Letters of counsel went to this man to make sure he had received the new birth.

From South Madras, India, came this comment: "The effect of hearing it stays with me for some time after that program. Every time you close your program with those consoling and soothing words, 'If your life is empty, it can be filled to overflowing,' I want this to happen to me." A follow-up specialist wrote him to help him place his faith in Christ as personal Saviour.

A man who described himself as "a heavy drinker and heavy smoker" in 1963 wrote to the CBMC in Toowoomba, Australia, sponsors of "Unshackled!" on a station there, urging that the program be continued. He said: "Just over twelve months ago it was through a series of these programs that I came to the Lord Jesus Christ. I came to know my sin and that I was in need of a Saviour. Often I suffered from blackouts lasting twenty-four hours or more from excessive drinking. I could find no purpose in life and often my weekly wages were gone in two or three days." This young man was enrolled in a theological college at last report!

Thus, as the late Dr. M. R. De Haan of the Radio Bible Class once put it, "The phenomenal response and acceptance of America's unique radio program, 'Unshackled!' is indeed the work of God. The ministry and outreach of this Lighthouse has been multiplied a thousand times by the open door of radio broadcasting."

Chapter 17

DOCTORING SKID ROW ILLS

IN HIS FIRST YEARS at the Mission Harry Saulnier was well on his way toward earning the title "Doc." While at the Commonwealth Edison Company he had taken a first aid course and had gotten a first aid certificate. So the word got around that the new superintendent had a big bottle of mercurochrome and could bandage a wound with the skill of a medic. As a result, men from the street suffering cuts and bruises incurred in fights or falls came in regularly for repairs.

"In more serious cases we'd stretch them out on one of the tables in the dining hall, bind them up, and send them over to Cook County Hospital," Saulnier recalls.

All of this was better than nothing, but it wasn't good enough. And for that reason the superintendent and the staff prayed for 11 years for professional help.

In 1951 two young medical students from the University of Illinois, Dean Smith and Jack Pollard, strolled into Saulnier's office and announced, "Mr. Saulnier, God has laid it on our hearts to open up a medical clinic here."

"That's an answer to prayer!" Saulnier shot back.

God had been burdening the hearts of members of the Christian Medical Society chapter at the university, they revealed, during the time prayers were going up from the Mission for help in ministering to the aches and pains of Skid Row.

Dr. Dean Smith, now a plastic surgeon in Grand Rapids, Michigan, vividly recalls how God worked out the details of setting up what today is an efficient, modernly-equipped medical clinic serving up to 45 persons a week:

"We were able to generate some enthusiasm among the Christian graduate physicians in the Chicago area who counseled us much. Dr. Gus Hemwall and Dr. John Elsen were some of those who counseled us and guided us. I can remember going with Dr. Hemwall to look over secondhand medical office furniture.

"Another problem was securing the approval of authorities at school. I remember having at least one interview with Dr. Andrew Ivy, then administrative director of the Medical School, and Dr. Stanley Olson, dean. Both of these men were quite warm and friendly and heartily endorsed our activity as long as it was properly supervised.

"As to the beginning of the Clinic itself, it reminded one much of the offering that Israel brought to Moses at the time the Tabernacle was to be built, when the Lord led such as were willing of heart to bring what they had to Him for the Tabernacle. After Mr. Saulnier arranged to have the rooms remodeled for the Clinic use, different members of our Christian Medical Society group contributed things: cabinets, diagnostic equipment, laboratory equipment. Our dental friends from the Dental School even supplied a secondhand dental chair.

"There was no shortage of help. Some of those who helped, besides Jack Pollard, now a radiologist in Boston, were James Peterson, Burton Sutherland, Al Tuftee, Bob Quackenbush, Zerne Chapman, and Del Nelson. When the work was further made known, there were Christian nurses from the various hospitals [members of the Nurses Christian Fellowship] and some nurses who were studying at Moody Bible Institute who came down and helped."

Until 1963 patients trudged up a long stairway to the second floor where the Clinic occupied three relatively small rooms. When the Men's Division and Mission chapel were moved to the old Loyal Hotel building, remodeling began in the original Mission building to provide more Clinic space. Today there's a professional look about the area, consisting of three medical examining rooms, two dental rooms, an X ray room, quarters for records and supplies, and a laboratory containing extra supplies and sterilizing equipment. In addition, there's a private dormitory with four beds where ailing staff personnel may rest. Eventually it will become a hospital ward when and if round-the-clock nursing service is available. Currently, a registered nurse —staff member Audrey Knutson—is on duty from 8:15 A.M. to 5:15 P.M.

Medical practice at the Clinic is confined largely to most dental problems, first aid, and treatment of minor ailments, including cuts, leg ulcers caused by excessive drinking of wine, colds, and stomachaches. Those needing more detailed diagnosis and therapy are referred to the Cook County Hospital or some other medical treatment center of the city's welfare department. War veterans, of course, are sent to a Veterans' Administration hospital if special treatment is needed.

Not only Skid Row cases but also mothers and children from the Women's and Children's Division are treated. They are examined during the early evening hours. Medical treatment is given Monday, Wednesday, and Friday evenings, and dental treatment on Tuesday and Thursday evenings. Christian medical students continue to make up the main part of the staff, though a licensed, qualified physician always in attendance guarantees the Clinic both legal and medical status and guards against errors in diagnosis and treatment. More than a dozen practicing physicians and dentists in the area give of their time, coming one or more times a month.

The evening I visited the Clinic five Northwestern University students and a physician were on duty, along with four nurses. A Moody Bible Institute student was there to counsel patients evidencing spiritual problems.

Some 20 patients, including mothers and children, waited for a nurse to come and call them to an examining room. I chatted with several to determine their reason for being at the Clinic:

A pale, gaunt young man from Detroit couldn't shake a cold. He worked on the waterfront and was one minute in a heated building and the next minute outside in the cold.

A white woman waited with her baby, who had diarrhea. The baby appeared to be about 18 months old and had definite Negroid features. The mother said her husband had been in the State Hospital for the past seven years and she was having a difficult time making ends meet. She had three other children.

A pleasant, heavyset man who said he is a welder had come for examination of a growth on his lip.

A Negro woman had come for treatment of sinusitis.

While ministering to the body, Clinic personnel also minister to the soul. In many cases there's little time to do an adequate counseling job, and for that reason a counselor is always on duty. But numerous times doctors, nurses and students have had opportunity to talk with patients about spiritual problems. Dr. Delbert Nelson of Chicago told of dealing with a man who had once been on the business staff at Harvard University. Nelson saw him a couple of times and talked to him about the sin that had dragged him to Skid Row. A man in his 40's, the patient made a profession of faith, and when Dr. Nelson last talked to him he was planning to return to his family.

Dr. John Elsen of Evanston, Illinois, who has been a sort of big brother to the Clinic personnel since the Clinic's inception, sums up the spiritual opportunities of this important phase of the Mission outreach: "We have had a number of men confess Christ in our Clinic, and there has been a great deal of spiritual growth on the part of many others. Probably the most notable thing that I have found over the years is the sense of companionship and willingness to listen on the part of both nurses and doctors in the Clinic. This is particularly true for men who have difficulty in maintaining their Christian testimony and have slipped off into drinking, etc., at times. This had been one of the most effective ministries in counseling and guiding these men on return. They many times feel more down and out than ever; and while we cannot condone their actions, we can show them that we are vitally concerned about them, even as Christ is."

Chapter 18

KEEPING THE LOWER LIGHTS BURNING

Go out quickly into the streets and lanes of the city, and bring in hither the poor, and the maimed, and the halt, and the blind (Luke 14:21*b*).

WHILE THE COMING of Harry Saulnier over a quarter of a century ago as keeper of the Old Lighthouse resulted in a much broader ministry sending the light to the four corners of the earth, Pacific Garden Mission must still be regarded basically as a Skid Row ministry. This was the original purpose, and it's still number one today despite the many facets of the work. However, some may actually wonder, for to the casual observer Skid Row seems to be vanishing along South State, especially with the addition of parking lots and the new Jones Commercial High School. But a walk along the street shows that it is much the same: the flophouses and honky-tonks are still there along with tattoo parlors, amusement palaces of "fun, art, and movies," theaters featuring nudist shows, and liquor stores where you can buy Five Star brandy at $1.25 a half pint, plus all sorts of other alcoholic beverages.

To complete the picture, pathetic figures still ply the sidewalk between dives, drowning their troubles in cheap wine and cursing the day they were born. But the light of the Mission still flashes through their dark, sin-swept world, calling them to hope, security, and a new life in Jesus Christ.

I talked with various veteran mission workers in direct contact with Skid Row men served by PGM. Some, I learned, are regulars who have been coming to the Old Lighthouse off and on for years. Yet the motto regarding these men is "Never give up on them." For there have been numerous cases of old-timers who finally trusted the Saviour after years of hearing the gospel and blossomed out in newness of life.

Among the old-timers they're praying for at PGM are such colorful characters as "Elmer Eder" who has been in and out of the Mission for more than 20 years. I saw him pass by the Mission door, a long green object in his hand. "He's an inventor," a worker explained. "He's invented a golf ball retriever and has been trying to get backers for it. First it was a rake made of Swedish steel. It looked good even to some of the fellows here, but Elmer insisted on managing the financial matters and that didn't work." A small, wiry man, Elmer, who professes to be saved, nonetheless can fight like a wildcat—except wildcats never hit with coke bottles and flowerpots, as Elmer has been known to do. Ask Joe Kurp, the two-ton night man, an ex-sparring partner of Jack Dempsey, who is glad he learned to duck in his fighting days.

"Bud Thompson," a Tennessean who wouldn't weigh 125 pounds soaking wet, according to Manfred Friedrich, has also been a periodic visitor for years. If he isn't in jail for drunkenness, he'll likely wind up at the Mission. One night in a fit of delirium tremens, he dreamed that he was in hell. Harry Saulnier was the chief. In his dream Thompson pleaded with Chief Saulnier for one more chance. Soon after, police carried him to the hospital to sew up an ugly gash he got in a fall. He got out immediately afterward and slept in an alley that night. Later he returned to the Mission, and each time he comes he is offered "one more chance."

Another old-timer that staff members pray for is "Phil Black," an artist, who "looks like a demon out of hell," as one man put it. His expression is constantly sarcastic, and he is a fighter when ruled by drink. Once he hit burly Manfred Friedrich six times. At one time it appeared Phil had made a stand for the Lord, and he worked in the Mission for a time, using his artistic ability to paint the Western mural on the walls of the Servicemen's Canteen. But soon he slipped back to the old life, falling into a worse state than ever.*

Thus, ministering to the flotsam of Skid Row brings its heartaches, but the happy stories on the other side of the ledger brighten the picture considerably. Day by day the Spirit of God is moving upon the hearts of men, and one by one they come to be made whole at the foot of the cross. In a typical year some 221,000 Skid Row men and women sign in and out of the Mission. Many of these, of course, are repeaters, but it is conservatively estimated the Mission annually proclaims the gospel to 200,000 drifters. In recent years, the harvests of souls among Skid Row people have been especially encouraging: 4368 in 1962, 4346 in 1963, and 3059 in 1964. The Mission has no way of knowing how many of those making professions actually "stick," but the percentage is high enough to keep the lower lights burning brightly.

The annual cost of maintaining the Skid Row ministry is considerable—186,000 dollars. (The total annual budget, including all phases of the PGM work, is 310,000 dollars.) Though the U.S. Government pours some 30 billion dollars each year into its new fight against poverty, the Mission receives no federal or local aid. Scores of churches include the Mission in their budgets, and certain other funds come in from Christian foundations and from legacies. But more than 85 percent of the funds are from individuals in the U.S., Canada, and elsewhere. A few, to be sure, send large gifts regularly, but such gifts are no more appreciated than the dollar or two dollars from a boy or girl, an elderly pensioner, or a shut-in. And scores of gifts come each month from all three groups.

"I am a boy 13 years old, but I am willing to give to Christ

---

*Though Elmer, Bud, and Phil are fictitious names, the men are real and the details true.

for the sake of other people," read one recent letter accompanied by a gift.

Letters from senior citizens often remind staff personnel of the widow whom Christ commended for giving her all: "I am sending a little gift for your wonderful work for the Lord. I am in my ninety-sixth year and am at the Covenant Home."

"I am old and have heart trouble and am not able to work. I get $57 per month Social Security, but I am sending you $5." "I am a widow. My income is $69.30 a month. Seven dollars isn't much but I want to help what I can."

Some of the gifts from the faithful seemingly stand little chance of getting through because of strangely worded addressing, but somehow Chicago postal employees manage to get this mail delivered. From Jamaica, West Indies, came a letter addressed in this fashion: "The City Garden Meschition, Chicago 5, Inonnia, U.S.A." A friend in Alaska, sending an anniversary gift, addressed his letter: "Pacific Guard and Mission, 87th Guard Anniversary, Chicago 5, Ill."

Some of those who write say they can't give but that they are praying. These letters are prized, along with the rest, for Harry Saulnier is constantly urging friends everywhere to pray regularly for the work "to turn back the powers of darkness that press in on us." In Arlington, Washington, four mothers meet every morning on schooldays and remember the Mission. Many shut-ins and elderly people, as well as the young and able-bodied, pray every day for the Old Lighthouse.

Even greater days lie ahead for the Mission, it would appear. With the completion of the section for families and homeless children, the Old Lighthouse will be at peak efficiency. But chances are Harry Saulnier won't let up. He hasn't said much about it, but another project has burdened his heart for years. "I've often wished we could have a farm where we could send the men who are saved, a place where we can work with them so that they will become established in the Lord," Harry told me. "But it's such a big undertaking. We're looking to God to find the place near Chicago and to tell us if and when we should add such a new division."

Keeping the Old Lighthouse in the Big City keeps all the keepers hopping. And it takes a lot of faith along the way.

PACIFIC GARDEN MISSION NEWS

Each month those who stand behind our work receive the NEWS, a sprightly news piece written and published in the finest tradition of present-day journalism. Conversion miracles. Thrilling statistics. Answers to prayer. These and many things more make this publication the very pulse beat of P.G.M.

There is no subcription charge. Those interested receive the NEWS simply by requesting it. A constant flow of letters attests to the blessings received. Send your name and address to the Mission today.

PACIFIC GARDEN MISSION presents

"Miracle on State Street"

A pre-maritally pregnant girl, an old man and a young sailor arrive at the Mission at different times and are saved. The three are reunited as a Christian home in a miraculous way. The dramatic story combines suspense, tears and joy . . . with a remarkable ending. 16mm, 28 minutes, sound and color.

"Out of the Night"

A young business executive lands on Skid Row through alcoholism, finds new life in Christ at the Mission and returns to his wife and establishes a Christian home. 16mm, 28 minutes, sound and color.

"The Street"

A stirring documentary depicting with shocking clarity the drama, despair and ultimate triumph through Christ of Skid Row alcoholics and dope addicts. 16mm, 35 minutes, sound and color.

"Around the Clock at PGM"

This dynamic filmstrip (automatic or hand operated) brings you right into the Old Lighthouse and shows you what goes on here during a typical 24-hour day. 35mm, 18 minutes, color and sound.

(all three films and the filmstrip are available on a rental or free will offering basis)

FACTS YOU SHOULD KNOW . . .
. . . about "UNSHACKLED!" P.G.M.'s Radio Broadcast

- Broadcast weekly on more than 735 stations, including 60 foreign outlets—write the Mission for free station log.
- Half-hour dramatic true life stories of men and women who have been unshackled and are now rejoicing in Christ.
- Does your local station air "UNSHACKLED!"? If not, write for further details!

PACIFIC GARDEN MISSION
646 S. State St., Chicago, IL 60605
(312) 922-1462

DATE DUE

920

Adair, James R

2526

The Old Lighthouse

DATE	ISSUED TO

920

2526

Adair, James R

The Old Lighthouse

First Baptist Church Library

GAYLORD FG

A. Harry Saulnier, present Superintendent, speaks with an inquirer. B. Col. George Clarke, Founder of PGM. C. Harry Monroe, Superintendent 1892-1912. D. Mel Tro[illegible] General Superintendent 1912-1918. E. Billy Sunday, famous evangelist converted at P[illegible] F. Scene from the PGM Dental Clinic. G. Easter service, 1896, with Harry Monroe presiding. H. New Year's Day service, 1966. I. The four buildings of the Pacific Garden Mission.

When I was a child, my dear Aurore, I was tormented by the fact that I wasn't able to hear what flowers said when they talked to each other. My botany professor assured me they said nothing. Whether he was deaf or he didn't want to tell me the truth, he swore they said nothing at all.

I knew he was wrong. I would hear them chattering, especially in the evening when the dew began to form; but they spoke too low for me to make out their words.

Furthermore, they were distrustful, and when I would walk by the flower beds or along the path in the meadow, they would warn each other with a sort of "shhh," which they passed from one to the other. It was as if they said from start to finish, "Watch out, be quiet! Here comes that curious little girl who listens to us."

But I persisted. I practiced walking very quietly without disturbing the smallest blade of grass, so they wouldn't hear me and so I could get very, very close. Then, by bending way down under the shade of the trees so they couldn't see my shadow, I finally heard some words clearly.

I had to pay close attention. The little voices were so soft and low that the least little breeze would carry them away, and the humming of sphinx moths and other night moths would cover their voices completely.

I don't know what language they were speaking. It wasn't my native French or the Latin I was studying at that time. But it so happened that I was able to understand it very well. It even seemed to me I could understand this language better than any I had heard before.

One evening, I managed to lie down on

the sand in a sheltered corner of the border and hear everything that was said near me. Everyone was talking throughout the garden, but I knew I couldn't catch more than one secret at a time. I stayed in the corner very quietly and here is what I heard from the poppies: "Ladies and gentlemen, it is time to be done with these trite remarks. All plants are equally noble; our family bows to no one and anyone who wants to can accept the royalty of the rose. But I proclaim that I've had enough of this and I give no person the right to say he or she is better born or more titled than I."

To this the chrysanthemums answered in unison that the poppy speaker was right. One of them, who was larger and more beautiful than the others, asked to speak and said: "I have never understood the airs the rose family puts on. How, I ask you, is a rose better made or prettier than I am? Nature and art got together to increase the number of our petals and the brilliance of our colors. We are even more opulent in shape, because the most beautiful rose has hardly more than two hundred petals and we have almost five hundred. As far as colors are concerned, we have purple and almost a true blue, something the rose will never have."

"As for me," said a large perennial larkspur, "I am the Prince Delphinium. I have the azure blue of the skies in my corolla and my many relatives have all the shades of pink. So the so-called queen of the flowers has a lot to be envious about and as for her highly praised fragrance . . ."

"Don't get into that!" blustered the poppy. "All that bragging about fragrance gets on my nerves. What, I ask you, is fragrance? A tradition established by gardeners and butterflies. Frankly, I think the rose smells terrible and I'm the one who is fragrant."

"We don't smell at all," said the chrysanthemum, "and that way we show good manners and good taste. Odors are indiscreet and boastful. Any plant who respects herself doesn't announce her arrival with a scent. Her beauty should suffice."

"I don't agree," cried a large, white poppy who gave out a strong smell. "Odors indicate wit and good health."

Laughter drowned out the voice of the big poppy. The carnations held their sides and the mignonettes were convulsed with laughter. But instead of getting angry he started again to criticize the shape and the color of the rose, who couldn't answer. All the rosebushes had just been pruned and the growing sprouts still had only small buds, tightly wrapped in their little, green blankets. A very richly dressed pansy bitterly criticized the many-petaled flowers, and, since the latter were a majority in the flower bed, they all began to get angry. But there was so much jealousy toward roses that they made peace with one another in order to scoff and jeer at *them* again. The pansy was even applauded when she compared a rose to a large, firm, round cabbage, preferring the cabbage because of her size and usefulness. All this foolishness that I was hearing exasperated me and suddenly, speaking their language and kicking those silly flowers, I screamed: "Be quiet! You're all talking nonsense. I expected to hear the wonders of poetry here. What a disappointment for me to hear about your rivalries, your boasting, and your petty jealousy!"

There was a prolonged silence and I left the flower bed.

I'll just go see, I said to myself, if wild flowers have more common sense than those cultivated ninnies, who, receiving their borrowed beauty from us, seem to have also taken on our prejudices and our shortcomings.

I crept along in the shadow of the bushy hedge, heading toward the meadow. I wanted to know if the spirea, who are called queens of the meadow, were also proud and jealous. But I stopped next to a tall wild rosebush, where the flowers were all talking to one another.

"Let's try to find out," I was thinking, "if the wild rose makes fun of the cabbage rose with a hundred petals and scorns the button rose."

I must tell you that, in my day, they hadn't created all the varieties of roses that learned gardeners have since produced by grafting and by developing new seeds. Nature wasn't poorer because of it. Our bushes were filled with numerous varieties of roses that were very hardy: the *canina*, so named because people thought it was a remedy for mad dog bites; the cinnamon rose; the musk rose; the *rubiginosa*, or the rusty rose, which is one of the prettiest; the Scotch rose; the *tomentosa*, or the cottony rose; the alpine rose, and so on. Back then, in our gardens, we had charming species that are almost lost today. There was a red-

and-white variegated rose that didn't have many petals but displayed her crown of stamens in a beautiful bright yellow and smelled like orange blossoms. It was as hardy as could be, fearing neither dry summers nor hard winters. There were also button roses, small and large varieties, which have become especially rare, and the little May rose, the most precocious and perhaps the most fragrant of all, which you cannot find today in the shops. We also had the damask, or French, rose, which we knew how to use and you can only get now in the south of France, and finally the hundred-petal rose, or rather, the cabbage rose. No one knows what country it comes from and people usually attribute its development to cultivation.

The cabbage rose—*centifolia*—was then, for me as well as for everyone, the ideal rose, and I wasn't convinced, as was my tutor, that it was a monster created by horticulturists. I read in my poetry books that the rose was, from the beginning of time, the ideal of beauty and fragrance. Today's tea roses, which don't even smell like roses, were unknown, as were all these charming varieties that change endlessly, and have fundamentally altered the standard of what a true rose should be.

I was studying botany at the time. I studied it in my own way. I had a very acute sense of smell and I expected the fragrance to be one of the essential qualities of the plant. My teacher, who took snuff, would not agree to this criterion of classification. He could no longer smell anything but tobacco, and when he sniffed another plant, it would make him sneeze shamefully. So I listened carefully to what the wild roses were saying over my head, because, from the very first, I could tell they were talking about the origins of the rose.

"Stay here, sweet West Wind," the wild roses were saying. "We have blossomed. The beautiful roses of the flower beds are still sleeping in their green buds. See, we are fresh and cheerful, and if you rock us a little, we will scatter our fragrance, which is as sweet as the fragrance of our famous queen."

Then I heard the West Wind say, "Be quiet, you are only children from the North. I'll stay and chat with you, but don't dare to compare yourselves to the queen of flowers."

"Dear West Wind, we respect and worship her," answered the flowers of the rosebush. "We know how jealous the other garden flowers are of her. They claim she is no better than we are, that she is our daughter and owes her beauty merely to grafting and cultivation. We're not very smart and we don't know how to answer them. Tell us, because you've been around longer than we have on this earth, tell us the true origin of the rose."

"I'll tell you, because it is my story, too. Listen and don't ever forget it."

And the West Wind began his story:

"Back in the times when beings and things of the universe still spoke the language of the gods, I was the eldest son of the King of Storms. My black wings touched the two extremities of the wide horizons. My immense head of hair was tangled in the clouds. My appearance was terrifying and dazzling. I had the power to gather the thick clouds of the setting sun and spread them like an impenetrable veil between the earth and the sun.

"For a long time I reigned with my father and brothers over the barren earth. Our mission was to destroy and disrupt. My brothers and I, unleashed to all four corners of this wretched little world, looked as if we would never allow life to appear on this misshapen cinder that today we call the land of the living. I was the strongest and the most violent of all. When my father, the king, was tired, he would spread above the clouds and give me the job of continuing the relentless destruction. But in the heart of this still, lifeless earth, a spirit was moving, a powerful goddess, the Spirit of Life, who wanted to be born. By crumbling mountains, filling up oceans, and piling up dust, suddenly one day she began to spring up everywhere. We increased our efforts but only managed to hasten the birth of a multitude of beings, who escaped us, either because they were so small or because they were so weak. Lowly little flexible plants, tiny floating shellfish, would find places for themselves in the still, warm surface of the earth's crust, in the silt, in the waters, in all kinds of debris. In vain, we would madly flood these upstart creations. Life constantly came into being and appeared in new forms, as if a patient and inventive genie of creation had decided to adapt the organs and the needs of all of these beings to the tormented environment we made for them.

"We began to tire of their resistance, which appeared to be passive but in reality was invincible. We destroyed entire races of living beings—others would appear, organized to withstand us without being killed. We were exhausted with rage. We retreated above the cloud cover to deliberate and ask our father for new strength.

"While he was giving us instructions, the earth, delivered for an instant from our fury, became covered with innumerable plants where myriads of animals, cleverly adapted within our different species, found shelter and food in huge forests or on the sides of mighty mountains, as well as in the purified waters of immense lakes.

"'Go,' said my father, the King of Storms, 'Here is the earth who has adorned herself like a bride to marry the sun. Put yourselves between them. Pile up enormous thunderheads, roar, and may your breath flatten the forests, level the mountains, and unleash the seas. Go and don't come back as long as there is a living being or a plant standing on this cursed arena where life wants to establish itself in spite of us.'

"We scattered like seeds of death over the two hemispheres. Like an eagle, I tore through the curtain of clouds and swept down on the ancient countries of the Far East. There deep valleys slope toward the ocean from the high Asiatic plateaus under a fiery sky and, bathed in a swamp of humidity, give birth to gigantic plants and fearsome animals. I had rested from my earlier tiredness, I felt endowed with an incomparable strength, and I was proud to bring disorder and death to all these weaklings trying to defy me. With one flap of a wing, I flattened an entire country; with one puff, I knocked down a whole forest, and I felt within me a blind, drunken joy, the joy of being stronger than all the forces of nature.

"Suddenly a perfume entered me as if I had inhaled something foreign into my body, and surprised by this new experience, I stopped to gather my senses. Then, for the first time, I saw a being who had appeared on the earth while I was gone, a new, delicate, almost imperceptible being—the rose!

"I swooped down to crush her. She bent over, lay down on the grass and said, 'Have pity on me! I am so beautiful and sweet! Sniff me and you will spare me.'

"I sniffed her and a sudden exhilaration overcame my fury. I lay down on the grass and fell asleep beside her.

"When I woke up, the rose had stood up again and was swaying softly, rocked by my now calmed breath.

"'Be my friend,' she said. 'Don't leave me again. When your terrible wings are folded, I love you, and I think you are beautiful. No doubt you are the King of the Forest. Your softened breath is a delicious song. Stay with me and take me with you, so I can go see the sun and the clouds close up.'

"I took the rose to my breast and flew away with her. But soon it seemed to me she was wilting. Listless, she could no longer talk to me; her fragrance, however, continued to enchant me. Afraid that I would destroy her, I flew quite slowly. I gently brushed the treetops, avoiding the least little bump. I climbed cautiously to the palace of dark clouds where my father was waiting for me.

"'What are you doing?' he said. 'And why is that forest I see on the shores of India still standing? Return immediately and wipe it out.'

"'Yes,' I answered, showing him the rose, 'but

let me entrust to you this treasure I want to save.'

"'Save!' he cried, roaring in anger. 'You want to save something?'

"And with one breath, he tore the rose from my hand and she disappeared into space, scattering her wilted petals.

"I lunged to try to capture at least a remnant; but the king, irritated and implacable, seized me in turn, turned me over his lap and violently tore off my wings. My feathers went flying into space to join the scattered petals of the rose.

"'You wretched child,' he told me, 'you felt pity! You are no longer my son. Go back to earth and join up with that disastrous Spirit of Life that defies me. We'll see if she can make anything of you, because now, thanks to me, you are nothing.'

"And throwing me into the pit of emptiness he forgot me forever.

"I tumbled as far as a clearing and lay exhausted beside the rose, who was happier and more fragrant than ever.

"What is this miracle? I thought you were dead and I cried for you. Do you have the gift of life after death?

"'Yes,' she answered, 'like all creatures whom

the Spirit of Life enriches. Look at these buds that surround me. This evening I will have lost my brilliance and I will work to renew myself, while my sisters charm you with their beauty and pour their perfumes over you in their day of celebration. Stay with us. Aren't you our companion and our friend?'

"I was so humiliated by my dethronement, that with my tears I watered the earth, to which I felt bound forever. The Spirit of Life felt my tears and was moved by them. She appeared to me in the form of a radiant angel and said, 'You felt pity, you pitied the rose. I want to have pity on you. Your father is powerful, but I am more powerful than he is. He can destroy, but it is I who create.'

"While she was saying this, the shining being touched me, and my body became like that of a beautiful child with a face the color of a rose. Butterfly wings sprouted from my shoulders and I started to flutter about with sheer delight.

"'Stay with the flowers, in the cool shelter of the forests,' said the goddess. 'For now, these canopies of greenery will hide and protect you. Later, when I have conquered the rage of the elements, you will be able to travel the earth, where you will be blessed by the people and celebrated by poets.'

"'As for you, charming rose, the first to be able to disarm anger with beauty, you are to be the symbol of the future reconciliation of forces that are enemies of nature. You will also be the educator of future races, because those civilized races will want to make everything serve their own needs. My most precious gifts—grace, gentleness, and beauty—will be in danger of seeming to have less value than money and power. Teach them, kind rose, that the greatest and most legitimate power is that which charms and reconciles. Now I give you the title that future generations will not dare take away from you. I proclaim you Queen of the Flowers. The ranks that I establish are divine and have only one means of expression—charm.'

"Since that day, I have lived in peace with the heavens, loved by people, animals, and plants. My free and divine beginnings allow me the choice of living where I please, but I am too much a friend of the earth and servant of the life that my beneficial breezes sustain, to leave this dear earth where my first and eternal love keeps me. Yes, my dear little ones, I am the rose's faithful lover and consequently your brother and your friend."

"In that case," cried all the little roses on the wild rosebush, "take us dancing and celebrate with us, singing praises to the queen, the hundred-petaled rose of the East."

The West Wind fluttered his pretty wings, and over my head there was a joyful dance, accompanied by the beating branches and clicking leaves acting as kettle drums and castanets. A few of the happy little ones tore their ball gowns and strewed their petals in my hair, but they didn't notice. They danced very beautifully and as they sang, "Long live the beautiful rose whose sweetness conquered the son of thunderstorms! Long live the good West Wind who remained a friend to the flowers!"

When I told my tutor what I had heard, he announced that I was sick and should be given medication. But my grandmother saved me from that by telling him, "I feel sorry for you if you have never heard what roses say. As for me, I miss the days when I was able to hear them. It's a talent that children have. Be careful not to confuse talent with illness."

The Bug-Eyed Fairy

Elsie had a very peculiar Irish governess. She was the nicest person in the world, but there were certain animals she found so unpleasant that she would fly into veritable fits of rage against them. If a bat entered her quarters in the evening, she would scream without apparent reason and become indignant toward anyone who would not chase after the poor creature. Since a lot of people are repulsed by bats, no one would have noticed her hostility toward them, except that she felt the same way about lovely birds: warblers, robins, swallows, and other insectivores, not to mention nightingales, which she called cruel beasts. Her name was Miss Barbara—but they called her "Bug-Eyed Fairy"—"Fairy" because she was very learned and very mysterious, and "Bug-Eyed" because she had huge, clear, bulging round eyes, which mischievous Elise compared to glass bottle stoppers.

However, Elsie didn't hate her governess, who was the epitome of indulgence and patience with Elsie. She just liked to make fun of Miss Barbara's peculiarities and especially her pretense of seeing better than everyone else, even though she could have won first prize for nearsightedness in a military medical contest. She didn't even know she was near an object unless she touched it with her nose, which, unfortunately, was extremely short.

One day when Miss Barbara had bumped her head on a half-opened door, Elsie's mother said, "Really, one of these days you're going to hurt yourself badly! I'm telling you, my dear Barbara, you should wear glasses."

Miss Barbara answered sharply, "Me? Glasses? Never! I'm afraid they'd spoil my vision!"

When they tried to make her understand that her vision couldn't get any worse, she protested, with an air of triumphant conviction, that she wouldn't trade "the treasures of her vision" with anybody. She saw the tiniest little objects the way others saw them through the strongest magnifying glasses; her eyes were two microscope lenses continually revealing marvels that no one else could see. The fact is, she could count the threads of the finest cloth and the stitches of the most delicate fabrics, while Elsie, who had so-called good eyes, saw absolutely nothing.

For a long time, they called her Mademoiselle Grenouille (Miss Frog), and then they called her Mademoiselle Hanneton (Miss Maybug), because she banged into things everywhere. Finally, the name Bug-Eyed Fairy prevailed because she was too well educated and too intelligent to be compared to an animal, and also because everyone, seeing the eyelet and the other marvelous embroidery that she knew how to do, would say, "She's a true fairy!"

Miss Barbara wasn't indifferent to this compliment, and she usually would reply, "Who knows? Maybe! Maybe!"

One day, Elsie asked her if she was serious when she said that, and Miss Barbara cleverly repeated, "Maybe, my dear child, maybe!"

That was all that was needed to arouse Elsie's curiosity. She no longer believed in fairies, for she was twelve years old. But she regretted not believing anymore, and you wouldn't have had to ask her twice for her to believe again.

The fact is, Miss Barbara had some strange habits. She hardly ate anything and hardly ever slept. They weren't even sure that she did sleep, because no one had ever seen her bed unmade. She said that she remade it herself each day, early in the morning when she woke up, because she could only sleep in a bed that was made to her liking. In the evening, as soon as Elsie left the parlor with her maid, who slept next to her, Miss Barbara would eagerly retire to the summerhouse that she had requested for her living quarters, and it was said you could see a light burning there until daybreak. It was even claimed that, at night, she would walk with a little lantern, talking out loud to invisible beings.

Elsie's maid talked about Miss Barbara's activities so much that, one fine evening, Elsie felt an irresistible desire to see them for herself, to discover the mysteries of the cottage. But how would she dare go to such a place at night? She would have to walk at least two hundred feet through a clump of lilacs over which a large cedar grew, and under this dual shadow, follow a narrow, winding path that was dark, dark, dark!

"Never," thought Elsie. "I'll never have the courage to do it."

The servants' silly gossip had frightened her, and she didn't chance it. But the next day she did risk asking Miss Barbara about what she did during her long evenings.

"I stay busy," the Bug-Eyed Fairy answered gently. "My whole day is dedicated to you; the evening belongs to me. I use it to work for my own betterment."

"So, you don't know everything, since you still study?"

"The more you study, the better you can see that you still know nothing."

"But what do you study so much? Latin? Greek?"

"I know Latin and Greek. I'm busy with other things."

"What? Don't you want to tell?"

"I look at things that only I can see."

"What do you see?"

"Please don't ask me to tell you; you'd want to see it too, and you wouldn't be able to or you'd see it poorly, which would be a disappointment to you."

"Is what you see very beautiful?"

"More beautiful than everything you have seen or will ever see in your dreams."

"Dear Miss Barbara, show it to me, I beg you!"

"No, my child, never! It's not up to me."

"Well, I will too see it!" shouted Elsie, becoming quite distraught. "I'll come to your house at night and you won't turn me out."

"I don't think you're likely to come. You would never dare come!"

"You mean I'll need courage to come to your nighttime ceremonies?"

"You'll need patience, and you have absolutely none."

This angered Elsie and she changed the subject. Later she returned to her argument and pestered the governess so much that Miss Barbara promised to take her to her summerhouse that evening, but she warned Elsie she would see nothing or would understand nothing that she might see. See! See something new, unknown! What curiosity, what excitement for an inquisitive little girl! Elsie didn't feel like eating her dinner. She bounced around on her chair uncontrollably, she counted the hours, the minutes. Finally, after the evening's occupations, she got permission from her mother to go to the summerhouse with her governess.

They were barely into the garden when they met someone who appeared to make Miss Barbara very nervous. It was only Mr. Bat, Elsie's brothers' tutor, a very inoffensive-looking man. He wasn't handsome: he was thin, with a pointy nose and ears, and always dressed from head to toe in black. He wore coats with tails, very pointy also. He was shy, even timid; after lessons, he would disappear as if he needed to hide. He never spoke at the table, and in the evening, while waiting to supervise the children's bedtime, he would walk in circles around the terrace in the garden, which was harmless but appeared to be an indication of a shallow mentality, given to foolish idleness. Miss Barbara didn't think of him that way. She was terrified of Mr. Bat, first of all because of his name. She claimed that when a person had the misfortune to have such a name, he should leave the country and take another name. She had all sorts of prejudices against him. She held it against him that he had a good appetite, and she thought he was gluttonous and cruel. She contended that his strange circular walks were an indication of the most harmful inclinations and concealed the most sinister intentions.

Therefore, when she saw him on the terrace, she shuddered. Elsie, who was clinging to Miss Barbara's arm, felt it tremble. What was so astonishing about the fact that Mr. Bat, who loved the fresh air, was outside until his pupils' bedtime? They went to bed later than Elsie, the youngest of the three. Miss Barbara was nonetheless shocked by this behavior, and walking past him, she couldn't keep from saying dryly, "Do you plan to stay out here all night?"

Mr. Bat started to run away, but, afraid of being impolite, he tried to answer with a question.

"Does my presence bother anyone, and do they want me to go back in?"

"I have no orders to give you," continued Miss Barbara sharply, "but I'm inclined to believe you'd be better off in the parlor with the family."

"I'm uncomfortable in the parlor," the tutor answered modestly. "My poor eyes suffer terribly from the heat and the bright light of the lamps."

"Oh! Your eyes can't stand the light? I knew it! Twilight is the most light your eyes need? Would you like to be able to fly in circles all night long?"

"Of course!" answered the tutor, trying to laugh and be pleasant. "I'm 'batty,' aren't I?"

"It's nothing to brag about!" cried Miss Barbara, trembling with anger.

And she dragged Elsie, dumbfounded, into the dark shadows of the little pathway.

"His eyes, his poor eyes!" repeated Miss Barbara, with a convulsive shrug of her shoulders. "I can't feel sorry for you, you savage beast!"

"You're very hard on that poor man," said Elsie. "His eyes really are so sensitive that he can no longer see in the light."

"No doubt, no doubt! But how he makes

up for it in the darkness! He's hemeralopic, and what's more, he's presbyopic."

Elsie didn't understand these epithets, which she supposed were degrading, and didn't dare ask for an explanation. She was still in the shadowy pathway, which she didn't like one bit, but she finally saw the tree-covered walk open in front of her. The summerhouse was appearing beyond it, whitened by the light of the rising moon, when suddenly she drew back, forcing Miss Barbara to draw back too.

"What is it?" asked the lady with the big eyes, who saw nothing at all.

"It's . . . it's nothing," answered Elsie, embarrassed. "I saw the dark form of a man in front of us, and now I can make out Mr. Bat crossing by the door to your summerhouse. He's walking in your flower border."

"Ah!" cried Miss Barbara indignantly. "I should have expected it. He follows me, he spies on me, he's trying to ruin my life. But don't be afraid, dear Elsie, I'll give him what he deserves."

Miss Barbara rushed forward.

"Aha! Sir," she said, talking to a large tree against which the moon cast strange shadows.

"When will you stop pestering me with your harassments?"

She was going to scold him properly, when Elsie interrupted her and led her toward the door to the summerhouse, saying, "Dear Miss Barbara, you're mistaken. You think you're talking to Mr. Bat but you're talking to your shadow. Mr. Bat is already gone. I don't see him anymore and I don't think he was trying to follow us."

"Frankly, I don't agree with you," answered the governess. "How can you explain the fact that he arrived ahead of us, since we left him behind, and we neither saw nor heard him pass by us?"

"He could have walked through the flower beds," answered Elsie. "It's the shortest way and it's the way I often go when the gardener isn't looking."

"No, no!" said Miss Barbara distressfully, "he went over the trees. Look, you can see far, look over your head! I bet he's lurking in front of my windows!"

Elsie looked and saw only the sky, but, after a minute, she saw the moving shadow of a huge bat pass back and forth on the cottage walls. She didn't want to say anything to Miss Barbara, whose obsessions were making Elsie impatient because they were keeping her from satisfying her curiosity. Elsie urged her to go into the summerhouse, saying that there were neither bats nor tutors spying on them.

"Besides," she added, entering the little parlor on the first floor, "if you're worried, we could close the windows and curtains very tightly."

"Now *that* is impossible!" answered Miss Barbara. "I'm giving a ball and my guests must come through the window."

"A ball!" cried Elsie, dumbfounded. "A ball in this little cottage? Guests who enter through the window? You're making fun of me, Miss Barbara."

"It's a ball, I say. A grand ball," answered Miss Barbara, lighting a lamp, which she placed on the windowsill. "Magnificent costumes, unbelievable luxury!"

"If that's true," said Elsie, shaken by her governess's confidence, "I can't stay here in this old dress I have on. You should have warned me. I would have put on my pink dress and my pearl necklace."

"Oh! My dear girl," answered Miss Barbara, placing a basket of flowers next to the lamp. "It would do you no good to cover yourself in gold and jewels—you could never compare with my guests."

Elsie, a little mortified, said nothing. Miss Barbara put some water and honey in a saucer and said, "I'm preparing the refreshments."

Then, suddenly, she cried out, "Here's one now! It's the princess moth, the *Nepticula marinicollella*, in her black velvet tunic crossed with a large band of gold. Her dress is of black lace with a long fringe. Let's present her with an elm leaf; it's the palace of her ancestors where she was born. Wait! Give me that leaf from the apple tree for her first cousin, the beautiful *Malella*, whose black dress has silver stripes and a skirt fringed in pearly white. Give me some flowering broom, to brighten the eyes of my dear *Cemiostoma spartifoliella*, who is approaching in her white gown with black and gold accents. Here are some roses for you, Marquise *Nepticula centifoliella*. Just look, dear Elsie! Look at this dark red tunic, trimmed in silver. And these two illustrious blue moth *Lavernides*: *lineela*, who is wearing an orange scarf embroidered in gold over her dress, while *schranckella* has an orange scarf striped with silver. What taste, what harmony in these gaudy colors, softened by the velvety fabrics, the transparency of the silky fringes, and the delightful patterns! The *Adelida panzerella* is wrapped in gold, embroidered with black; her skirt is in lilac with gold fringe. Finally, here's the pyralid moth *rosella*, one of the most simply dressed, who has an overdress of bright pink tinted with white on the borders. What a pleasant effect the underdress of light brown has! She has only one fault, which is that she's a little too tall. But here's a group of really exquisite little creatures. These are the Tineidae, or clothes moths, some dressed in brown and studded with diamonds, others in white with pearls on gauze. *Dispunctella* has ten drops of gold on her silver dress. Here are some important people of rather imposing size—the Adelidae family with their antennae twenty times longer than their bodies. Their clothes are green-gold with red or violet highlights, which remind you of the necklaces of the most beautiful hummingbirds.

"And now, look! Look at the crowd pushing to get in! There are more and still more coming! Elsie, you won't know which one of these queens of the evening to admire the most for the splendor and the exquisite taste of her attire. The tiniest details of the bodice, the antennae, and feet are unbelievably delicate, and I don't think you have ever seen such perfect creatures anywhere. Now, notice the grace of the movements, the crazy and charming haste in flight, the flexibility of their antennae, with which they talk to each other, the gentleness of their bearing. Elsie, isn't it an incredible celebration, and aren't all other creatures ugly, freakish, and sorry-looking in comparison?"

"I'll say anything to make you happy," answered a disappointed Elsie, "but to tell the truth, I see nothing, or practically nothing of what you're describing so enthusiastically. I can see little microscopic butterflies flying around those flowers and the lamp, but I can hardly make out bright specks and dark specks, and I'm afraid you're drawing on your imagination for the brilliance you like to dress them in."

"She doesn't see! She can't make them out!" the Bug-Eyed Fairy cried unhappily. "Poor little thing! I knew it! I warned you that your disability would keep you from seeing the joys I relish. Fortunately, I know how to compensate for your weak vision. Here is an instrument that I, myself, never use, which I borrowed from your parents for you. Take it and look."

She gave Elsie a very strong magnifying glass, which caused Elsie some difficulty, since she had never used one. Finally, after a few tries, she succeeded in making out the real and surprising beauty of one of the little creatures. She focused on another and saw that Miss Barbara has not misled her: gold, purple, amethyst, garnet, orange, pearl, and pink combined to form symmetrical adornments on the coats and dresses of these almost imperceptible dignitaries. She innocently asked why so much richness and beauty were lavished on creatures who lived only a few days at the most and who flew at night, barely visible to humans.

"There it is!" answered the Bug-Eyed Fairy, laughing. "Always the same question! My dear Elsie, grown-ups ask the same question, which means they don't have any better idea of the laws of the universe than children. They believe everything was created for them and what they don't see or don't understand shouldn't exist. But I, the Bug-Eyed Fairy, as they call me, know that what is simply beautiful is as important as what is useful to people, and I rejoice when I contemplate marvelous things or creatures that no one dreams of making use of. There are thousands and thousands of millions of my dear little moths spread over the earth. They live modestly with their families on little leaves, and no one has yet thought of harassing them."

"That's true," said Elsie. "But birds, warblers, and nightingales eat them, not to mention bats!"

"Bats! Oh! You just reminded me! The light that attracts my poor little friends and allows me to study them also attracts bats—horrible beasts who prowl around all night long, mouths open, swallowing everything they run into. Come, the ball is over, let's put out the lamp. I'll light my lantern, since the moon has set, and I'll take you back to the house."

As they walked down the front steps of the summerhouse, Miss Barbara added, "I warned you, Elsie. You have been disappointed in your expectations, you only imperfectly saw my little night fairies and their fantastic dance around my flowers. With a magnifying glass you can only see one object at a time, and when the object is alive, you only see it at rest. But I see my whole, dear little world at once; none of its elegance and extravagance escapes me. I showed you very little of it today. It was too cool this evening and the wind wasn't coming from the right direction. On stormy nights, I see thousands of millions take refuge in my home, or I pay them a surprise visit in their shelters of foliage or flowers. I have told you the names of a few of them, but there are vast numbers of others, which, depending on the season, are born to a short existence of ecstasy, finery, and celebration. We don't know all of them, even though some very patient and knowledgeable people study them carefully and have published huge volumes where they are wonderfully portrayed—and enlarged for people with weak eyes. But these books are incomplete, and every gifted and well-intentioned person can add to the scientific catalog through new discoveries and observations. As for me, I've found a large number that have not yet had their names or their pictures published, and I'm trying hard to make up for the ingratitude and disdain that science has shown them. It is true they are so very, very small, that few people bother to look at them."

"Are there any smaller than the ones you

have shown me?" asked Elsie, who, seeing that Miss Barbara had stopped on the steps, leaned on the handrail.

Even though Elsie had stayed up later than usual, she hadn't had quite the surprise and good time that she had expected, and she had begun to feel sleepy.

"There are infinitely small beings, which should not be treated disrespectfully," replied Miss Barbara, who didn't notice her pupil's sleepiness. "There are some that can't be seen by humans even when they are enlarged as much as possible by instruments. At least that is what I presume and believe, and I see more than most people can see. Who can say at what size, visible to us, the life of the universe stops? Who can prove that fleas don't have fleas, which in turn nurture fleas which nurture others, and so on into infinity? As far as moths are concerned, since the smallest we can perceive are unquestionably more beautiful than the large ones, there is no reason a throng of others doesn't exist, still more beautiful and smaller, which scientists would never suspect."

Miss Barbara got this far in her argument without realizing that Elsie, who had slipped down to the steps of the summerhouse, was sound asleep. Suddenly an unexpected bump knocked the little lantern from the governess's hands, making it fall into Elsie's lap. She woke with a start.

"A bat! A bat!" cried Miss Barbara, beside herself as she tried to gather up the smashed, extinguished lantern.

Elsie jumped up, not knowing where she was.

"There! There!" screamed Miss Barbara. "On your skirt. The horrible beast fell too, I saw it fall, it's on you!"

Elsie wasn't afraid of bats, but she knew that a slight impact can make them dizzy, and they have sharp little teeth to bite you if you try to touch them. Noticing a black spot on her dress, she grabbed it with her handkerchief, saying, "I've got it. Calm down, Miss Barbara, I've got it all right."

"Kill it! Smother it, Elsie! Squeeze very hard and smother that horrible spirit, that miserable tutor who's plaguing me!"

Elsie didn't understand her governess's hysteria. She didn't like to kill, and she thought bats very useful, since they destroy a multitude of mosquitoes and harmful insects. She shook her handkerchief instinctively to let the poor animal escape—but what a surprise, and how frightened she was, to see Mr. Bat escape from the handkerchief and rush at Miss Barbara, as if he wanted to devour her!

Elsie fled across the flower beds, chased by an insurmountable terror. But, after a few minutes, she had second thoughts and went back to help her unfortunate governess. Miss Barbara had disappeared and the bat was flying in circles around the summerhouse.

"My goodness!" cried Elsie hopelessly, "that cruel beast has swallowed my poor fairy! Oh! If only I'd known, I'd have saved her life."

The bat disappeared and Mr. Bat appeared in front of Elsie.

"My dear child," he said to her, "it is all well and good to save the lives of the poor persecuted people. Don't regret a good deed. Miss Barbara is quite all right. Hearing her cry out, I ran over here, thinking one or the other of you was in grave danger. Your governess took refuge in the house and barricaded the door, while showering me with abuse I don't deserve. Since she abandoned you to what she considers great danger, would you like me to take you to your maid, if you won't be afraid of me?"

"Really, I've never been afraid of you, Mr. Bat," answered Elsie. "You're not wicked, but you are very peculiar."

"Me? Peculiar? Who would make you think I have any kind of peculiarity?"

"But . . . I held you in my handkerchief a minute ago, Mr. Bat, and let me tell you that you risk your life too easily, because, if I had listened to Miss Barbara, it would have been the end of you!"

"Dear Miss Elsie," answered the tutor, laughing, "I now understand what happened, and I bless you for having saved me from the hatred of that poor fairy, who isn't wicked either, but who is very much more peculiar than I am!"

After Elsie had had a good night's sleep, she thought it very unlikely that Mr. Bat had the power to change from man to beast at will. At lunch, she noticed that he gobbled down rare slices of beef with sheer delight, while Miss Barbara had only some tea. She decided the tutor wasn't the type to treat himself to microscopic insects, and that the governess's diet was likely to cause hallucinations.

The
Talking
Oak

Once upon a time in the forest of Cernas, in central France, there was a big, old oak tree, which could very well have been five hundred years old. Lightning had struck it several times, and it had had to grow a new crown, a little flattened, but thick and green. This oak tree had had a bad reputation for a long time. The oldest people in the neighboring village were still saying that in their youth this oak would talk—and would threaten those who wanted to rest in its shade. They told the story of two travelers who had been struck by lightning when they were looking for shelter. One of them had died immediately; the other had escaped in time and was only stunned because he had been warned by a voice that had cried out to him, "Get away, quickly!"

The story was so old that people hardly believed it anymore, and even though the tree still bore the name "Talking Oak," young shepherds would come near it quite fearlessly. After Emmi's adventure, however, it developed a reputation of being bewitched more than ever.

Emmi was a poor little swineherd, orphaned and very unhappy, partly because he was poorly housed, poorly fed, and poorly dressed, but even more because he hated the pigs that poverty forced him to care for. He was afraid of them, and the pigs, who are more shrewd than they seem, could sense that he wasn't in control. He went out in the morning, leading them in search of acorns in the forest. In the evening he would bring them back to the farm. How pitiful it was to see him, covered in dirty rags, his head bare, his hair standing on end from the wind, his poor little face pale, thin, dirty, sad, afraid, and suffering, chasing his herd of squealing beasts, who looked at him with sidelong glances, heads lowered and always threatening. To see him run after them on the dark moors, in the red mist of early dusk, you would have thought of a marsh fire chased by a gust of wind.

This poor little swineherd could have been lovable and good-looking, however, if he had been cared for, clean, and happy like you, my dear children, who are reading my story. But he didn't even know how to read; he knew nothing, and he could barely speak to ask for what he needed. Since he was timid, he didn't always do that. Whose fault was it if everyone forgot him?

One evening the pigs returned to the barn by themselves, and the swineherd did not appear at suppertime. His absence was noticed only after the turnip soup had been eaten, and the farmer's wife sent one of the boys to call him. The boy came back to say that Emmi was neither in the barn nor in the loft, where he slept in the hay. They thought he had gone to see his aunt, who lived nearby, and they went to bed without giving him another thought.

The next morning, they went to his aunt's house, and were surprised to learn Emmi had not spent the night with her. He hadn't appeared in the village since the night before. They inquired about him in the neighborhood; no one had seen him. They looked in vain in the forest. They thought the wild boars and the wolves had eaten him. However, they found neither his weeding hoe—a kind of forked prod with a short handle that swineherds use—nor a single rag of his poor clothes; they decided he had left the neighborhood to live the life of a wanderer. The farmer said it was no great loss; the child was good for nothing, didn't like his pigs, and didn't know how to make them like him.

A new swineherd was hired for the rest of the year, but Emmi's disappearance frightened all the boys in the neighborhood. The last time Emmi had been seen, he had been near the Talking Oak, and that was probably where something bad had happened to him. The new swineherd took care never to lead his herd over there, and the other children were wary of playing near it.

You ask me what became of Emmi? Patience, I am going to tell you.

The last time he had gone into the forest with his animals, he had noticed a clump of wild sweet peas in bloom a short distance from the big oak tree. The wild sweet pea, or tuberous groundnut, is that pretty papilionaceous plant you have seen that has butterfly-shaped flowers in pink clusters. The tubers are as big as hazelnuts, a little bitter even though they are sweet. Poor children are fond of them; it is a food that costs nothing. But only pigs, who like them too, think of fighting for them. When people talk about the ancient hermits living on roots, you can be sure that the most sought-after food in their austere diet, here in central France, was the tuber of this pea vine.

Emmi knew very well that the groundnuts could not yet be good to eat, because it was only the beginning of autumn, but he wanted to mark the spot so he could come and dig in the dirt when the stalks and the flowers were dry. He was followed by a young pig who began to dig; he was threatening to uproot everything, when Emmi, annoyed to see the wanton destruction of the gluttonous beast, smacked him a good one on the snout with his hoe. The iron on the hoe was newly sharpened and cut the pig's nose slightly, and the pig let out a cry of alarm. You know how animals stand by each other, and how certain distress calls put them all in a rage against a common enemy. Besides, the pigs had had a grudge against Emmi for a long time because he never lavished flattery or compliments on them. They got together, each trying to squeal louder than the other, and surrounded him, trying to eat him. The poor child ran for his life, but they followed him. These beasts, you know, can run frightfully fast; he barely had time to reach the big oak tree, scramble up its gnarled trunk, and hide in its branches. The savage herd stayed at the foot of the tree, squealing, threatening, trying to uproot it. But the Talking Oak had tremendous roots that could hardly take a herd of pigs seriously. The attackers, however, didn't give up trying until after the sun set. Then they decided to go back to the farm, and little Emmi, certain they would eat him if he went with them, decided never to return.

He was well aware that the oak was considered a bewitched tree, but he had been the victim of real, living people too often to be very much afraid of spirits. All his life he had known only poverty and beatings. His aunt was very hard on him: she forced him to guard the farmer's pigs, though he had always been afraid of them. When he went to see her, begging her to take him back, she greeted him, as they say, with a good beating. So, he was really afraid of her, and his only desire was to become a shepherd on another farm where the people might be less stingy and not so mean to him.

During the first few minutes after the pigs left, Emmi was just happy to be rid of their fierce squealing and threats, and he decided to spend the night where he was. He still had some bread in his unbleached cloth sack, because during the siege he had endured, he hadn't wanted to eat. He ate half of the bread and saved the rest for his next meal; after that, he would have to trust in the grace of God!

Children can sleep anywhere. However, Emmi hardly slept at all. He was sickly, often feverish, and would dream rather than rest his mind while he slept. He settled in as best he could between two main branches that were covered with moss, and he really wanted to sleep, but the wind, which was making the leaves moan and the branches creak, frightened him. He began to think about evil spirits, so much so that he thought he heard a shrill, angry voice say several times, "Go away, get away from here!"

At first Emmi, shaking with fear and with a lump in his throat, couldn't think of answering. But, as the wind died down, the voice of the oak softened and seemed to whisper in his ear in a motherly and affectionate tone, "Go away, Emmi, go away!" Emmi felt brave enough to answer, "Oak tree, my beautiful oak, don't send me away. If I climb down, the wolves who are out at night will eat me."

"Go, Emmi, go!" said the voice even more softly.

"My good Talking Oak tree," Emmi said again in a beseeching voice, "don't send me to the wolves. You saved me from the pigs, you were kind to me, be kind again. I am a poor unhappy child, and I could not, would not, hurt you. Let me stay tonight; if you ask me, I will go away tomorrow morning."

The voice didn't answer, and the moon gave

a silvery sheen to the leaves. Emmi concluded that he would be allowed to stay, or that he had dreamed the words he thought he heard. He fell asleep, and, strangely, he had no more dreams and didn't wake up until daybreak. He then climbed down and shook off the dew, which had soaked his poor clothes.

"I must return to my village," he said to himself. "I'll tell my aunt that my pigs tried to eat me, that I had to spend the night in a tree, and she will let me find another kind of work."

He ate the rest of his bread, but when he started back home, he wanted to thank the oak tree who had protected him during the day and through the night.

"Goodbye and thank you, my good oak tree," he said, kissing the bark. "I will no longer be afraid of you, and I will return to thank you again."

He crossed the moor and was heading toward his aunt's cottage, when he heard voices from behind the farm's garden wall.

"To top it off," one of the boys was saying, "our swineherd hasn't come back. He hasn't been seen at his aunt's, and he's abandoned his herd.

He's heartless and lazy and I'm going to give him a good kicking with my hard wooden shoe, to punish him for making me lead his animals to the fields today in his place."

"What difference does it make to you, if you have to take the pigs?" asked the other boy.

"It's a disgrace at my age," said the first boy. "It's well enough for a ten-year-old, like little Emmi, but when you're twelve, you're entitled to watch the cows, or at the very least, the calves."

The two boys were interrupted by their father.

"Let's get going," he said. "Get to work! As for that wretched swineherd, if the wolves ate him, too bad—but if I find him alive, I'll tan his hide. It won't do him any good to go crying to his aunt. She's decided to make him sleep with the pigs to teach him not to put on airs and turn up his nose."

Emmi, terrified by this threat, considered himself warned. He hid in a stack of wheat, where he spent the day. Toward evening, a goat returning to the barn lingered to nibble on some grass and let Emmi milk her. When he had filled and drunk from his wooden bowl two or three times, he buried himself deeper into the bundles of grain until nightfall. When it was completely dark and everyone was in bed, he slipped up to his loft and took a few things that belonged to him: some coins he had earned that the farmer had given him the day before and his aunt hadn't yet had time to snatch from him, a goat skin and a sheep skin he used in the winter, a new knife, a little earthenware pot, and some very ragged underwear. He put them all in his sack, went down to the barnyard, climbed the fence, and tiptoed away, so as not to make any noise. But as he passed by the pig barn, the wretched beasts smelled him or heard him and started to squeal angrily. Emmi was afraid that the farmers, wakened from their first hours of sleep, would be hot on his heels. He set off at a run and didn't stop until he was at the bottom of the Talking Oak.

"Here I am, back again, my good friend," he told the tree. "Let me spend one more night in your branches. Tell me if that's all right with you!"

The oak did not answer. The air was calm, not a leaf was moving. Emmi thought that silence meant consent. Loaded down as he was, he skillfully hoisted himself up to the large fork in the tree where he had spent the preceding night, and he slept there quite soundly.

When day came, he began to look for a good place to hide his money and his baggage, because he still hadn't decided how to leave the area without being seen and sent back to the farm against his will. He climbed up higher, above the fork in the tree. He then discovered in the main trunk of the big tree a black hole made by lightning a very long time ago. The bark around it had thickened, and in the back of this hiding place there were ashes and thin splinters of wood broken by the lightning.

"Really," the child said to himself, "here's a very soft and very warm bed, where I can sleep without any fear of falling if I dream. It's not large, but it's big enough for me. Let's see first if some nasty animal lives in it."

He rummaged around inside this refuge and saw that it had been struck from above, creating an opening that would let in a little dampness if it rained. He could see that it would be easy enough to close the hole with some moss. An owl had made its nest in the opening.

"I won't bother you," thought Emmi, "but I

will close the opening between us. That way, we will each have our own separate place."

When he had prepared his little nest for the following night and secured his belongings, he sat down in his hole, his legs resting outside on a branch, and began vaguely to consider the possibility of living in a tree. But he wished the tree were in the middle of the forest instead of near the edge, in plain sight of the shepherds and swineherds who brought their animals there. He had no way of knowing that, as a result of his disappearance, the tree had become a fearsome thing, and no one would come near it anymore.

Emmi began to get hungry, and even though he was a light eater, he felt the effects of not having eaten anything solid the day before. Should he go dig up the still green groundnuts he had noticed just a few feet from there? Or should he go as far as the chestnut trees growing farther on in the forest?

As he started to climb down, he saw that the branch he was standing on wasn't a part of his oak. It was a branch from a neighboring oak that intertwined its beautiful strong boughs with those of the Talking Oak. Emmi ventured onto this branch and reached the next oak, which also had a neighboring tree that was easy to reach. Light as a squirrel, he thus ventured from tree to tree until he reached the chestnut trees, where he gathered many nuts. The chestnuts were still small and not very ripe, but he wasn't particular. He came down to earth, you might say, to cook them in a deserted and well-hidden place where charcoal vendors had earlier cooked some chestnuts. In the circle made by their fire there were a lot of tiny scraps of half-burned chestnut shells. Emmi had no trouble making a pile and setting fire to it by hitting a stone with the blunt edge of his knife. He fed the sparks with dry leaves, while determining to gather a supply of mushrooms that grow on the bark of decrepit old trees, of which there were many in the forest. These mushrooms are very combustible and can be used as tinder. With water from a little stream he could cook the chestnuts in his little earthenware pot with holes in the lid, which was made for just that purpose. It's a piece of equipment every shepherd in this part of the country owns.

Emmi had often returned to the farm only

in the evenings, because of the great distance he had to take his animals, and was therefore used to feeding himself. It was not hard for him to gather his dessert of wild raspberries and blackberries from the bushes of the little clearing.

"Now I've found my kitchen and my dining room," he thought.

And he began to clean out the little stream of water that was nearby. With his hoe, he pulled out the rotting grasses, dug a little reservoir, cleared a little waterfall that the water was making in the clay, and purified it with sand and pebbles. This work kept him busy until sunset. He gathered his pot and his hoe, and climbing back on the branches he had already found to be solid, he returned on his squirrel path, climbing and jumping from tree to tree until he reached his oak. He brought a bushy armload of ferns and very dry moss back with him, with which he made his bed in the hole he had already cleaned out. He could hear his neighbor the owl fretting and grumbling above his head.

"Either it will move away," he thought, "or it will get used to me. The good oak tree doesn't belong to it any more than it belongs to me."

Used to living alone, Emmi didn't miss anyone. For several days he was especially happy just to be rid of the company of pigs.

When he saw the season of the chestnut harvest approaching, he built up his own stock, which he buried in the sand, where they kept until spring. He accumulated a number of groundnuts from the fallow fields, and he made snares to catch larks by gathering horsehair left here and there on the bushes. He collected enough tufts of wool from the thorns on the hedges to make himself a sort of pillow. Later, he made himself a distaff and a spindle and learned all by himself how to spin yarn. He made knitting needles with some wire that he found near a poorly repaired fence; they repaired it again and he stripped it a second time to make rabbit traps. Thus, he managed to make stockings and eat meat. He became an expert hunter; on the lookout day and night for small game, initiated in all the mysteries of the moor and the forest, he set his traps skillfully and wanted for nothing.

Emmi even had as much bread as he wanted, thanks to an old beggar woman, who came by the foot of the oak tree every week and put down her full beggar's bag, so she could rest. Emmi would watch out for her, climb down from his tree, his head covered with his goat skin, and give her a piece of small game in exchange for part of her bread. If she was afraid of him, her fear was expressed only by a foolish laugh and an annoying submissiveness.

And so the seasons passed—winter, which was very mild, and the following summer, which was hot and stormy. In this solitude, absorbed by the constant worry of surviving and protecting his freedom, Emmi had no time to be bored. The farm people might have called him lazy, but he knew very well that it was a lot harder surviving alone than if he had stayed on the farm. He also acquired more knowledge, courage, and foresight than he would have in ordinary life. Nevertheless, when his unusual life was perfectly regulated to suit him and took less time and care, he began to think and to feel his little conscience ask him certain embarrassing questions. Could he always live like this, depending on the forest without being of service to anyone and without pleasing any of his fellow human beings? He began to take a liking to old Catiche, the beggar woman who gave up her bread in exchange for rabbits and braces of meadowlarks. Since she couldn't remember anything and hardly talked at all and consequently told no one about their meetings, he began to speak openly to her, and she no longer feared him. There was pleasure in her laughter when she saw him come down from his tree. Emmi himself was surprised to share her pleasure. He didn't admit it, but he felt that the presence of a human being, as decrepit as she was, was a sort of blessing to someone who had been sentenced to a solitary life. One day, he tried to talk to her and asked her where she lived. She suddenly stopped laughing, and said to him in a clear and serious voice, "Do you want to come with me, boy?"

"Where?"

"To my house. If you would like to be my son, I'll make you rich and happy."

Emmi was amazed to hear old Catiche speak distinctly and reasonably. Curious, he wanted to believe her, but a gust of wind shook the branches over his head, and he heard the voice of the oak tree say to him, "Don't go with her!"

"Good evening and goodbye," he said to the old woman. "My tree doesn't want me to leave it."

"Your tree's a fool," she answered. "Or rather you're the fool to believe a tree."

"Do you think that trees don't talk? You're very much mistaken!"

"All trees talk when the wind pounces on them, but they don't know what they're saying; they aren't really saying anything."

Emmi was angered by this rational explanation of a marvelous phenomenon. He answered Catiche, "You're the one who's rambling on, old lady. Maybe all trees are like you, but my tree, at least, knows what it wants and what it's saying."

The old woman shrugged her shoulders, gathered up her beggar's bag, and went away, laughing once again.

Emmi wondered if she was acting or if she just had moments of clear-headedness. He let her go, but he followed her, slipping from tree to tree without her knowing it. She wasn't going very fast and she walked all bent over, her head forward, her mouth half-open, staring straight ahead. However, her tired appearance didn't keep her from going on, without hurrying up or slowing down. So she walked through the forest for a good three hours, until she came to a poor little settlement perched on a hill. Behind it, there were more woods as far as you could see. Emmi saw her enter a sad little hut separated from the other dwellings, which, even if they seemed less shabby, were nothing more than a cluster of huts. He dared not venture farther than the edge of the forest and retraced his steps, thoroughly convinced that if Catiche had a "home," it was poorer and uglier than the hole in the talking tree.

He went back to the large oak, where he didn't arrive until evening, overcome with exhaustion but happy to be home. From this trip, he had learned more about the size of the forest and that there was a village nearby. It seemed to be much poorer than Cernas, where Emmi had grown up. The surrounding heath had not a trace of farming, and the few animals that he had seen grazing around the huts were nothing but skin and bones. So, he would not find a better life there than the one he had here.

At the end of the week, Catiche arrived at the oak tree at the usual time. She was returning from Cernas, and he asked for news of his aunt to see whether the old woman would answer as she had the last time. She very clearly replied, "Nanette has remarried, and if you go back to her, she will try to kill you to get rid of you."

"Are you serious?" asked Emmi. "Are you telling me the truth?"

"I'm telling the truth. Your only choice now is to return to your master and live with the pigs, or come live with me, which'd be better than you think. You can't keep living in the forest. It's been sold, and they'll probably chop down these old trees, your oak tree right along with them. Believe me, little one. You can't live anywhere without earning money. Come with me. You'll help me earn a lot, and when I die, I'll leave you what I have."

Emmie was so astonished to hear this that he looked up at his tree and listened as if he were expecting advice.

"Leave this old log alone," continued Catiche. "Don't be so foolish—just come with me."

Since the tree said nothing, Emmi followed the old woman, who revealed her secret to him as they went.

"I was born far from here, poor like you and orphan. I was raised in poverty and was beaten often. I too was a swineherd and, like you, I was afraid of pigs. Like you, I ran away, but crossing a dilapidated old bridge over a river, I fell into the water. They thought I was dead when they pulled me out. They carried me to a good doctor, who brought me back to life. But I had lost my mind, I was deaf, and I could barely talk anymore. He kept me out of the kindness of his heart, and since he wasn't rich, the parish priest took up a collection for me, and the ladies brought me clothes, wine, sweets, everything I needed. I began to feel better, I was so well cared for! I ate good meat, I drank good sweetened wine, in the winter I had a fire in my room. I was treated like a princess, and the doctor was happy. He would say, 'Look at her. She hears what you're telling her. She's finding the words to speak again. In two or three months she will be able to work and earn an honest living.' And all the beautiful ladies would argue over who would take me home.

"So, it wasn't hard for me to find a place as soon as I was well, but I didn't like to work, and my employers weren't happy with me. I might have liked being a lady's maid, but I didn't know how to sew or arrange hair; they made me fetch water from the well and pluck the chickens, which I didn't like. I left that place, thinking I would be better off elsewhere. But the next was even worse. They called me dirty and lazy. My old doctor had died. I was turned out of house after house. Having been everyone's darling, now I was more wretched than before. I'd developed a taste for happiness, now people gave me so little that I barely had enough to eat. They thought I was too big and looked too healthy to be a beggar. They said to me, 'Go to work, you loafer! It's a shame, at your age, to roam the streets when you could be clearing fields for thirty sous a day.'

"Then I pretended to be lame to make people believe I couldn't work, but they thought I was still too strong not to be able to work. So I remembered when everyone had pitied me. I learned how to act the way I did back then, giggling instead of speaking, and I played my character so well that money and bread began to pour into my beggar's bag. I've been doing this for forty years, without ever meeting a refusal. Those who can't give me money give me more cheese, fruit, or bread than I can carry. With what's leftover, I raise chickens, which I send to market, and they bring in a lot of money. I have a nice house in a village. The region is poor, but the people aren't. We're all beggars and cripples, or so we say, and each one does his rounds in a place where the others have agreed not to go that day. Each one goes about his business in his own way, but no one does as well as I do, because I'm best at giving the impression I can't earn a living."

"The fact is," replied Emmi, "I never would've thought you could talk as you do."

"Yes, yes," answered Catiche, laughing, "you wanted to startle me, coming down from your tree dressed like a werewolf, to get some bread. I pretended to be afraid, but I recognized you and I said to myself, 'There's a poor boy who'll one day come to Oursines-les-Bois and who'll be very happy to eat my soup.'"

As they were talking, Emmi and Catiche arrived at Oursines-les-Bois; that was the name of the place that Emmi had seen before where this so-called crazy woman lived.

There wasn't a soul in the gloomy village. Animals were grazing here and there, unattended, on rocky soil overgrown with thistles. Disgusting filth in the muddy lanes, which served as streets, a vile stench rising from all the huts, torn laundry drying on the bushes, rotten thatched roofs with nettles growing in them, a look of cynical neglect, of pretended or voluntary poverty—it was enough to turn Emmi's stomach with disgust. He was used to lush greenery and good smells in the forest. However, he followed Catiche into her hut of hard-packed earth, more like a pigsty than a dwelling. The inside was completely different: the walls were decorated with straw matting, and the bed had a mattress and good wool blankets. There were plenty of provisions of every kind—wheat, bacon, vegetables and fruits, casks of wine, and even sealed bottles. In the backyard, the rack of chicken cages was full of plump poultry and ducks fattened on bread and bran.

"You see," Catiche said to Emmi, "that I am much richer than your aunt. She gives me charity every week, and if I wanted to, I could wear better clothes than hers. Do you want to see my cupboards? Come back inside, you must be hungry. I'll give you a dinner the likes of which you've never seen in all your life."

Indeed, while Emmi admired the contents of her cupboards, the old woman lit the fire and pulled a goat's head from her beggar's bag, which she fried with all kinds of leftovers, sparing neither salt, nor rancid butter, nor rotting vegetables—proceeds from her last trip. I don't know what kind of dish she made, but Emmi ate it, more surprised than pleased. She forced him to wash it down with a half-bottle of cheap wine. He had never drunk wine before, and he didn't like it, but he drank it anyway. To set an example, the old woman drank a whole bottle, got tipsy, and became very talkative. She bragged about knowing how to steal even better than how to beg and went so far as to show him her purse, which she kept buried under a stone in the hearth and which contained gold coins from every period of the century. There were at least two thousand francs. Emmi, not knowing how to count, didn't appreciate the beggar woman's wealth as much as she would have liked.

After showing him everything, she said, "Now, I don't think you want to leave me anymore. I need a boy, and if you want to be in my service, I will make you my heir."

"No, thank you," answered the child, "I don't want to beg."

"Very well, then, you'll steal for me."

Emmi wanted to get angry, but the old woman had talked about taking him to Mauvert the next day, where a big fair was being held. Since he wanted to see the country and find out about places where he could earn an honest living, he answered without showing his anger, "I couldn't steal, I never learned how."

"You're lying," answered Catiche. "You steal your small game and fruit rather handily in the forest of Cernas. Do you believe these things don't belong to anyone? Don't you know that anyone who doesn't work lives at the expense of someone else? This forest has been pretty much abandoned for a long time. The owner was a rich old man who didn't care about anything anymore and didn't even have it guarded. Now that he is dead, all that is going to change, and even if you hide like a rat in tree holes, they'll grab you by the collar and take you to jail."

"Well, then," answered Emmi, "why do you want to teach me to steal for you?"

"Because, when you know how to do it, you'll never be caught. You think about it. It's getting late, and we have to get up at daybreak tomorrow to go to the fair. I'll make a bed for you on my trunk, a good bed with a comforter and a blanket. For the first time in your life, you'll sleep like a prince."

Emmi dared not refuse. When old Catiche wasn't pretending to be an idiot, there was something frightening in her look and in her voice. He went to bed and at first was surprised he was so comfortable, but after a while, he was surprised to be so uncomfortable. The huge feather mattress was suffocating him. The blanket, the lack of fresh air, the bad cooking odors, and the wine he had drunk gave him a fever. He got up, alarmed, saying that he wanted to sleep outside, and that he would die if he had to spend the night closed in.

But Catiche was snoring, and the door was barricaded. Emmi resigned himself to sleeping stretched out on the table, really missing his mossy bed in the oak tree.

The next day, Catiche gave him a basket of eggs and six chickens to sell, ordering him to follow her at a distance and to pretend not to know her.

"If they knew that I sell," she told him, "they would no longer give me anything."

She told him the price he must get before handing over her merchandise, adding that she would be watching him, and that if he didn't bring her the money faithfully, she could force him to give it to her.

"If you don't trust me," Emmi answered, insulted, "carry your merchandise yourself and let me go."

"Don't try to run away," said the old woman. "I could find you wherever you go. Don't talk back and do as I say."

As she insisted, he followed her at a distance, and soon noticed the road was full of beggars, each one more repulsive than the last. They were the inhabitants of Oursines, all going together to take a cure in a miraculous fountain that day. All were crippled or covered with hideous sores. All left the fountain healthy and cheerful. The miracle wasn't hard to explain. All their ailments were faked and would come back after a few weeks, to be healed on the next holiday.

Emmi sold his eggs and chickens and quickly took the money to the old woman. Turning his back on her, he escaped through the crowd, wide-eyed, wondering and marveling at everything.

He saw acrobats do amazing stunts and he lingered a while to gaze at their sequined suits and gilded headbands. He heard an interesting conversation going on next to him. It was Catiche's voice talking to the husky voice of the leader of the acrobats. The only thing separating him from them was the tent.

"If you don't mind giving him wine to drink," Catiche was saying, "you'll persuade him to do anything you want. He's an innocent little thing who's of no use to me and who intends to live alone in the forest, where he's been perched for a whole year in an old tree. He's as nimble and agile as a monkey, he weighs no more than a baby goat, and you will have him doing the most difficult stunts."

"And you say he's not out for the money?" asked the acrobat.

"No, he doesn't care about money. You feed him and he won't have sense enough to ask for anything else."

"But will he want to run away?"

"Bah! If you beat him, he won't even try."

"Go get him for me, I want to see him."

"And you'll give me twenty francs?"

"Yes, if I can use him."

Catiche left the tent and found herself face-to-face with Emmi. She signaled him to follow her.

"No, I won't," he told her. "I heard your bargain. I'm not as innocent as you think. I won't go with those people and be beaten."

"Oh, yes, you will," answered Catiche, taking his hand in her iron grip and pulling him toward to tent.

"I don't want to, I don't want to!" cried the child, struggling. With his free hand, he grabbed the shirt of a man near him who was watching the scene.

The man turned around, and, speaking to Catiche, asked her if this child were hers.

"No, no," shouted Emmi, "she isn't my mother, she's no relation to me, she wants to sell me to those actors for twenty francs!"

"And you don't want to?"

"No, I don't want to! Get her claws off me. Look! She's making me bleed."

"What's goin' on with this woman and this child?" The good policeman, Erambert, had been attracted by Emmi's cries and Catiche's yells.

"Bah! It's nothing," answered the peasant whom Emmi was still holding by the shirt. "It's a poor woman who wants to sell a boy to tightrope walkers; but we'll stop her easily, officer. We won't need you."

"You always need the police, my friend. I want to know what's goin' on here." And turning to Emmi: "Speak, young man. Tell me what's happenin'."

At the sight of the policeman, old Catiche had let go of Emmi and tried to escape, but the magnificent Erambert grabbed her by the arm. She quickly began to laugh and make faces, pretending once more to be an idiot. However, just when Emmi started to answer, she flashed a beseeching look at him that was filled with tremendous fear. Since Emmi had been taught to fear policemen, he thought that Erambert would cut off her head with his long sword. So he took pity on her and answered, "Let her go, sir, she's a crazy, idiotic woman. She frightened me, but she didn't want to hurt me."

"Don't you know her? Isn't she Catiche? A woman who pretends to be what she isn't? Tell the truth."

Another look from the beggar woman gave Emmi the courage to lie to save her life. "I know her," he said. "She is innocent."

"I'll find out what's goin' on with her," answered the good policeman, letting Catiche go. "Go on about your business, old woman, but don't forget that I've had my eye on you for a long time."

Catiche escaped, and the policeman moved on. Emmi, who was more afraid of him than of the old woman, still clutched old Vincent's shirt. That was the name of the peasant who had been there to protect him. He had a good, sweet, and happy face.

"Well, now, son," said this kind old man to Emmi, "are you finally going to let go of me? You have nothing more to fear; what do you want from me? Are you trying to make a living? Do you want some money?"

"No, thank you," said Emmi. "It's just that I'm afraid of all these people and I'm all alone and don't know where to turn."

"Where would you like to go?"

"I would like to return to my forest in Cernas without going by Oursines-les-Bois."

"You live in Cernas? It's easy enough to take you there since I'm going into the forest shortly. I'm going to have supper under the arbor. Wait here by the village crucifix and I'll come back and get you."

Emmi thought that the village cross was too close to the acrobat's tent; he would rather have followed Vincent under the arbor. Also, he needed something to eat before the trip.

"If you aren't ashamed of me," he told him, "let me eat my bread and cheese beside you. I have enough to pay my share. Here, take my purse, you pay for both of us, because I wish to pay for your dinner also."

"I'll be darned!" Old Vincent exclaimed, laughing. "We've got a very honest and generous boy here. But my stomach is empty and your purse is hardly full. Come, sit down here. Take back your money. I've got enough for both of us."

While they were eating together, Vincent made Emmi tell his whole story. When it was finished, Vincent said to him, "I see that you have a good head and a good heart, because you didn't let yourself be tempted by Catiche's money, and at the same time you didn't want to send her to prison. Forget about her and don't leave the forest again, since you're getting along fine there. Only you can decide whether you want to live there all alone. As it happens, I'm going to the forest to build shelters for about twenty workers who are getting ready to cut down the trees between Cernas and Planchette."

"Oh! Are you going to cut down the forest?" asked Emmi, dismayed.

"No! We're only going to clear one part, which isn't near the shelter of your Talking Oak, and I know they won't go near the old trees any time soon. So don't worry, no one will bother you. But if you want my advice, my boy, you will come and work with us. You aren't strong enough to handle a hooked-blade saw or a logging axe, but if you're agile, you'll easily be able to get the ropes ready and bundle the firewood, as well as help the workers, who always need a boy to run errands and bring meals. The logging company belongs to me. The workers are on piece rate, which means they're paid according to the amount of work they do. I suggest you let me decide what to pay you, and I advise you to accept. Old Catiche was right to tell you that when you don't want to work, you have to be a thief or a beggar. Since you don't want to be either, you'd better jump at this chance to take this work I'm offering. It's a good opportunity."

Emmi accepted joyfully. Vincent inspired total confidence. Emmi put himself at Vincent's disposal and together they took the road into the forest.

It was dark when they arrived at the logging area in the hills. Even though Vincent knew the roads quite well, he would have had a hard time finding the place if Emmi, who had learned to see like a cat at night, hadn't shown him the shortest way. They found a shelter already prepared by workers who had come the night before. It consisted of tree trunks with their branches lopped off placed as gables, and a roof of thick layers of moss and grass. Emmi was introduced to the workers and given a warm welcome. He ate some hot soup and slept soundly.

The next day, he began his apprenticeship: light the fire, cook, wash dishes, fetch water, and the rest of the time help build new huts for the twenty other workers who were expected. Vincent, who supervised everything, was amazed at

Emmi's intelligence, skill, and quickness. Emmi wasn't the one learning to do everything from scratch, rather, he was teaching the smartest ones. Everyone exclaimed that he wasn't a boy but a frenzied spirit that the good fairies of the forest had sent to serve them. Since Emmi was obedient and modest, talented and resourceful, the men took a liking to him, and the toughest woodcutters spoke to him gently and politely.

After five days, Emmi asked Vincent if he was free to take Sunday off and go where he wanted.

"You're free," answered the good man, "but if you listen to me, you'll go back to see your aunt and the people of your village. If it's true your aunt doesn't care about taking you back, she'll be happy to know you're in a position to earn your own living without her being involved. If you think they'll beat you at the farm for leaving your herd, I'll go with you to calm them down and protect you. You can be sure, my boy, that work is the best passport and it cleanses everything."

Emmi thanked him for the good advice, and followed it. His aunt, who had thought him dead, was afraid when she saw him. Without relating his adventures, Emmi let her know he was working with the woodcutters and would never again be dependent on her. Vincent confirmed his story and declared that he regarded the boy as his own and had a good deal of respect for him. He spoke the same way at the farm, where they were invited to drink and eat. Nanette came to hug Emmi in front of everyone and brought him some old clothes and a half dozen cheeses. In short, when Emmi left with the old woodcutter, he was reconciled with everyone, and free from all blame and reproach.

When they had crossed the moor, Emmi said to Vincent, "Would you mind at all if I went to spend the night in my oak tree? I promise you I'll be in the cutting area on the hill before the sun rises."

"Do what you want," answered the woodcutter. "But where'd you get such an idea, to live in a tree?"

Emmi tried to make him understand that he had a loyal friendship with the oak tree, and Vincent listened to him, smiling, a little surprised by this notion but inclined to accept and understand it. He accompanied Emmi to the tree, where they wished each other a good night and went their separate ways. How happy Emmi was to be at home again.

The next morning Emmi arrived at the logging area on time. He worked there all summer and the entire winter that followed. Every Saturday night, he would sleep in his oak tree. On Sundays, he would pay a short visit to the people of Cernas and return to his tree until Monday morning. He grew taller but stayed thin and nimble. He kept himself very clean and had a nice-looking little face, which was alert and kind of pleasing to everyone. Vincent taught him to read and count. People had high hopes for his intelligence, and his aunt, who had no children, hoped to keep him with her to bring her honor and profit, because he was a person of good counsel and seemed to get along no matter what he did.

But Emmi loved only the woods. He had learned to see and hear things that no one else could see or hear. On long winter nights, he especially loved the area where the pines grew, where the piled-up snow formed wonderful, beautiful, white shapes, gently laid down along their black branches. The branches, when rocked by the breeze, seemed to move and talk mysteriously among themselves. Most often they seemed to sleep, and he would look at them with a kind of frightened respect. He was afraid to say a word, to make a move that would awaken the beautiful fairies of the night and of the silence.

When ice imprisoned the little stream, he would break it to drink, but carefully, so as not to destroy the crystal castle his little waterfall had formed. He liked to look at candelabra of frost along the forest paths and the iridescent icicles in the morning sun.

On some evenings the transparent architecture of the bare trees stood like black lace against the red sky or the pearly background of clouds lit by the moon. And, in summer, what warm murmuring, what beautiful bird concerts under the foliage! He made war with the rats and snakes who ate eggs and baby birds, but he protected the many inhabitants of his old oak tree so well that they all knew him and let him mingle with them. He would not allow ants to settle in his neighborhood, but he would let the woodpecker work in the wood of the tree to dig out gnawing insects that destroy it. He chased caterpillars from the leaves. He did not spare the voracious Maybugs. To tell the truth, the oak tree had never been so healthy and had never displayed such rich and cool greenery.

Emmi was fussy about where he made his bed and only slept really well in his tree. Yet, he had to leave this dear forest when the wood had been cut and carried away. Emmi followed Vincent, who moved ten miles off by Oursines, to begin another cutting on another property.

Since the day of the fair, Emmi had not returned to this repugnant place and had not seen Catiche. Was she dead? Was she in prison? No one knew anything. Many beggars disappear without anyone being able to say what became of them. No one looks for them or misses them.

Emmie had not forgotten that Catiche had brought him bread and the sound of a human voice every week when he was completely alone. He confided in Vincent that he wanted to find out what had happened to her, and they stopped at Oursines to ask. It was holiday time in that den of thieves. People were drinking and singing, banging on pots. Two women, their hair flying in the wind, were fighting in a doorway; children splashed about in a filthy puddle. As soon as the two strangers appeared, the children fled like a flock of wild ducks. They ran from hut to hut to warn the inhabitants. All noise stopped and doors were closed. The frightened poultry hid in the bushes.

"Since these people don't want anyone to see their merrymaking," said Old Vincent, "and since you know where Catiche lives, let's go right there."

They knocked several times without an answer. Finally, a broken voice told them to enter and they pushed open the door. Catiche, pale, skinny, and frightening, was seated in a large chair by the fire, her dried-up hands gripping her knees. Recognizing Emmi, she showed an expression of joy.

"Finally you are here," she said. "Now I can die in peace!"

She explained to them that she was paralyzed. Her neighbors came to get her up in the morning and put her to bed at night and brought her something to eat when they felt like it.

"I don't need anything," she added, "but I

have something that worries me. It's my money. It's here under the stone where I put my feet. This money is meant for Emmi, who has a good heart and saved me from prison when I wanted to sell him to bad people. But as soon as I'm dead, my neighbors will search everywhere and will find my treasure. That's what keeps me from sleeping. You must have this money, Emmi, and take it far away from here. If I die, you keep it. I'm giving it to you. Didn't I promise it to you? If I get my health back, you'll bring it back to me; you're honest, I know you. It will always be yours, but I'll have the pleasure of seeing it and counting it right up to my last hour."

At first Emmi refused. It was stolen money, which disgusted him, but Vincent offered to take charge of it in order to return it to her on demand, or to put it in Emmi's name, if she happened to die without claiming it. Vincent was well known throughout the area as a fair man who had accumulated some wealth honestly. Catiche, who had wandered about everywhere and heard everything, knew very well that he could be trusted. She asked him to close the doors of her hut very tightly, then move her chair back, since she could not move herself, and pull up the stone in the hearth. There was quite a bit more than she had shown Emmi the first time. There were five leather purses and about five thousand francs in gold. She wanted to keep only three hundred francs to pay her neighbors for their care and to have herself buried.

As Emmi looked disdainfully at this treasure, Catiche told him, "You will learn someday that poverty is an evil disease. If I hadn't been born in this poverty, I wouldn't have done what I did."

"If you repent," Vincent told her, "God will pardon you."

"I've been sorry," she replied, "ever since I became paralyzed, because I'm dying of worry and loneliness. I dislike my neighbors as much as they dislike me. Now I think it would have been better if I had lived differently."

Emmi promised to come back and see her and then went with Vincent to his new work. He missed the forest near Cernas, but he understood duty and did his work faithfully. After a week he returned to Catiche. He arrived as they were carrying her coffin away on a little cart pulled by a donkey. Emmi followed it for about a half a mile to the parish church, and attended the burial.

When he returned to the cutting area, Old Vincent told him, "You're too young to have so much money. You won't know how to put it to good use, or it'll get stolen. If you let me be your guardian, I'll invest it and pay you an allowance from it until you are old enough."

"Do what you think is right," answered Emmi. "I'll rely on you. But if the money's stolen, as the old woman boasted, wouldn't it be better to try to return it?"

"Who can we return it to? It's been stolen penny by penny, because this woman received charity by deceiving everyone and pinching here and there from no one knows who. We don't know what things she stole and no one dreams of getting them back. The money is not for you to feel guilty about. The shame is in those who make poor use of it. Catiche was a *champie*, what the peasants call a foundling; she had no family, she left no heirs. She gave you her fortune, not to thank you for doing something bad, but because you forgave her for the harm she wanted to do to you. So, I consider it a well-earned inheritance, and that by giving it to you, the old woman did one good deed in her life. I don't want to hide the fact that with the income I'll pay you, you won't have to work much, but, if I'm not mistaken, you're a very good boy and you'll keep on working your heart out, as if you had nothing."

"I'll do as you advise," answered Emmi. "All I ask is to stay with you and obey your orders."

The honest young man had no reason to regret the confidence and friendship he felt for his mentor. The latter always considered him a son and treated him as a good father would. When Emmi became a man, he married one of the old woodcutter's granddaughters. Since he hadn't touched his capital, to which interest had been added yearly, he was rich by farmers' standards. His wife was pretty, brave, and good. Throughout the countryside this young couple was greatly admired. Since Emmi had acquired knowledge and showed intelligence in his work, the owner of the Cernas forest chose him as its general manager and had a pretty house built for him in the most beautiful spot in the old cluster of trees, right next to the Talking Oak.

Emmi had become too big to sleep in his former shelter, and so much bark had grown that the little lodging was practically closed off. When Emmi, as an old man, saw that the opening would soon be completely closed, he wrote with a steel-pointed tool on a copper plaque his name, the date of his stay in the tree, and the main circumstances of his story. At the end he put this prayer:

> Fire from the sky and wind from the mountain, spare my friend, the old oak. Let it see my grandchildren and also their children grow up. Old oak who spoke to me, say a good word to them, too, from time to time, so they will love you as I have loved you.

Emmi slipped this inscribed plaque into the hole where he had slept and dreamed for so long.

The slot closed completely. Emmi passed away but the oak still lives. It no longer talks, or, if it talks, there are no longer ears capable of understanding it. People are no longer afraid of it, but Emmi's story spread, and thanks to the fine reputation he left behind, the oak is still respected and honored.

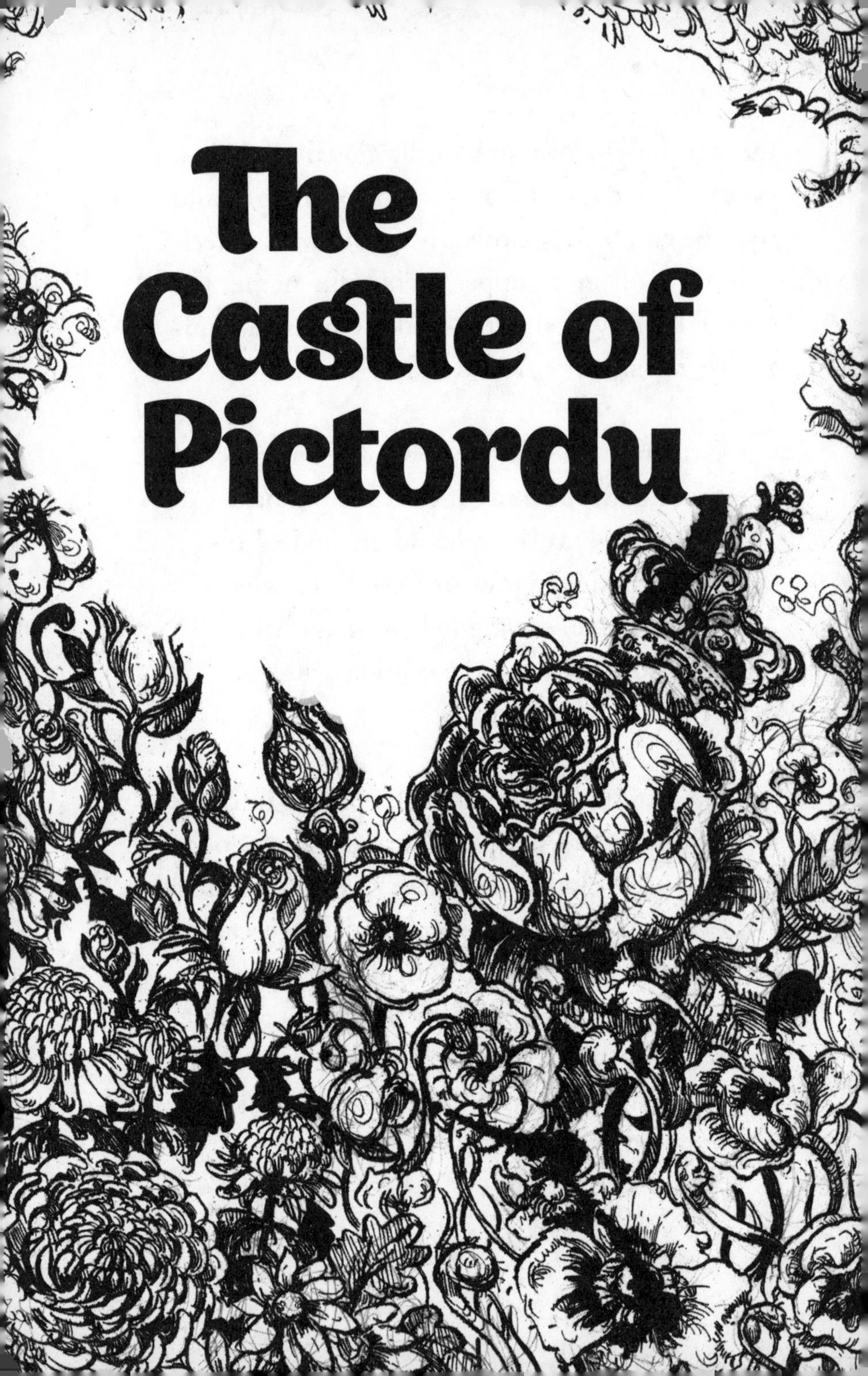
The Castle of Pictordu

The Talking Statue

The abandoned castle of Pictordu lay deep in the heart of a primitive region of southern France called, at the time, the province of Gévaudan. It was there all by itself, in a wilderness of forest and mountains. It looked very, very sad, and worn out, like someone who has entertained many important people and given beautiful parties, and then finds herself dying—poor, sick, and abandoned.

The distinguished Mr. Flochardet, a painter famous in the south of France, was traveling in a coach on a road that followed along a little river. He had with him his only daughter, Diane, eight years old, who had been a student at the convent of the Visitandines of Mende. The little girl had been running a childhood fever every other day for three months. The doctor had recommended the fresh air of her birthplace, so Flochardet was taking her to a pretty villa that he owned near Arles.

After leaving Mende, father and daughter had made a detour to visit a relative, and they were planning to spend the next night at Saint-Jean-Gardonenque, known today as Saint-Jean-de-Gard.

This was in the eighteenth century, long before there were trains. Life was slower than it is now. They would not arrive home for another two days. The trip was more difficult still because the road was in terrible shape. Mr. Flochardet had climbed out to walk beside the coachman, who was also on foot.

"What is that in front of us?" he asked. "Is it a ruin or an outcropping of white rocks?"

"Sir," said the coachman. "Don't you recognize the Castle of Pictordu?"

"How could I recognize it? I'm seeing it for the first time. I have never taken this road and I never will again. It is ghastly and we are making no progress."

"Be patient, monsieur. This old road is straighter than the new one. You would still have eighteen miles to go before nightfall if you had taken it. This way, you have no more than a mile."

"The castle appears to be very large and grand still. Why doesn't anyone live there anymore?"

"Because the owner, who inherited it, doesn't have the money to repair it. It once belonged to a rich nobleman who had wild goings-on—dances, spectacles, games, feasts, what have you. He spent a fortune and his descendants have never recovered, nor has the castle. It still looks fine on the outside, but one of these days it will tumble into the river, and onto this road we're taking."

"As long as it lets us pass this evening, let it crumble if it wants to! But why the strange name—Pictordu?"

"Because of that crooked rock you see rising above the forest behind the castle. It looks as if it's been twisted by fire. They say that in olden times the entire countryside burned. This is said to be volcanic country. I'll bet you've never seen anything like it, have you?"

"As a matter of fact, I have. I've seen many such rocks. But that doesn't interest me right now. I beg you, my friend, get back on your seat and drive as fast as you can."

"I'm sorry, sir, not yet. We have to get past the park, where there are a lot of broken stones and I'll have to lead the horses carefully. Don't be concerned about the little girl; there is no danger."

"That may be," replied Flochardet, "but I would still like to carry her in my arms. Tell me when we're getting close."

"We're there now, sir. Do as you please."

The artist had the driver stop the coach, so that he might lift Diane out. She was sleepy and beginning to feel faint from her fever.

"Climb those stairs," said the coachman. "Cross the terrace and we'll be at the bend in the road at the same time."

Flochardet climbed the stairway, still carrying his daughter. In spite of its dilapidated state, it was truly a grand stairway, with a balustrade that had once been very beautiful and elegant statues still standing at intervals. The terrace, once paved, had become a garden of wildflowers that grew between the cracked stones and mixed with costly shrubs that had been planted in urns. Scarlet honeysuckle harmonized with enormous clumps of wild roses; jasmine was blooming among the brambles. Cedars of Lebanon stood above native firs and hardy holm oaks. Ivy had spread out like a carpet or hung in garlands; strawberry plants, nestled in the steps, formed arabesques up to the pedestals of the statues. This terrace, overrun with wild vegetation, had perhaps never been so beautiful, but Flochardet was a portrait painter and wasn't too fond of nature. Besides, this profusion of wild plants made walking at dusk difficult. He was afraid the thorns would scratch his daughter's pretty face. He continued on, shielding her as best he could, when from below he heard the noise of horses' hooves reverberating on the stones, and the voice of the coachman, who was moaning, groaning, and swearing, as if he were in trouble.

What should he do? How could he rush to the man's aid with a sick child in his arms? With her sweetness and good sense, little Diane helped him out of the predicament. The coachman's cries had wakened her completely, and she recognized the need to get the poor man out of danger.

"Go on, Papa," she said to her father. "I'm fine here. This garden is so pretty—I really like it. Leave your coat with me. I'll stay right here and won't move. You'll find me by this large urn. Don't worry."

Flochardet wrapped her in his coat and ran to see what had happened. The coachman wasn't hurt, but in trying to get over the rubble, he had overturned the coach, and the wheels were completely broken. One of the horses had fallen and injured his knee. The coachman was desperate. You had to feel sorry for him, but Flochardet couldn't help getting needlessly angry. What was going to happen now, with night falling and a little girl too heavy to carry for six miles—three hours of walking? He left the coachman to fend for himself and returned to Diane.

Instead of finding her asleep at the foot of the large urn, as he had expected, he saw her coming to meet him, very much awake and almost cheerful.

"Papa," she said to him, "I heard everything from the edge of the terrace. I was troubled by your worrying, when the lady called to me by name. I looked up and saw that she was pointing toward the castle. It was as if she were telling me to go in. Let's. I'm sure she'll be happy and we'll feel at home in her house."

"What lady are you talking about, my child? The castle is deserted, and I see no one here."

"Don't you see the lady? That's because it's starting to get dark. But I can still see her very well. Look! She's still showing us the door to enter her house."

Flochardet looked at what Diane was showing him. He saw a life-size statue that represented an allegorical figure, Hospitality perhaps, that, with an elegant and gracious gesture, really did seem to be pointing to the entrance of the castle.

"What you think is a lady is really a statue," he said to his daughter, "and you dreamed she was talking to you."

"No, Papa, I didn't dream it. We must do what she wants."

Flochardet didn't want to argue with the sick child. He glanced at the ornate facade of the castle, which, with its necklace of climbing plants hanging from the balconies and its carved stone, seemed magnificent and still sturdy.

"Indeed," he said to himself, "it can be a shelter until we find something better. I'll easily find a corner where my little girl will be able to rest while I work something out."

He followed Diane, who was resolutely pulling him by the hand through a grand courtyard surrounded by a colonnade. Continuing straight ahead, they entered an immense room, which, to tell the truth, was nothing but a bed of wild mint and common horehound with whitish leaves, surrounded by columns, more than one of which were lying on the ground. The others supported the remains of a cupola riddled with a thousand holes. The ruin did not seem very inviting to Flochardet, and he was going to turn back when the coachman caught up with them.

"Follow me, sir," he said. "There's a little lodge over here that's still sturdy where you can spend the night quite comfortably."

"Do we have to spend the night here? Isn't

there a way to reach, if not the village, at least some farm or country house?"

"Impossible, sir. There's no house we could reach tonight. The mountain is too rugged and my poor horses are both in bad shape. I don't know how we'll get out of here, even in broad daylight. For goodness' sake! The first thing to do is find a place for the young lady to sleep. I'm going to find you a room that still has doors and shutters and a ceiling that won't collapse. As for me, I've found a sort of stable for my animals, and since I have my little sack of oats for them, and you have some food for yourself, we won't starve to death tonight. I'll bring you all your things and the cushions from the coach to sleep on. One night will pass quickly."

"All right," Flochardet agreed. "Let's do as you think best, since you've recovered your spirits. Surely there's some caretaker you know here who will offer hospitality?"

"There is no caretaker. The Pictordu castle takes care of itself. For one thing, there's nothing here to steal. In addition . . . But I'll tell you about that later. Here's the door of what was once the baths. I know how to open it. Enter here, monsieur; there are neither rats, owls, nor snakes. Wait for me. You've nothing to fear."

While talking and walking through several more-or-less ruined main buildings, they had come to a sort of low, heavy, austere pavilion. Like the rest of the castle, it dated back to the Renaissance. But while the other buildings offered a capricious mixture of different styles of architecture, this pavilion, situated in a cloistered courtyard, was a small-scale imitation of an ancient Roman public bath, its interior fairly well enclosed and well preserved.

The coachman had brought one of the lanterns with its candle from the coach. He struck a light, and Flochardet checked to be sure that the shelter would be acceptable. He sat on the base of a column and tried to hold Diane in his lap while the coachman went to get the cushions and their belongings.

"No thank you, Papa," she said. "I'm very happy to spend the night in this pretty castle. I don't feel sick here. Let's go help the coachman so it won't take as long. I'm sure you're hungry and I can't wait to taste the cakes and fruits you packed in the little basket for me."

When Flochardet realized that his sick little girl was so brave, he took her with him back to the coach, and she was able to make herself useful. In a quarter of an hour, the cushions, coats, boxes, baskets—in a word, everything that was in the coach—had been carried to the bath pavilion of the old castle. Diane didn't forget her doll, whose arm had been broken during the adventure. She wanted to cry, but seeing that her papa had lost some more precious things that had also broken, she had the courage not to complain. The coachman found consolation in noticing that two bottles of good wine had escaped the disaster, and he gazed at them lovingly as he carried them.

"Well," Flochardet said to him, "since you've found us shelter after all, and since you seem dedicated to our service . . . What is your name?"

"Romanèche, sir!"

"Well, Romanèche, you'll dine with us and you'll sleep in this big room, if you wish."

"No, sir, I'll go take care of my horses. But I'll not refuse a glass of wine, especially after a misfortune. And I'll wait on you. Perhaps the little girl would like some water. I know where the spring is. I'll prepare her bed. I know how to take care of children, I have some of my own!"

Having spoken, kind Romanèche took care of everything. The dinner consisted of cold chicken, bread, ham, and some sweets, which Diane enjoyed nibbling. They had neither chairs nor tables, but, in the middle of the room, a marble pool formed a small amphitheater with terraced steps where they could sit comfortably. The spring that had once fed the bath and still bubbled up in the cloister provided excellent water, which Diane drank from her little silver goblet. Flochardet gave one of the bottles of wine to Romanèche; they made do without glasses.

While he ate, the painter observed his daughter. She was cheerful and would have gladly chattered on instead of sleeping, but when she was no longer hungry, he encouraged her to lie down. The two men made a very adequate little bed for her with the cushions and coats in a marble waterway at the edge of the pool. The weather was superb; it was the middle of summer, and the moon was rising. Besides, there was one candle left and the place was not gloomy at all. The interior had been painted with a fresco. You could still see birds fluttering about in the garlands on the domed ceiling, trying to catch butterflies bigger than themselves. On the walls nymphs danced in circles, hand in hand. One was missing a leg, another her hands, another her head. Stretched out on her improvised bed, with her doll in her arms, lying quietly and waiting for sleep, Diane studied the injured dancers and decided they were in a festive mood, nevertheless.

The Veiled Lady

When Mr. Flochardet was satisfied that his daughter was sleeping, he said to the coachman, now acting as butler and cleaning up the remains of the dinner, "So explain to me why this castle takes care of itself; you implied there was a specific reason for that."

Romanèche hesitated a moment, but his courteous passenger's good wine had put him in the mood to chat and this is what he said: "I'm sure you're going to make fun of me, sir. You educated people just don't believe in some things."

"I understand what you're trying to say, my

good man. I don't believe in the supernatural, I admit. But I do like magical stories. This castle must have a legend; tell it to me—I won't make fun of you."

"Very well, sir, here it is. I told you the Castle of Pictordu took care of itself. That was a manner of speaking. It is guarded by the Veiled Lady."

"Who is the Veiled Lady?"

"Aha! That no one knows! Some say she's a living person who dresses in old-fashioned clothes; others say she's the spirit of a princess who lived a long time ago and comes back here every night."

"Will we have the pleasure of seeing her?"

"No, sir, you won't see her. She's a very polite lady who wants people to come to her home. She sometimes invites passersby to come in, and if they don't notice her, she overturns their coaches or makes their horses fall. Or, if they're on foot, she makes so many rocks fall on the road that they can't get by. She must have shouted some sort of invitation that we didn't hear, from the top of the castle or the terrace. Now, you can say what you want, but the accident we had wasn't very natural, and if you had insisted on continuing on your way, something worse would have happened."

"Very good. Now I understand why you found it impossible to take us elsewhere."

"Somewhere else, even in the village, you'd have been worse off, less well looked after. And the dinner . . . well, I thought it was excellent!"

"It was very satisfactory, and I'm not unhappy to be here; but I want to know all about the Veiled Lady. When you enter her home without an invitation, isn't she very unhappy?"

"She doesn't get angry and she doesn't show herself. You never see her. No one has ever seen her. She's not wicked and has never hurt anybody. But you hear a voice crying to you, 'Leave!' And whether you want to or not, you feel forced to obey, as if something as strong as forty pairs of horses were dragging you."

"That could very well happen to us, since she hasn't invited us at all."

"Pardon me, sir—I'm sure she must have called us, but we weren't paying attention."

Flochardet then remembered that little Diana believed she had heard the statue call her from the terrace.

"Speak more softly," he said to the coachman. "The child dreamed something like that, and she shouldn't believe in such fantasies."

"Oh!" cried Romanèche, "She heard! . . . Well, that's it, sir! The Veiled Lady loves children, and when she saw you passing without heeding her invitation, she overturned the coach."

"And ruined the horses? That's a shabby trick for someone so hospitable!"

"To tell you the truth, monsieur, my horses aren't hurt very badly; a little blood is all. It was the coach she was aiming for. But if we can repair it tomorrow, or get another, your journey will only be delayed a few hours, since you were supposed to spend the night in Saint-Jean-Gardonnenque. Perhaps you're expected somewhere, and you're afraid of worrying people if you don't get there on a certain day?"

"Absolutely," Flochardet answered, just a little fearful that the lady with the veil might have some new whim. "First thing in the morning, we'll have to see about making up the lost time."

In fact, Flochardet was not expected home on a certain day. His wife didn't know Diane had been taken sick at the convent, and she was not anticipating the pleasure of seeing her again before school vacation.

"Well, now," Flochardet said to Romanèche, "I believe it's time to turn in. Do you want to sleep here? It's all right with me, if you're more comfortable here than with your horses."

"Thank you, monsieur, you're too kind," Romanèche answered, "but I can sleep with them. It's habit, you know. Are you afraid of staying alone with the little girl?"

"Afraid? No, since I won't be seeing the Lady. By the way, could you tell me how they know she's veiled, since no one has ever seen her?"

"I don't know, monsieur. It's an old story. I didn't make it up. I believe in it without fretting over it. I'm not a coward, and besides, I've never done anything to upset the castle's spirit."

"Well, then, good evening and good night," said Flochardet. "Be here promptly at daybreak without fail; get us out of here quickly and smoothly, and you won't be sorry."

Flochardet, left alone with Diane, went over to her and touched her cheeks and her little hands. He was surprised and happy to find them cool. He tried to take her pulse, even though he knew little about children's fevers. Diane gave him a kiss, saying, "Don't worry, Papa, I'm just fine; it's my doll who has a fever. Don't disturb her."

Diane was sweet and loving; she never complained. Her father was delighted that she seemed so calm and playful, as well.

Mr. Flochardet was no more than forty years old, a handsome, friendly, rich, well-bred gentleman. He had earned a lot of money painting very refined, sophisticated portraits, which ladies always thought looked true to life, because he made them look beautiful and young. In reality, all of Flochardet's portraits looked alike. There was always a very pretty classic head that he reproduced again and again, changing it very little. He had only to finish it by copying the clothes and hair styles of his models. The precision of the details made up the entire personality of the portraits. He excelled in copying the shade of a dress, the movement of a curl of hair, the lightness of a ribbon, and in very many of his portraits you could immediately recognize the likeness of a cushion or a parrot placed next to the model. He wasn't without talent. But he was without originality, genius, or a feeling for true life. He was very successful. Elegant middle-class ladies preferred him to a great master who might have had the impertinence to reproduce a wart or accentuate a wrinkle.

After a first marriage of two years, he had married for a second time, this time a young woman, poor but from a good family, who considered him the greatest artist in the universe. She was certainly not foolish by nature, but she was so very, very pretty that she had never found the time to think deeply and educate herself. In addition, she had shied away from the task of raising her husband's daughter herself. That's why she had made him send Diane to a convent, with the idea that since she was an only child, she would be happier with little playmates her own age than at home alone. She didn't learn to play with Diane and entertain her herself, or if she had learned, she was always too busy. It took her quite a while to dress ten times a day and each time to make herself more beautiful.

Flochardet was a good father and a good husband. He liked Mrs. Flochardet to be a bit frivolous, because she primped all day to please him. It was also, she told herself, useful to him, for it allowed him to study the feminine finery that he used to advantage in his painting.

While sleeping near the pool of the old castle, Flochardet pondered these things—his wife's clothes and her beauty, his sick daughter who might already be cured, his rich clients, the work that he was late getting back to. He thought about the accident with the coach, the peculiar coincidence of the coachman's fantastic story and little Diane's hallucination, the Veiled Lady and the country people's need to believe in the supernatural, even if their fantasies weren't caused by fear. While meditating on these different impressions, he fell into a deep sleep and even snored a little.

Diane was sleeping too, wasn't she? Well, I confess I really don't know. I allowed this digression about her father and mother at the risk of making you impatient, because you must know why Diane was, as a rule, a quiet and dreamy little girl. She had spent her babyhood all alone with her nanny, who loved her but who spoke very little, and she had been obliged to sort out in her little head, as best she could, the ideas that came to her. So you won't be surprised by what I'm going to tell you next about her. For now, I must tell you how her mind was awakened and set to work in the Castle of Pictordu.

When she heard her papa snoring, she opened her eyes and looked around. It was dark in the great round room, but since the domed ceiling wasn't very high and one of the lanterns from the coach, that had been hung on the wall, still gave out a dim flickering light, Diane could dimly make out one or two of the dancers of antiquity who were positioned in front of her. The best preserved but at the same time the most mutilated was a tall woman whose dress had a certain freshness, who bare arms and legs were very well drawn, but whose face, damaged by humidity, had completely disappeared. While not quite asleep, Diane had vaguely heard what the coachman had told Mr. Flochardet about the Veiled Lady, and little by little she began to dream that this body without a face must have some connection with the castle's legend.

"I don't know," she thought, "why my papa considers it a fantasy. I am really very sure the lady spoke to me on the terrace, and with a very sweet, very pretty voice. I would be happy if she wanted to talk to me again. If I weren't afraid of upsetting Papa, who thinks I'm still sick, I would even go see her, if she's still there."

She was just thinking this when the lantern went out and she saw a large, beautiful blue light, just like the moon's, cross the room. And in this soft ray of light, she saw that the ancient dancer had left the wall and was coming toward her.

Don't think Diane was afraid; it was an exquisite figure. Her dress fell in a thousand graceful folds over her beautiful body and seemed to be sprinkled with silver sequins. A jeweled belt held the light fabric at her waist. A shimmering gauze veil was wrapped around her hair, which escaped onto her snow-white shoulders in blond curls. You couldn't make out her face through the gauze, but what looked like two pale rays of light shone through instead of eyes. Her bare legs and her arms, uncovered to the shoulders, were a perfection of beauty. Indeed, the obscure and faded nymph from the wall had become a living woman, lovely to look at.

She came right up to the child and, without touching her father, stretched out next to her, leaned over Diane's forehead, and gave her a kiss. What I mean is that Diane heard the soft sound of her lips but felt nothing. The little girl threw her arms around the lady's neck to return the kiss and hold her, but she only kissed a shadow.

"So are you made only of mist," she said, "since I can't feel you? Talk to me, at least, so I know if it was you who spoke to me before."

"It was I," the Lady answered. "Do you want to come for a walk with me?"

"I'd like to, but take away my fever, so my papa won't worry anymore."

"Don't worry, you won't be sick with me. Give me your hand."

The child held out her hand confidently, and even though she didn't feel the fairy's hand, it seemed to her that a pleasant coolness passed through her entire being.

They left the room together.

"Where do you want to go?" asked the Lady.

"Wherever you want," the little girl answered.

"Do you want to go back to the terrace?"

"The terrace seemed so pretty with all of its bushes and tall grass full of little flowers."

"Don't you want to see inside my castle, which is even more beautiful?"

"The roof is caved in and it's in ruins!"

"That's where you're wrong. It appears that way to those who are not authorized to see it."

"Would you let *me* see it?"

"Certainly. Look!"

Immediately, the ruins in which Diane thought she was standing became a beautiful gallery with a gold-embossed ceiling. Between each large window, crystal lamps lighted big, beautiful black marble statues carrying torches. Other statues, some bronze, others white marble or jasper, others completely gilded, appeared on their ornately carved pedestals. Under her feet, a mosaic floor depicting arrangements of flowers and birds extended as far as the little traveler's eyes could see. At the same time, the sounds of far away music could be heard. Diane, who loved music, began to jump and run, impatient to see dancing, for there was no doubt in her mind the fairy was taking her to a ball.

"Do you like to dance, then?" the fairy asked her.

"No," she replied. "I've never learned to dance. I think my legs are too weak. But I love to see anything pretty and I want to see you dance in a circle again, the way I saw you in the painting."

They arrived at a large hall filled with lighted mirrors, and the fairy disappeared; but immediately Diane saw a number of people just like her, dressed in green and wearing gauze veils, hundreds of them, leaping nimbly in all of the large mirrors to the sounds of an unseen orchestra. She delighted in watching the circle dance until her eyes tired and it seemed to her she was sleeping. She felt herself awakened by the cool hand of the fairy, and she was in another room, even more exquisite and grand. There was a beautifully carved, massive gold table in the middle of the room loaded with extraordinary fruits, flowers, cakes, and candies, piled up to the ceiling.

"Take what you want," said the fairy.

"I don't want anything," Diane replied, "unless you have some very cold water. I'm as hot as if I'd been dancing."

The fairy blew on her through the veil, and Diane felt rested and no longer thirsty.

"You're fine. What do you want to see now?"

"Everything you think I should see."

"Don't you have any idea?"

"Do you want to show me the gods?"

The fairy did not seem surprised by this

request. Diane had once had an old mythology book with very ugly pictures that had seemed very beautiful at first but had displeased her in the end. She had longed to see something better and thought the fairy would probably have beautiful pictures. The fairy led her into a room hung with paintings representing life-size mythological characters. At first Diane looked at them with astonishment, and then with the desire to see them move.

"Have them come over here near us," she said to the fairy.

Immediately, all these gods and goddesses left their frames and began to walk around. Then they rose very high and whirled around the ceiling like birds chasing one another. They were going so fast Diane could no longer distinguish one from another. She thought she recognized a few she had seen in her book: graceful Hebe, the goddess of youth, with her goblet, proud Juno with her peacock, kind Mercury with his little hat, Flora with all her garlands. But all this mention made her tired again.

"It's too hot here," she said to the fairy. "Take me to your garden."

At that very instant she was on the terrace; but it was no longer the uncultivated, wild place she had crossed to enter the castle. It had flower beds, paths made of multicolored pebbles like a mosaic, and urns spilling over with flowers that made a thousand designs, resembling a rich carpet. The statues were singing a beautiful hymn in honor of the moon, and Diane wished she could see the moon goddess, whom she was named after. Instantly, the goddess Diana appeared in the sky in the form of a silver cloud. She was very, very large and held a shining bow. Little by little she became smaller, and then so small you would have thought she was a swallow. She came nearer and became big again. Diane tired of following her with her eyes and said to the fairy, "Now, I want to kiss you."

"Does that mean you want to sleep?" asked the fairy, taking her in her arms. "Well, then, sleep. But when you wake up, don't forget anything I've shown you."

Diane fell into a deep sleep. Later, when she opened her eyes, she was once again lying in the marble waterway, holding the little hand of her doll. The bluish dawn had replaced the blue moon. Mr. Flochardet had risen and opened his overnight bag. He was quietly trimming his beard, because in those days a man of the world, no matter where he was, would have been embarrassed not to be freshly shaven first thing in the morning.

The Young Lady of Pictordu

Diane got up, put her shoes back on (she had taken them off when she went to sleep), fastened the hooks on her dress, and asked her papa to lend her the mirror so that she might tidy up a bit while he went with Romanèche to prepare for their departure. Folchardet, knowing she was clean and neat, left her alone, reminding her that if she went out she should be careful in the castle's rubble and watch where she was walking.

Diane washed up, put everything back neatly in her toilet kit, and seeing her father wasn't back yet, wandered through the castle, hoping to find once again all the beautiful things she had seen with the fairy during the night. But she couldn't even find the right rooms. The spiral staircases were broken and the steps were loose, unsupported on the sides by the crumbling tower walls. The rooms of the upper floor had collapsed onto the floor beneath and she could no longer tell what belonged to the main building. She could clearly see that all the structures had been richly decorated; some inside walls still had traces of painting. There were remnants of gilding on broken marble; very beautiful fireplaces still attached to walls were standing in the emptiness. The floor was littered with all kinds of debris. There were sparkling fragments of stained-glass windows strewed over the green of the wild plants and little marble hands, which had belonged to statues of Cupid, and bronze Zephyr's wings, once gilded, that had fallen from a candelabra. There were shreds of tapestry, gnawed by rats, but still showing the faint outline of a queen or a vase filled with flowers. It was an entire world of riches and pleasures fallen to fragments and dust.

Diane couldn't understand why such a grand castle, whose facade still stood magnificently on the slope of the ravine, should have been abandoned. What I'm seeing right now must be a dream, she thought. They tell me that when I have a fever, my mind wanders a bit. But I didn't have one last night; I was seeing things as they really are. I don't feel sick, but the fairy told me you can only see the castle when she allows it, and I must be content to see it the way she is showing it to me right now.

After looking in vain for the beautiful rooms, the great galleries, the paintings and statues, the gold table loaded with sweets—all the marvelous things among which she had spent the night, Diane went into the garden and found only nettles, brambles, large Aaron's rod, and lilies. Some instinct convinced her that these plants weren't uglier than the others, and the overgrown flower beds pleased her just as they were, stripped of their symmetrical design and their colorful stonework. She gathered some colored pebbles from the paths, put them in her pockets, and continued along the edge of the terrace, looking amid the tangle of shrubs for the statue that had spoken to her the night before. She found it standing next to a large vase, with its arm stretching toward the entrance to the castle, but it was no longer talking. How could it have spoken? It had no mouth, it had no face. The only thing left was the back of its head with a remnant of cloth wrapped around the stone hair. The other statues were even more mutilated by the weather, neglect, and stones thrown by foolish children. They were all missing one or two arms, and some were lying stretched out on violet thistles and yellow toadflax.

Looking very closely at the one that had spoken to her, Diane thought she recognized the likeness of her kind fairy. At the same time she associated the statue with the dancer painted in the room where she had slept. She could easily imagine anything she wanted about the figures since all the gods and goddesses in Renaissance art had been copied from ancient Greek and Roman figures. By coincidence, the faces of the two figures had been removed, so Diane's association, if not correct, was at least plausible.

Tired of walking, she went to look for her father and found him below the terrace, trying to speed up the repairs to the coach. Romanèche had found a wheelwright from the neighborhood, a good country fellow, but without the best equipment. "We must be patient, little girl," Romanèche told her. "I've found you some brown bread, which isn't bad at all, some very fresh cream, and some cherries. I took it all to your big bedroom. If you want to go back and have some breakfast, you won't be bored."

"I'm not bored at all," Diane answered, "but I'll go eat a little. Thank you for thinking of me."

"How do you feel?" her father asked. "How did you sleep?"

"I didn't sleep a lot, Papa, but I couldn't have enjoyed myself more."

"Enjoyed yourself dreaming, you mean? You had happy dreams? Well, that's a good sign. Go and eat."

Watching her walk away, Flochardet thought admiringly of his pale, thin child, who bothered no one with her sickness and showed a quiet little happiness in every situation.

I don't understand, he thought, why my wife believed we had to send her away from the house, where she made so little noise and was so easy to please. I know my sister, the abbess of the Visitandines of Mende, is very good to her, but my wife should be even nicer to her.

Diane returned to the bath pavilion, and since she knew how to read, she noticed a faint inscription carved over the door. She succeeded in deciphering it: BATHS OF DIANA.

"Well!" she said to herself, laughing, "Is this really my own room here? I would very much like to bathe here, but the water has stopped flowing. I must be satisfied with eating and sleeping here."

She enjoyed the food Romanèche had put on the steps of the pool for her, and then she wanted to draw.

You won't believe this, but she hardly knew how; her father had never given her lessons. He gave her paper and pencils when she wanted them, to do her childish scribbling in a corner of his studio. She would try to copy the portraits she saw him doing. He thought these attempts were very funny and laughed at them uproariously, but he didn't believe she had the least bit of talent for drawing. He had made up his mind not to pressure her into following his career.

At the convent where Diane had just spent a year, they didn't teach drawing. In those days, you only got an education in art in order to earn a living at it. Flochardet, being rich, aimed to make his daughter into a real young lady, that is to say, a pretty woman who knew how to primp and prattle, without straining to be anything more.

But Diane loved drawing with a passion, and she had never looked at a painting or a statue without examining it very carefully. In the chapel of her own convent, there had been some small statues of saints and a few paintings that had more or less pleased her. I don't know why, but looking at the fresco in the Baths of Diana in the Castle of Pictordu, and vaguely remembering everything the fairy had shown her in the night, she was convinced that the paintings in the convent were worthless, and that now she had something very beautiful in front of her.

She remembered that her father had said, putting two sketchbooks in his suitcase, "This little one will be for you, if you still have a taste for wasting paper."

She went to get the sketchbook, sharpened a pencil with her little pocketknife, and began to copy the nymph in the green dress, on which the morning sun cast a fresh light. Then she noticed the figure wasn't dancing at all. She was moving majestically, marking the tempo with steps that were soft, not too lively, because her two feet were resting on the cloud carrying her, and her hands, intertwined in those of her sisters, were not pulling them along to speed up the dance. Maybe she's a muse, Diane thought. She hadn't forgotten her mythology, even though such profane tales were forbidden in the convent.

As she daydreamed, Diane sketched on and on. Unhappy with her first drawing, she made a second, and then another, and another, until the sketchbook was half-filled. When she had gotten that far, she still wasn't happy. She was about to continue when a little hand was placed on her shoulder. Turning around with a start, Diane saw behind her a little girl about ten years old, rather poorly dressed but pretty and nice-looking. She was studying Diane's drawing and said to her mockingly, "So, you enjoy drawing pretty ladies in books, do you?"

"Yes," Diane answered. "Do you?"

"Me? Oh, no, never! My father forbids it. I don't spoil his books."

"My papa gave me this one for my own fun," Diane replied.

"Really? Is he rich, then?"

"Rich? Goodness, I don't know!"

"You don't know what it means to be rich?"

"Not really. I've never thought about it."

"Then that's because you're rich. I know very well what it's like to be poor."

"If you're poor . . . I have nothing to give you, but I'll go ask Papa . . ."

"Oh! Do you think I'm a beggar? You're certainly not very polite! Is it because I'm wearing just a calico dress while you have a silk shirt? For your information, I'm very much above you anyway. You're only a painter's daughter, but I'm Miss Blanche de Pictordu, daughter of the Marquis de Pictordu."

"How do you know so much about me?" asked Diane, very much unimpressed by these distinctions she did not understand.

"I just saw your papa in the courtyard of my castle, where he was talking with my father. I know you spent the night here. Your father apologized and my father, who is a real lord, invited him to come to a house in better shape than this abandoned castle. I'm warning you because you're going to come and eat at our new house."

"I'll go wherever my papa wants," Diane answered, "but I'd like to know why you say this castle is abandoned. I think it's still very beautiful and you don't know everything that's in it."

In a sad and haughty manner, Miss Blanche de Pictordu said, "Inside there are grass snakes, bats, and nettles. You don't have to make fun of me. I know we lost our ancestors' fortune and we have to live like country squires. But my papa taught me that that doesn't make us less important, because no one can say we're not the only true Pictordus."

Diane was more and more confused by this little girl's ideas and tone of voice. She naively asked if she were the Veiled Lady's daughter.

This question seemed to irritate the young lady of the castle.

"I'll have you know the Veiled Lady doesn't exist," she answered dryly, "and only ignorant and foolish people believe in such stupid stories. I'm not the daughter of a ghost. My mother came from as good a family as my father's."

Diane, feeling too ignorant to answer, made no reply. Her father came to tell her to get ready to leave. The coach was fixed. The Marquis de Pictordu insisted that the painter accept his dinner invitation. In those days people dined at noon.

The marquis's new home was at the end of the ravine on the road to Saint-Jean-Gardonenque. Occasionally, the marquis would go for a walk in the ruins of his ancestor's castle, and that day, having come by chance, he proved to be very kind and hospitable to these travelers delayed by an accident.

Flochardet quietly urged Diane to put on a fresh dress before he closed the suitcases, but Diane, in spite of her simplicity, was very tactful. She could easily see that Blanche de Pictordu was jealous of her plain traveling clothes. She didn't want to anger her further by making herself more beautiful. She asked her father to let her stay as she was, and she even took off a little turquoise brooch that fastened the black velvet around her neck and put it into her pocket.

When the coach was packed again, the marquis and his daughter, who had come on foot, climbed in with Diane and Flochardet, and half an hour later they all arrived at the new house.

It was a little farmhouse with the family coat of arms on the wall of the loft and very modest living quarters. The marquis was a rather narrow-minded man, not very well educated, but he was well-bred, very hospitable, and devout. He was incapable of resigning himself to the fact that he was one of the least important nobles of his province. He took pride in the fact that, by birth, he ranked above the eight important barons of Gévaudan. He felt bitterness toward no one and thought it was reasonable that a painter could get rich by working. He expressed the high esteem in which he held Flochardet, whose fame he was aware of, and welcomed him as best he could. But he couldn't help apologizing constantly for his lack of wealth, adding that, in this decadent world, nobility without money was no longer respected.

It wasn't that the marquis was sullen. He was bored and only wanted to be amused, but it was wrong of him always to talk about his situation in front of his daughter. Little Blanche had been born proud and envious, and had become bitter. It was really too bad, since she could have been a charming girl, as happy as any other, if she had been satisfied with her lot in life. Her father was very good to her and, all in all, the only things she lacked were unimportant.

Dinner was adequate and well served by a large peasant woman who was Blanche's nanny and the only servant in the house.

They talked about a lot of things that didn't interest Diane. But when the conversation turned to the old castle she had left so regretfully, a fact she didn't dare mention, she listened as hard as she could.

Her father said to the marquis, "Since you complain about your financial difficulties, I'm surprised at the neglect in which you've left those antique artworks. You could have sold them for good money."

"Are there really works of art in my castle?" asked the marquis.

"There were before all the roofs caved in. I saw a lot of pieces that, had they been saved in time, could have been sent to Italy where people still have a liking for old things."

"Yes," replied the marquis, "with a little money, I could have saved something, I know, but I didn't have even that little bit of money. I would have had to send for an artist, tell him to choose and evaluate; and then the packing, the freight, a trustworthy person to accompany them

. . . You understand that I couldn't do the work of a merchant!"

"But isn't there someone in the vicinity who would want some tapestries or statues?"

"No one. Rich people today look down on that old junk. They keep up with what's in fashion, and Chinese ornaments, rococo things, powdered shepherdesses are in style; no one likes nymphs and muses anymore. You need curlicues, ornate and overdone. Don't you agree?"

"I never criticize what's in fashion," replied the painter. "I am, by profession, its blind and devoted servant. However, styles change, and it's possible a liking for the old Valois style from the Renaissance will come back. If you've saved any ornamental pieces from your castle, keep them; a time might come when they'll be valuable."

"I've saved nothing," replied the marquis. "When I was born, my father had already let everything fall apart, through scorn and also from pride. Nothing would have convinced him to sell one stone from his castle, and he didn't move out until it almost fell on his head. More humble and more submissive to the will of God, I came to live in this little farmhouse, the only property of any worth left from our immense holdings."

Diane tried to understand what she was hearing and thought she succeeded. It gave her a guilty conscience. From her pocket she pulled a handful of the little multicolored pebbles she had picked up on the terrace, and giving them to Mr. Flochardet, said, "Papa, here's what I took from the castle garden. I thought they were just ordinary stones; but since you told the marquis he was wrong to let it go to waste, I must return his things. I didn't mean to steal."

The marquis was touched by Diane's kindness, and putting the pebbles back in the child's hand, said, "Keep these as a souvenir of us. I'm sorry, my dear little girl, but these are pieces of glass and worthless fragments of marble. I wish I had more to offer you."

Diane hesitated to take back the playthings so graciously offered to her. When she had pulled everything out of her pocket so hastily, she had also pulled out the little turquoise brooch. She looked at her father, indicating Blanche to him. From where she stood Blanche was eyeing the jewel and looked as though she were eager to touch it. Flochardet understood the good intentions of his daughter, and presenting the pin to Miss de Pictordu, he said, "Diane asks you to accept these little cut stones in exchange for your pretty pebbles, so you will have a souvenir of each other."

Blanche blushed until her ears were crimson. She was too proud simply to accept it, but her desire for this pretty turquoise made her heart pound.

"You will make my daughter very sad if you refuse," Flochardet told her.

Blanche seized the jewel nervously, almost tore it from the painter's hands, and ran away without taking the time to thank him, she was so afraid her father would order her to refuse it.

Perhaps that's what he would have done if he'd hoped to be obeyed, but knowing the temperament of his child, he didn't want his guests to be witness to a disagreeable scene. He begged Flochardet to forgive an uncivilized little girl's brusque manners and thanked him for her.

When dinner was over, Flochardet, who wanted to travel the rest of the day, said good-bye to the marquis, inviting him to honor Flochardet with a visit if he were ever in the south of France. The marquis thanked his guest for the lovely time they had spent together, and they shook hands. Ordered by her father, Blanche came grudgingly to give Diane a cold kiss. She had the turquoise brooch at her neck and held it with her hand, as if she were afraid someone would take it from her. Diane couldn't help thinking she was very foolish, but she forgave her in consideration of the good marquis, who had had the coach's baskets filled with his best cakes and most beautiful fruit.

Little Bacchus

The rest of the trip was without incident.

Diane no longer had a fever, and she almost had her color back when Flochardet put her into her stepmother's arms, saying, "I'm bringing her back to you because she was sick. I think she is already cured, but we'll have to see if the fever comes back."

Diane was so happy to be back in her parents' home it was as if she were drunk for several days. Mrs. Flochardet was overjoyed too, and took good care of her at first. She seemed to love Diane very much. She gave her a thousand little presents and played with her as she would with a pretty doll. Diane let her hair be curled, let herself be dressed up, and showed no impatience with all the time devoted to her grooming.

Without realizing it, however, she was really very bored spending all this time on her person. She stifled yawns and would become faint when she had to stand in front of a mirror, trying out hairstyles and trying on clothes. She didn't know how to groom herself to her stepmother's liking, and when she tried to make herself plainer and follow her own taste, she was scolded and chastised as if she had committed a serious mistake. She had wanted to busy herself doing something else, learning anything at all. She asked a lot of questions, but Mrs. Flochardet thought her questions were foolish and inappropriate, and that it was not worthwhile for her to be so curious about serious things. Diane had to hide from her stepmother her great desire to learn to draw. Mrs. Laura Flochardet was looking forward to the day when her husband had made his fortune and there wouldn't be any more painting in the house.

Then she could take on the imposing manners of a great lady.

Diane began to become extremely bored and miss the convent, which she hadn't liked very well, but where at least they supervised the use of her time. She became pale again, her step listless, and the fever returned every other day around sundown and lasted until morning.

Then her stepmother worried herself sick and pestered her to take a lot of medicine, on the advice of all the beautiful ladies who came to visit. Every day they thought up a new way to cure the fever, and since they followed up on nothing, nothing succeeded. The child continued to submit to everything and tried to reassure her parents, saying she wasn't feeling sick.

Mr. Flochardet was even more upset than his wife. Forced to work every hour of the day at his painting, he spent the evening at his daughter's bedside and, hearing her rambling, was afraid she might go mad.

Luckily, one of his friends was a good elderly doctor, who had better judgment. He knew Mrs. Flochardet very well and observed the way she treated the child. One day, he said to Mr. Flochardet, "You must leave this little girl alone, throw away all those bottles and pills give her only what I prescribe, and don't argue when she wants something. She is very sensible. Don't you see that the idleness to which you've condemned her, for fear of making her sick, is making her even more ill? She is bored; let her find something to do, and when she shows a distinct preference for a field of study, help her to devote herself to it. Above all, don't make her into a little model for trying on clothes. It's a strain, not a pleasure, for her. Leave her waist and her hair free, and, if Mrs. Flochardet can't endure seeing Diane like that, try to distract her—busy her with other things."

Mr. Flochardet understood, and knowing it would be difficult to persuade Mrs. Flochardet, he saw to it she was distracted. He told her the child was not seriously ill, and encouraged her to resume her life of visiting, walking with her friends, dining in town, and spending her evenings dancing or in conversation. He had no trouble convincing her. Diane was free to do what she wanted, as in the past.

So Diane once again asked for and obtained

permission to slip into her father's studio when he was working, and to reappear in her little corner, sometimes studying the canvas, sometimes the sitter. But she no longer tried to produce her scribblings, so nobody would laugh at her expense. She knew now that painting was an art, and it was necessary to study it to know it.

Her desire to learn to paint remained so strong that it was almost an obsession, but she no longer talked about it. She was afraid her father would tell her, as he had before, that she had no talent for it, and that her stepmother would be against it.

But Mr. Flochardet did not try to thwart her. Old Dr. Féron, having advised Flochardet to observe her leanings, expected her to show her former taste for portrait drawing and had put a supply of pencils and paper at her disposal. Diane didn't use them. Instead she studied her father's works and sketches, and dreamed.

She often thought of the Pictordu castle. Since it was sometimes discussed in her presence as that ruin where Flochardet had been obliged to spend a night, she no longer dared to believe in everything the veiled fairy had shown her. She was sorry she had seen it in such a confusing way, perhaps distorted by fever, and she wished, if it had been a dream, that she could dream it again. But you never dream what you want to dream, and the muse from the goddess Diana's baths didn't come back to summon her.

One day when Diane was straightening up her toys, because she was a very tidy person, she came across the little colored stones from the Pictordu flower beds. Among the stones, there was a ball of hardened sand, about the size of a nut, that she had picked up to use as a marble. She tried, for the first time, to use it, but in tossing it, she saw the sand break away and reveal a real marble. But this marble was no longer perfectly round; it was, rather, oval with bumps and hollows. Diane examined it and recognized it as the head from a statuette of a child. The face looked so pretty to her that she couldn't stop looking at it, turning it over, putting it first in the sun, then in shadow, thinking she might always find a new beauty there.

She had been absorbed in looking at it for an hour when the doctor, who had come in very quietly and was watching her, said to her in a friendly voice, "What are you looking at with so much pleasure, my little Diane?"

"I don't know," she replied, blushing. "Look for yourself, my dear friend. I think it's the face of a little Cupid."

"It's more likely a young Bacchus, because there are grapevines in his hair. So, where did you find it?"

"In some sand and stones, at that old castle my father was just telling you about yesterday."

"Well, let me see it!" answered the doctor, putting on his glasses. "It's really very pretty! It's an antique."

"Does that mean it's something that's out of style today? Mama Laura says that antiques are very ugly."

"I'm just the opposite. I think everything new is ugly."

At that moment, Mr. Flochardet came in. He had finished a portrait sitting, and, before beginning another, he came to greet the doctor and ask him how he thought the little girl was doing.

"I think she's doing very well," answered Dr. Féron, "and she's even saner than you, because she admires this little fragment of antique statuary. I'll wager you don't like it at all."

After having them explain how this object had turned up in Diane's hands, Mr. Flochardet examined it indifferently and, throwing it back on the table, said, "It's not any more poorly made than anything else from that era, if it really is an antique. I wouldn't know how to appraise it as you would. You have a passion for these scraps and believe yourself qualified to judge. I don't deny your expertise and scholarship, dear doctor, but such debris is so worn, so misshapen, that you often see it through the eyes of a believer. I admit that it would be impossible for me to do likewise, and all of these so-called masterpieces of Greek or Roman art impresses me as much as Diane's dolls when a nose is broken or their cheeks are scratched."

"Philistine!" said the doctor angrily. "You dare to compare . . . Ah, yes! You're a frivolous artist! You are only well versed in laces and muffs. You have no idea what real life is!"

Flochardet was used to the doctor's outbursts. He greeted them with laughter, and since his servant had come to announce that the carriage of his next client, the Marquise de Sept-Pointes, was coming into the courtyard, he left, still laughing.

"You are wicked today, my good friend," said

Diane, scandalized. "My papa is a great artist. Everyone says so."

"That's why he shouldn't talk foolishness," answered the doctor, still very upset.

"If what he says isn't true, he's only joking."

"Apparently! Let's forget about it. But you . . . you think this little head is pretty, don't you?"

"Oh! Very pretty! Really, I love it!"

"Do you know why?"

"No."

"Try to say why."

"It's laughing, it's happy, it's young, it's like a real child."

"And yet, it is the likeness of a god?"

"You said so, the god of the wine harvest."

"So it's not a child like any other? The person who made it thought that this child should be stronger and prouder than just any child. See how the neck is attached, the strength and elegance of the nape, the slightly wild hair on a low, wide forehead, yet noble still. But I'm telling you too much, you aren't ready to understand."

"Keep talking, my good friend. Maybe I will understand!"

"It doesn't tire you out to pay attention?"

"Not at all, I like it."

"All right. You should know that Greek artists had a feeling for greatness, and they put it in the smallest of things. Do you remember seeing my little collection of statues?"

"Of course—I remember them very well, also the beautiful collections in town, but no one has ever talked to me about them."

"Come and spend a morning at my house and I will help you understand how, with the simplest methods and barely adequate molds, these artists always made great and beautiful statues. You will also see Roman busts from a more recent era. The Romans were great artists, too! Not as noble, not as pure as the Greeks, but always true to life, and feeling life in what is really life."

"I don't understand anymore!" sighed Diane. "And I would so much like to know what you mean by life."

"It's very easy. Your dress, your shoe, your comb—are they living things?"

"Oh! Of course not!"

"Well, when you see a person in a picture or a statue whose face is not living, you can be certain it's not much better than the face of your doll, and that all the details of its clothing or jewels don't make it alive. All you have here is just a head without a body, very worn from friction. It lives, nonetheless, because the person who shaped it out of this little piece of marble had the will and the skill to make it live. Now do you understand?"

"I think maybe a little bit, but tell me more."

"No, that's enough for today. We'll talk about this another day. Don't lose . . ."

"My little head? Oh! No danger of that. I love it too much. It was given to me by someone I will never forget."

"And who is that?"

"The lady who . . . the lady . . . but I can't tell you about it!"

"You have secrets?"

"Well, yes. I don't want to tell!"

"Even me, your old friend?"

"Will you make fun of me?"

"I swear to you I won't."

"But you'll say it was the fever."

"What if I did say that?"

"It would upset me."

"So, I won't say it. Tell me."

Diane told him about all her visions and

delights at the Pictordu castle, and the doctor listened to her without laughing, without looking skeptical. His questions even helped her to remember better and make herself understood. For him it was an interesting study of the phenomenon of fever in the imagination of a child with a disposition toward poetry, and consequently toward magic. He didn't think he ought to disillusion her. He left her in doubt, as he had found her. He didn't want to assure her that what she had seen and heard was certain and real. He pretended he didn't know, either, whether she had dreamed or not, and the state of uncertainty in which he left her was, for her, a joy. Leaving her, the doctor said to himself, "We don't know what wrong we do to children by making fun of their inclinations and the damage that we can do them by suppressing their abilities. This little girl is a born artist, and her father doesn't see it. God save her from his lessons! He will distort her gift and make her dislike art."

Luckily for Diane, her excellent father hadn't thought to make her work, and seeing how frail she was, he had made up his mind not to occupy her with anything. She spent more than one morning at the doctor's home. She saw his antiques—busts, statues, medals, cameos, and engravings—over and over again. He was a serious amateur and a good critic, even though he had never picked up a pencil; he helped her understand, and that was all Diane needed to make her want to copy what she saw. So she drew a lot at his house while he was making his rounds.

I would be misleading you, my children, if I told you she drew well. She was too young and often left to her own devices. But she had already acquired one important thing: she understood that her sketches were not good. Before, she was happy with everything that her pencil produced. With her imagination and her lack of knowledge, she would see charming people instead of the monkeys she had just drawn. And when she had made a ball with four sticks coming down from it, she thought she had made a sheep or a horse. Now those easy illusions had vanished , and every time she made a sketch, the doctor told her, in vain: "Well, it's not bad."

But she would say to herself, "No, it is bad. I can see it's bad."

She sometimes thought that the fever was

keeping her from seeing properly, and she continually begged her good friend to cure her. Little by little, he succeeded, and then, feeling stronger and happier, she wasn't in such a hurry to know how to draw. She forgot her pencils and spent her time walking in the garden or in the country, enjoying everything, gathering her strength, and sleeping very well at night.

The Lost Face

The Flochardets left town in May and went to the country. Diane always enjoyed herself very much there.

One day when she was picking violets on the edge of a little wood between her father's garden and a neighbor lady's, she heard talking very near at hand. Looking through the branches, she saw her stepmother, visiting with the lady. Her stepmother was wearing a pretty silk shawl over a pink taffeta dress. The neighbor was dressed more sensibly for a walk in the wood, where Mama Laura had met her. Both were seated on a bench.

Diane went to greet them, and then she stopped, intimidated. She wasn't unsociable, but Mama Laura had become so cold and indifferent toward her that Diane no longer knew if her stepmother was happy to see her. So she withdrew, unsure and saddened, not wanting to run away, and went back to picking violets, waiting to be called.

As she was bent over behind the bushes, the ladies couldn't see her and Diane heard Mama Laura saying to her friend: "I thought she would come and curtsy to you, but she hid to get out of it. The poor child is so ill-mannered since they forbade me to train her! What do you expect, my dear? Her father is weak, and controlled by that Dr. Féron, who's a funny old grump. He has declared that the girl should receive no education at all. So you see the beautiful results!"

"That's too bad," said the other lady. "She's pretty and seems sweet. I often see her near my flower bed. She touches nothing and greets me politely when she sees me. If she were tidied up, she would be just fine."

"Ah yes, tidied up! My dear, can you imagine that the old doctor has forbidden her to wear a corset! Not a whalebone on her body! How can she help but be hunchbacked?"

"She's not hunchbacked. On the contrary, she is well formed, but you could dress her without tightening her waist and maybe put some trimmings on her skirts."

"Pooh! She's the one who doesn't want it. That child hates primping. She gets that from her mother, who was a common person, more concerned with her kitchen than looking gracious and fitting in."

"I knew her mother," answered the neighbor. "She was a fine woman, sensible and very distinguished, I assure you."

"Oh? I suppose. I'm just going by hearsay. Mr. Flochardet has her portrait hidden somewhere. He's never shown it to me. He doesn't want me to talk to him about her, and after all, it doesn't matter to me! Let them raise the child the way they want to, since it doesn't concern me! I could have loved her, though, if they had given me the responsibility of making her presentable . . . but . . ."

"So she's sullen and disagreeable?"

"No, my dear, she's worse than that; she's simple, absent-minded, and a little feeble-minded I think."

"Poor little thing! Don't they teach her anything?"

"Nothing at all! She doesn't even know how to tie a ribbon or put a flower in her hair."

"I thought she liked to draw?"

"Yes, she likes that, but her father says she has no taste and understands nothing about painting. And since she understands nothing about anything else . . ."

Diane heard no more. She had put her hands over her ears and fled farther into the woods to hide her tears. She felt a very deep sadness, without really knowing why. Was it humiliation at being thought stupid or discouragement at being considered incompetent by her father? Wasn't it rather the sorrow of discovering she wasn't loved?

"But my papa loves me," she said to herself. "I'm sure of it. Maybe he thinks I'm stupid and clumsy . . . but he doesn't love me less for it. It's Mama Laura who despises me and doesn't care about me."

Up until then, Diane had done her best to love Mama Laura. At that moment, she felt she was nothing to her stepmother, and for the first time, she thought about her real mother and tried very hard to remember her; but it was next to impossible. She had still been in her cradle when her mother had died. She very vaguely remembered her father's marriage to Mama Laura. The only thing she had noticed that day was her nanny's sadness. She remembered hearing her say several times when looking at Diane, "Poor little thing! This woman will bring her unhappiness."

Mama Laura had kissed Diane and offered her candy. The child had not paid any more attention to her nanny's distress. Now she began to understand it, hearing her stepmother's bitter words about her and about her dead mother, about whom no one had ever told her anything. She began to dream about her mother with a completely new fervency and sadness. It was as if she were discovering a dormant feeling within herself, deep in her heart. She fell down on the grass, repeating in a voice broken by sobs, "Mama! Mama!"

Then she heard someone calling to her in a soft voice through the blooming lilac bushes.

It was her nanny, dear Geoffrette, who picked her up, saying, "I've been looking for you for a good quarter of an hour. You shouldn't sleep on the grass like that, the ground is still cold. Here, I brought you something to eat. Get up, or you'll get sick! Come over here, eat in the sun."

Geoffrette could see that Diane was very upset. She succeeded in distracting the child, but that evening she again had a little fever and all night long she had confused and tiring dreams. In the morning she felt a little better, opened her eyes, and saw that the day was beginning to break. Through her blue curtain, her room looked all blue and she couldn't make anything out. Little by little she saw more clearly a person standing at the foot of her bed.

"Is that you, Nanny?" she said. But the person gave no answer and Diane heard Geoffrette cough in her bed. So who was this person who seemed to be watching over Diane?

"Is that you, Mama Laura?" she said, forgetting her stepmother's harsh words and only wanting to love her again.

The person still didn't answer and Diane noticed there was a veil over her face.

"Oh!" she said joyfully. "I recognize you! You're my good fairy from the castle! You're finally here! Did you come to be my mother?"

"Yes," answered the Veiled Lady, in her beautiful voice that reverberated like crystal.

"And you'll love me?"

"Yes, if you'll love me."

"Oh! I would love to love you!"

"Do you want to go for a walk with me?"

"Of course, right away, but I'm weak!"

"I'll carry you."

"Oh, yes. Let's go!"

"What do you want to see?"

"My mother."

"Your mother? . . . I'm your mother."

"Really? Then take off your veil so I can see your face."

"You know very well I no longer have a face!"

"Oh no! So I'll never see it?"

"That depends on you. You will see it the day you give it back to me."

"Oh, goodness, what does that mean? How will I do that?"

"You will have to find it again."

At about nine o'clock, the doctor, who had

been called by Geoffrette, came into Diane's room with her father. The child had no fever, it had broken. They nursed her that day and the following night she was very quiet. Two days later, she had recovered again and she returned to her walks and her carefree life.

Looking for the Face

One beautiful day of that year, the observant doctor noticed a change in the family. Mama Laura couldn't hide her wish to see Diane sent back to the convent. It wasn't that she hated Diane—Mama Laura wasn't evil. She was just vain, and she accused Diane of being stupid only because she was stupid herself. She was hurt not to have charge of Diane, humiliated at not having this toy at her disposal. Flochardet didn't know what to think anymore. He was torn between his wife's nagging and the doctor's advice, anxiously wondering whether Diane was intelligent beyond her years, as Dr. Féron claimed, or if she was wild and uneducated, as Mama Laura insinuated. He wondered if, for her own good, it wouldn't be better to send her back to the care of his sister, the nun in Mende.

As for Diane, her happiness had returned along with her unspoiled good nature. But she no longer loved her stepmother and no longer tried to make herself loved. She had become indifferent toward this beautiful woman. She was thinking about entirely different things.

Her desire to be educated had begun to torment her, and it wasn't just drawing she wanted to learn. It is impossible to study any kind of art without touching on the causes of its decline and progress, not to mention the entire history of the human race. Therefore, Dr. Féron had decided to seriously teach the little girl. He asked Flochardet to let Diane and her nanny come and spend her days with him, since the two families lived next door to each other, in town as well as in the country. He was getting ready to retire anyway and was thinking of turning his practice over to his nephew, who had just finished his studies and was very intelligent. The doctor had raised him as his son, but he had always wanted to have a daughter to share his fortune with also.

Flochardet didn't think he had the right to

refuse his daughter such a wonderful future. He was all the more willing because at the rate Mama Laura was spending money, he feared his own fortune would sooner or later be depleted. He gave in and Mama Laura was most delighted. She even found it much more convenient for the little girl to live with Geoffrette at the doctor's house. Flochardet gave in again, and Diane moved into a charming, well-furnished little room just for her with Geoffrette next door. She became very happy, very studious, and very healthy.

At twelve, Diane was still a charming child, simple, happy, good to everyone, never bragging or calling attention to herself. However, she was very solidly educated for her age, and her mind had serious and passionate aspects that no one knew about. She painted very pleasant pictures. She had learned a little about the mechanics of painting such pictures by watching her father work. But she no longer showed them to anyone, because once when the doctor had said they were very good, her father had said they were very bad. Diane felt the doctor, who was a good critic, understood nothing of execution. He had cultivated in her a love for what was beautiful, but he couldn't show her how to create it. She also felt her father had a system completely contrary to the doctor's theories, that he never thought anything good that was different from his method, and that he could be mistaken without knowing it.

But could Diane know if she were mistaken? What should she think of her father's talent, which the doctor criticized with such apparent accuracy? And what should she think about the doctor's criticism, a man who couldn't even hold a pencil or trace a line? This dilemma tormented her so deeply that she became slightly ill again. The doctor cared for her without becoming too concerned, but he tried to discover the psychological causes of her bouts of fever.

The doctor made up his mind to coax the truth from his dear adopted daughter, and, though she preferred not to talk about it, she couldn't resist his gentle questions.

"All right," she told him, "I admit it. I have an obsession. I have to find a face, and I can't find it!"

"What face? Still the Veiled Lady? Has that childhood fantasy come back to the reasonable young lady I see before me now?"

"Unfortunately, my friend, the fantasy has never left me since the Veiled Lady said, 'I am your mother and you will see my face when you give it back to me.' I didn't understand right away, but little by little I've discovered I must find and draw a face I've never seen—my mother's—and that's what I'm looking for. They tell me she was beautiful. Maybe it will be impossible for me to make anything that approaches her beauty, unless I have a lot of talent. I would like to have talent, but it's not coming. I am very unhappy with myself, I tear up or scribble over everything I do. All the faces I draw are ugly or insignificant. I watch how my father goes about making his clients more beautiful. I can see that he does and I know that's the reason for his success. How do I feel about those faces? When I look at his models, who are certainly not all beautiful—there are even women whose looks have faded and very ugly men who come to him to be painted—I think the ugliest faces are . . . how can I put it? . . . more acceptable than the conventional faces my father gives them. The people who pose are themselves, there is something original about each one, and that is exactly what my father believes he should take away from them—and they are happy it's taken away. As for me, in my head, I paint them just as they are, and I know if I knew how to paint, I would do just the opposite of what my father does. That's what is tormenting and saddening me, because I know he has talent and I don't."

"He has talent and you don't, that's certain," answered the doctor, "but you will have. You are too upset for it to come to you, and when you do have it—I don't want to say you'll have more than he does, I know nothing about it—it will be talent of another nature, because you see with other eyes. So, he can't teach you anything; you must find out for yourself, and you must take your time. You are trying to go too quickly, and by doing so, you risk not having any talent at all. You get a fever and you don't feel well.

"As for the face you're looking for, it's easy to get it for you if it will rid you of the Veiled Lady you're obsessed with. Your father has a very good miniature of your mother that looks very much like her. He didn't do it and he doesn't like it, because it's not his style. He shows it to no one and claims it's not she at all. I think it looks just like her and I'll ask him for it to show you."

At that moment, Diane's only desire was to see her mother's features. She thanked the doctor profusely and accepted his offer, overcome with joy. Dr. Féron promised she would see the miniature the next day. He made her promise to relax until then and from now on work with less passion and more patience.

She kept her word as well as possible. But as soon as she fell asleep that night, she saw the Veiled Lady again, who suggested a trip to Pictordu Castle. Diane agreed but she was afraid. As they entered through the courtyard, the castle fell down all around them. It didn't hurt them, though, any more than if it had been a little gust of snow. The ground was littered with cameos, each more beautiful than the next, falling from the clouds.

"Quickly," said the Veiled Lady. "Let's look for my face! It must be in here, it's up to you to recognize it. If you don't find it, too bad for you, you'll never know what I look like!"

Diane looked for a long time, until at last she found in her hand a shining carnelian. Against the red background the profile of an ideal beauty was carved in unpolished white, her hair pulled back with a ribbon and a star on her forehead. At first the little head seemed to Diane to be the size of a ring's setting, but as she looked at it, it grew and grew and filled the entire hollow of her hand.

"Finally!" the fairy cried out. "There I am! That's me, your muse, your mother, and you are going to see you're not mistaken." She began to untie her veil, but Diane couldn't see her face, because the vision vanished, and she woke up distraught.

When she got up in the morning, the doctor came to her room carrying a Moroccan leather box with gold hinges that he was going to open, believing he would give her sweet pleasure. But she cried out, pushing it away,

"No, no, my dear friend! I must not see it yet! She doesn't want me to. I must find it by myself. If not, she'll leave me forever!"

"As you wish," answered the doctor. "You have your own ideas that I don't always understand, but I don't want to argue with you. I'll leave you this locket, it's yours. Your father was going to give it to you. You'll look at it when the fairy who talks to you in your dreams gives you permission, or when you no longer believe in fairies. That will happen soon enough, since now you are at the age where you can distinguish dream from reality."

Diane thanked Dr. Féron for his wise words and the beautiful gift he had brought her. She kissed the locket, and, without opening it, hid it carefully in her desk, after swearing to herself she would wait for permission from the mysterious muse—and she kept her word. She resisted the desire to know the dear face, and she once again began looking for it at the end of her pencil. But she also kept her word to her good friend; she worked more patiently, no longer insisting on immediate success. She endeavored to copy models, without hoping to succeed in creating something beautiful overnight.

A strange idea helped her to be patient: she thought she remembered perfectly the beautiful cameo profile she had seen and touched in her dream. It was always before her eyes, and always the same, every time she wanted to think about it. But she refrained from thinking about it for too long at a time or too often, because then it seemed to flicker and threaten to disappear.

The Face Rediscovered

Diane continued to learn and to be happy, when one day—she was then about fifteen—she saw that her father was sad and changed.

"Are you sick, dear Papa?" she asked, kissing him. "You're not wearing your usual face."

"Pooh!" Flochardet answered, rather sharply. "Do you think you know something about faces?"

"I try, Papa. I do what I can," Diane replied. In her father's voice she could hear his ridicule of her unfortunate passion for art.

"You do what you can!" said Flochardet, looking at her sadly. "Why do you have this foolish idea stuck in your head that you'll be an artist? You don't need to be. You've found a second father, wiser and happier than the first. You want to have the worries of working, when you don't have to! Why? What for?"

"I can't answer that, Papa. It's out of my control, but if it makes you angry that I try, I'll give it up no matter how sad it would make me."

"No, no. Have a good time. Do what you want. Dream the impossible. That's the happiness of youth. Later, you will learn that talent won't save you from inevitable fate and misfortune."

"Oh my goodness! You're very unhappy, aren't you?" cried Diane, throwing herself into his arms. "Is it true? How? Why? You must tell me. I don't want to be happy anymore if you're not."

"Don't worry about anything," Flochardet answered, giving her a tender kiss. "I said that to test you. I'm not unhappy at all. I thought you no longer loved me because . . . because I neglected your education and entrusted it to someone else. Maybe you thought I was a frivolous father, indifferent and led by the nose . . ."

"Oh no, no, Papa. I love you and I've never thought that. Why on earth would I have thought that?"

"Because I've thought it myself from time to time. I blamed myself for certain things. Now I take comfort in knowing that if I should have some financial disaster, you won't be affected by it."

Diane tried to question her father further. He changed the subject and started to work again, but he was upset, impatient, and seemed disgusted with what he was painting. Suddenly, he threw down his brush angrily and said, "It's not going well today. I'd just as soon wreck the canvas, and for two sous, I'd break it in two. Come and take a walk with me!"

As they were getting ready to leave, Mama Laura came in, as dressed up as usual, but her face was different.

"What?" she said to her husband. "You're going out when you're supposed to deliver the portrait this evening?"

"And what if I don't deliver it until tomorrow?" Flochardet answered coldly. "Am I a slave to my customers?"

"No, but . . . you must collect the money for that painting tonight, because tomorrow morning . . ."

"Oh, yes! Your seamstress, your fabric merchant. They're out of patience, I know, and if we don't satisfy them, there'll be another scandal."

Mama Laura noticed Diane's eyes, wide with astonishment and fear.

"My dear child," she said. "You bother your father too much, you're keeping him from his work, and he must work, especially today. Leave him alone."

"You're sending me away?" cried Diane, dumbfounded and dismayed.

"No, never!" Mr. Flochardet shouted, sitting her down next to him. "Stay! You're not the one who's bothering me!"

"So, *I'm* in the way," Mama Laura responded. "I understand and I know what to do."

"Do whatever you want," Flochardet replied in an icy tone.

She left and Diane burst into tears.

"What's the matter?" her father said to her, trying to smile. "What does it matter to you if I quarrel a little from time to time with Mama Laura? She isn't your mother. Do you love her so dearly?"

"You're unhappy," Diane answered, sobbing. "My father is unhappy and I didn't know it!"

Again assuming his usual carefree tone of voice, he said, "No, a person isn't unhappy because of his annoyances. I have some rather serious ones, I admit, but I'll work it out. I'll work harder, that's all. I thought I'd be able to slow down a little. I've made quite a bit of money, about two hundred thousand francs. In the provinces, that's a very comfortable living, but I have to tell you, since you'll find out sooner or later, we've spent money like water. It was foolish of me to have a house built; the costs have been much higher than the estimates. In short, we'll have to sell it, and at a loss, since the creditors want their money right away."

"Now you won't be shocked to hear that I'm bankrupt. Don't be too distressed; people always exaggerate. I'll sell what I have, and my debts will be paid, my honor will be intact, and you'll have no reason to be ashamed of your father, rest assured! And besides, I'll make everything right. I'm still young and strong, I'll raise my prices a little, and my customers will just have to accept them. With time, I sincerely hope to save enough to give you a reasonable dowry if you're not in too much of a hurry to marry. In that case the doctor will make me a loan."

"Oh, let's not talk about me," cried Diane. "I've never thought of marriage and I'm not interested in what will happen to me in the future. Let's just talk about you. Is this pretty house in town that you love so much, that you've fixed up so nicely, where you are so very comfortable, going to be sold? No, that can't be. Where will you work? And your country home . . . where will you live, then?"

Flochardet, seeing Diane was more concerned for him than he wanted her to be, tried to reassure her, telling her that perhaps he could get new extensions on the loans. But she was worried that he would overwork. She feared he would become ill. She pretended to calm down, but only to please him, and she went home completely despondent and spent the evening crying inwardly. She dared not tell the doctor how sad she was; she didn't want to hear him blame and criticize her father. She played chess with her old friend and retired to her room to cry freely.

She slept little and didn't dream at all. In the morning, she started to work as usual, trying to keep herself busy. But she always returned to the cruel thought that Mama Laura would kill her father by making him work too hard, and if her own poor mother had lived, he would still be sensible and happy.

Then she mourned for her mother in her heart, not as before, when she missed her mother only on account of herself; she missed her now for the happiness her mother could have given her father and had taken away with her.

And she sketched mechanically, without thinking about what her hands were doing. She called out to her mother from the depths of her soul, saying, "Where are you? Do you see what's happening? Can't you tell me anything I could do to save and console someone who is overwhelmed and devastated by another?"

Suddenly, she felt a breath of warm air in her hair and a voice as gentle as the morning breeze murmur in her ear, "I am here. You have found me."

Diane trembled and turned around; there was no one behind her. The only movement in her room was the shadow of the linden tree leaves stirred by the wind, against the white pine floor. She looked at her paper; a very delicate silhouette was drawn there. It was she who had drawn it; she added details and shaped the face, still without attaching much importance to it. Then she filled in the hair, drew a ribbon around it, and added a star in memory of the magnificent cameo she had dreamed of. Then she looked at the drawing indifferently, while Geoffrette, who had just come in, scurried about the room, picking up a few things.

"Well, my child," said the good woman as she came closer, "are you happy with your work this morning?"

"Not any more than usual, Geoffrette. I don't even really know what I'm doing . . . But what's the matter with you? You're pale and are you crying?"

"Oh, my Lord!" cried Geoffrette. "How can it be? You didn't draw that face, did you? Did you look at the portrait, then? And you copied it?"

"What portrait? I didn't copy anything!"

"Then . . . then . . . is it a vision? A miracle? Doctor, come and see, come and see this! What do you think of this?"

"What? What is it?" said the doctor, who was coming to call Diane to lunch. "Why is Geoffrette shouting about a miracle?"

And looking at Diane's drawing, he added, "She copied the locket! But that's very well done, my girl; do you know how good it is? It's even astonishing, and the resemblance is striking. The poor young woman! It's as if I were looking at her.

Keep up the good work, my girl! You will paint better than your father. This one is beautiful and alive."

Diane, dumbfounded, was looking at her drawing and saw the exact picture of the cameo from her dream, the one she had kept in her mind, but it was the work of her imagination, and undoubtedly the resemblance that Geoffrette and the doctor found was also a case of imagination. She didn't want to tell them she had never opened the locket: she was afraid they'd make her open it, and she didn't think she was worthy, yet, of that reward.

During lunch, however, she asked her friend if he really thought the portrait of her mother was a good likeness.

"How would I have recognized her," he said, "if it weren't? You know I don't indulge you. Geoffrette," he added, "go fetch that drawing for me. I want to see it again."

Geoffrette obeyed, and the doctor again examined it attentively, as he enjoyed his coffee. He said no more. He seemed absorbed, and Diane wondered anxiously if he were not reconsidering his first impression. At that moment, Mr. Flochardet, who sometimes came to have coffee with the doctor, was announced.

"What are you looking at there?" he said to Dr. Féron, after kissing his daughter.

"Look for yourself," answered the doctor.

Mr. Flochardet leaned toward the drawing and grew pale.

"It's she," he said with emotion. "Yes, it surely is that dear and worthy creature whom—without telling anyone—I think about constantly, now more than ever! But who drew this portrait, Doctor? It's a copy of that locket I gave to you for Diane. Only it's infinitely better expressed and better rendered. The likeness is more dignified and more true to life. It's very remarkable and I don't have a single student capable of drawing anything like it. Tell me! Tell me who drew this?"

"It's . . . it's . . ." said the doctor with a shrewd hesitation, "a young student of . . . of mine, with all due respect to you!"

Flochardet looked at his daughter, who had turned toward the window to hide her emotions, and then he looked at the doctor questioningly. He understood. He turned again to the drawing, very much surprised, perhaps trying to find something in it to criticize. But he found nothing to correct, because he was in that frame of mind when you're no longer sure of yourself and are forced to admit you might be wrong about something very serious.

Diane dared not turn around, afraid she might be dreaming. She focused her attention on the window to hide her turmoil, indifferent to the ruby rays of the bright sun striking her head and penetrating her eyes like red-hot needles. In this dazzling light, she saw a marvelously beautiful, tall, white figure, whose greenish dress shimmered like emerald dust. It was the muse of her dreams, it was the good fairy, the Veiled Lady, but she no longer had the veil over her face, it floated around her like a golden aura. And her beautiful face, which was the same as the cameo seen in the dream, was exactly like the one Diane had drawn, the one Flochardet was contemplating on the sketching paper with mixed admiration and terror.

Diane stretched out her arms toward this shining figure, who was smiling and who said to her as she drifted away, "You will see me again!"

Diane, breathless and ecstatic, fell into a chair

in the bay window, choking back a joyful cry. Flochardet and the doctor rushed to her, thinking she was sick, but she reassured them. Not telling them of the vision she had just seen, she asked her father if he really was a little happy with her work.

"I'm not only happy," he answered, "I'm delighted and overwhelmed. I owe you an apology, my daughter; you're burning with enthusiasm, and with that, you have a knowledge of drawing way beyond your years. Continue without wearing yourself out; work, hope, doubt yourself often. That's good for you. But I don't doubt your talent any longer and I am very happy!"

They hugged each other and cried. Then Flochardet asked his daughter to let him talk business with the doctor, and she retired to her room, where she was all alone. Diane took out the Moroccan leather box she had tied with a black satin ribbon so she wouldn't be tempted to open it too soon. She finally opened it, kneeled on a cushion, and kissed the locket before looking at it. Then, she closed her eyes so she could remember the ideal image of the one who had promised to come back. She saw her again, very clearly, and certain of her consent, she finally looked at the portrait. Sure enough, it was the same face she had drawn; it was the muse, it was the cameo, it was the dream, and it was at the same time her mother. It was reality discovered through poetry, feeling, and imagination.

Diane didn't wonder how this marvelous experience had happened to her. She just accepted it, and didn't try to figure out how to explain it using her reason, as she would later try to do. I think she did the right thing. When you're still very young, it is better to believe in friendly divinities than to believe too much in yourself.

The Collapse

I'll not tell you what happened day-by-day in the two years that followed. Diane continued to work at her drawing bravely and modestly, often asking her father's advice with tender humility. But he wasn't always prepared to understand what he himself had been incapable of doing. Without realizing it, Diane was going in a direction exactly the opposite of his.

The area where she lived had a lot of fragments of antique statuary, which people were now beginning to appreciate, as French tastes were beginning to take a new turn. Engraving was spreading and popularizing precious finds from Herculaneum and Pompeii: paintings, urns, statues, furniture, all sorts of things. And an "elegant simplicity," as they used to say, was starting to replace Chinese-style knickknacks, overly elaborate table legs and feet, and other excesses. People were becoming more familiar with Italy, they traveled more, and if they still appreciated Watteau's beautiful colors and pleasing extravagance, they were no less in love with Etruscan urns and Greek medallions. They didn't exactly return to a taste for the old Valois style, which today we call Renaissance; they took up a new style, less original, but still charming. They made furniture in what we now call Louis XVI style, which before they called antique reproductions. They were very beautiful, although not faithfully reproduced, and they were very impressive. Women began to lower their colossal hairdos and fluff their hair, still powdered, casually around their foreheads. Men curled their whiskers and tied their long hair back with simple ribbons, instead of catching it up in a net as before. Some even fastened up braids with tortoiseshell combs. Flochardet was wearing his hair like that in his studio and painting portraits in which the clothing and hair were much less complicated than in those that had brought him so much fame.

But Flochardet was not really keeping up with the new tastes. As his business fell off, he tried to increase his rates at a time when people were less inclined to pay a lot of money. Since he would have been humiliated to accept a lower price, he watched his clientele rapidly diminish. His situation became very grave. Unable to control her spending, Mama Laura had taken her small assets from their combined resources and retired to her parents' home in Nîmes, where she stayed three-quarters of the year, spending the little money she had on new dresses.

Diane, seeing her father abandoned, sad, and alone, returned home to live with him and shared her time between him and the doctor. They let all the servants go except for Geoffrette, who did the cooking. Diane put his house and his business in order, but she could manage only to delay the disaster to come. When she realized the dimensions of her father's financial ruin, she went to ask the kind doctor for help.

"My dear friend," she said to him, "do you know that my father is ruined?"

"Yes, I know," the doctor answered, "completely ruined! He needs two hundred thousand francs and no one wants to lend it to him."

Diane begged the doctor for the loan, but the doctor was hesitant, sure that Flochardet's wife would come back and spend all the money once again. He had another solution to offer. The next day, when the town house and the country house were put up for auction, Dr. Féron bought them both. In his will, he planned to divide his entire fortune between Diane and his nephew. He didn't want Diane to have to choose between a struggle with her father or being forced into bankruptcy by him.

"My friend," he said to Flochardet, "I'm sorry I couldn't save you from this catastrophe. Now all your property's lost, but since I've acquired it, you'll live peacefully and debt-free from now on. You'll live with your daughter, to whom I'm renting what was your house and is now mine.

She'll put more than half of the building—the part you once used just for balls and parties—to good use by subletting it. What you earn together from your clientele will meet your expenses, since she expects to work side by side with you, and as she progresses, your studio will be back in fashion. That's not an unlikely scenario. I know public opinion is in her favor, and if she had wanted them, she would already have had many orders and great success."

Flochardet knew the doctor was right, and being naturally self-confident, he hoped to win back his clients and his independence, once it was certain his debts were settled.

Return to Pictordu

Indeed, there was new public support for Flochardet. In the provinces people don't like unstable situations, and besides, in the face of possible bankruptcy, almost everyone is worried, because almost everyone is more or less affected by it. When all his property had been rapidly liquidated and they saw the brave artist, completely penniless, cheerfully waiting in front of his canvas for the kindly faces of his fellow citizens, those smiling faces arrived. After a thousand tokens of respect and interest, more or less delicately expressed, they put him straight to work.

At his side, Diane waited calmly, resolutely, at her easel, for the men and women to bring her their children. She announced she had chosen this specialty so she wouldn't need to compete with her father. They brought her the entire younger generation from town and from the castles in the vicinity—the hope of their families, the pride of their mothers, a generation of youngsters who were almost all beautiful, because, we must not forget, Arles is full of beautiful people.

Diane displayed extraordinary composure, but in her heart, she felt she was too inexperienced to do well. Once again she called on her mother's miraculous assistance, even though she was now an adult. The beautiful muse and her mother were now one and the same in her thoughts.

One night, the first time she dared, she looked in her desk for the little head of the Bacchus found at Pictordu. Since that time she had learned to appreciate it, and she thought it was even more charming than it had seemed to her before. "Dear little god," she said to him, "you, too, have revealed life in art to me. Inspire me now! Teach me the secret of truth that a great, unknown artist has put in you. I'm willing to be unknown as he is, if, like him, I leave something as beautiful as you."

Diane didn't dare try using paints at first. She began with pastel pencils, which were very much in fashion at that time. On her first attempt, she drew a portrait so remarkable and charming that people talked about it for miles around. From then on, customers came to her at the same time her father's clientele came back to him. Aristocrats and middle-class people loved to meet in this very dignified studio where father and daughter worked together, one chatting with a cheerful wit, after years of sadness or preoccupation which had put people off; the other quiet and unassuming, unaware of her beauty and behaving in a manner that would make no one jealous. They remembered Mama Laura's scatterbrained airs, her silly costumes, and sharp tongue, and they weren't sorry to be rid of her. They had come there before to twitter about nothing, just to be in fashion;

now they came to talk seriously, and to cultivate good taste.

After one year, Flochardet and his daughter, living modestly but without great deprivations, were in a position to pay their rent to the doctor. He took the money and invested it in Diane's name. In his will, he had made her the owner of the entire purchase, but he refrained from telling her, as much to protect Flochardet's dignity and stimulate Diane's courage as to keep Mama Laura at a distance.

In spite of the doctor's caution, Mama Laura returned home when she found out the debts had been paid and business was going well. She didn't enjoy living with her parents, who had little money and were frugal. She saw practically no one there and she couldn't wear her beautiful clothes. So she returned, and Diane made it her duty to welcome her warmly. At first Mrs. Flochardet appeared touched, but soon she wanted to mingle with the high society that frequented her husband's studio. Her presence cast a chill over it, and her gossip was no longer fitting. The clients were annoyed with her for showing off her beautiful dresses and jewelry, which she should have sold to speed up payment on the household debts. They thought she was too comfortable and that she had an inconsiderate attitude toward Diane that was not at all appropriate. They made her feel she was no longer liked by anyone. Mrs. Flochardet became very resentful, exiled herself from the studio, and tried to renew friendships elsewhere. It was useless. She was a faded rose, her beauty had gone the way of her triumphs. People became even more critical of her. She was received coldly and very few of the calls she made were returned.

She then became a hypocrite in an attempt to redeem herself. Like a widow giving up her beautiful clothes, she took on the good behavior and sober appearance of a deeply religious person. Since she wasn't sincere, she became worse playing this role. Before she had only been selfish and frivolous; now she became envious and wicked. She had nothing good to say about anyone, slandered them, denigrated everything, and disrupted the family with her recriminations, her complaining, her touchiness, and her bitter character.

Diane continued to endure her stepmother

with unchanging sweetness. Seeing that her father still had some affection for the frivolous woman, she did everything she possibly could to fit her into the household. There was one thing she was able to refuse: Mama Laura's frantic desire to put the house back the way it was. Counting on the money her husband was earning again, she wanted to evict the renters and invite guests as she did before. Diane held firm, and from that moment on she was treated as an enemy by her stepmother, labeled a tyrant, and denounced as a miser to whoever would listen.

Diane suffered terribly from this persecution, and many times she was on the verge of returning to live with the doctor so she could work in peace. But she refrained, knowing her father would be unhappy without her.

One day she had a visit from a young lady whom she recognized right away, since she had a good memory for faces. She was Viscountess Blanche de Pictordu, recently married to one of her cousins. She was still pretty, still poor and unhappy with her lot in life, but still proud of her name, which she had the satisfaction of not giving up. She introduced her young husband to

Diane. He was a simple boy with a common, silly face. But he was a true Pictordu, from the oldest branch, and Blanche would not have understood that someone else might have been more worthy of her.

In spite of her stubborn ideas, Blanche had become more sociable, and since, in all other areas, she had a certain wit, she was very kind to Diane, complimented her talent, and didn't try to disparage Diane's profession the way she had before. Diane was happy to see her again; her name and her person refreshed her sweetest childhood memories. To encourage her to come back, Diane asked to draw her portrait. Blanche flushed with pleasure, as she had the time she received the turquoise brooch. She knew she was pretty, and to see her face drawn by a skillful hand was exhilarating; but she was poor, and Diane understood her hesitation.

"I'm asking you as a favor," she told Blanche. "To reproduce a perfect face is a satisfaction I don't experience every day, and since it's difficult, it will encourage me to improve."

Basically, Diane wanted only to pay an old sentimental debt to the memory of Pictordu.

Blanche couldn't understand this mysterious sensitivity; she credited it to her own charms. She let herself be begged a little and claimed she had other obligations, even though she was afraid she'd be believed. She had only a few days to spend in Arles; her financial situation didn't allow her to stay long in an expensive city, and her husband, busy with farming and hunting, urged her to return to the country where they lived.

"I'll only make a simple sketch with three colors: white, black, and red," Diane told her. "If I'm successful, it could be very pretty, and I'll only ask you to sit for one morning."

Blanche agreed to return, and the next day she arrived in a pretty sky-blue dress with the turquoise brooch on a ribbon around her neck.

Diane was inspired; she drew one of her best portraits, and the viscountess found herself so pretty that tears of gratitude filled the long black eyelashes encircling her blue eyes. She kissed Diane and begged her to come visit her in her castle.

"In the Castle of Pictordu?" Diane asked with surprise. "You told me you still lived with your father. Have you rebuilt the old manor?"

"Not completely," the viscountess replied. "That wouldn't have been possible for us; but we have restored a small pavilion and we'll be moving in next month. There is a guest room. It would be so kind of you to be the first guest to use it."

The offer was sincere. Blanche added that her father would be happy to see Diane again, as well as Mr. Flochardet, whom he still remembered fondly and referred to as "his friend Flochardet" when he heard people talking about his beautiful work.

Diane really wanted to see Pictordu again, and she promised to do her best to visit the following month, with or without her father. He had been encouraging her for a long time to take a little trip for enjoyment, if only to go visit her old aunt, the nun, in Mende, with Geoffrette. Pictordu was practically on the way, and surely she could make a detour.

It took two whole days to get to Saint-Jean-Gardonenque. Dr. Marcelin Féron, the doctor's nephew, now a well-known doctor himself, offered to accompany Diane and Geoffrette to the city, where they spent the night. From there, he went to visit one of his friends living in the vicinity, while Diane, ecstatic to have found the good coachman, Romanèche, took the road to Pictordu with Geoffrette in a rented carriage. A few necessary repairs had been made to the terrible road, and the travelers arrived safely in the evening, at the lower terrace of the castle.

The entrance was no longer there. The entrance to the repaired pavilion, once the Baths of Diana, was farther down. But Diane wanted to be alone when she saw the statue that had talked to her. She was afraid she wouldn't be able to find it again. So she sent Romanèche and Geoffrette on ahead, and, stepping over a small fence that had just been put up, she nimbly climbed the uneven, broken steps of the great stairway.

It was about four o'clock in the afternoon; the sun was beginning to cast its slanting light on everything. Before discovering her beloved statue, Diane saw its shadow against the sand of the terrace, and her heart leapt with joy. She ran to it and gazed in astonishment. She remembered it as huge, but, in reality, it was barely life-size. Was it as beautiful and monumental as Diane had remembered? No, it was a little overdone, and the folds of the dress were too detailed and too stiff, but it was elegant and graceful, and Diane, not wanting to criticize, threw it a kiss, naively sorry the statue didn't return it.

The terrace was in the same state of abandon as before. Diane saw that no one ever walked there. She later learned that Blanche, who was terrified of snakes and treated the most innocent grass snakes as poisonous vipers, never went into the ruins and permitted no one else to go there. Nevertheless, she lived right in the middle of this rubble, and Diane was both surprised, and very glad, to see that the solitude and disarray that had once charmed her remained unchanged.

She admired the jumble of dense foliage and dead trees, magnificent wild plants and once cultivated plants, both sorts now equally free and unruly. She loved the disorder of the stones, where moss had invaded the natural rocks and also the cut stones. She saw again the stream of pure water that had once fed the fountains and waterfalls and was now rippling discreetly between the grass and the stones. She contemplated the elegant Renaissance facade of the castle, where the live ivy entwined with garlands of ivy cut out of stone. A few windows, finely worked, a few small spires perhaps had disappeared. Diane didn't remember each detail exactly, but everything together still had the cheerful and noble aspect that buildings from that brilliant era retain even in their decay.

The Statue's Speech

Diane found the path to the bath pavilion right away. Blanche, alerted by the arrival of the carriage, ran to meet her and greeted her warmly, then led her into the pavilion where she had spent a night she would never forget. Alas! Everything had changed. Of the great round room, they had made a sort of drawing room, from which the pool had disappeared. They had cut out the marble to make a mantle for the fireplace; the vaulted ceiling decorated with garlands had been transformed into a harsh blue sky. Her precious nymphs, horror of horrors, were no longer dancing in lively, dignified circles around the circular wall. The living room, its walls covered in an orange cloth with large bouquets of flowers on it, was now square, and the cut-off corner areas were used as little bedrooms.

The arcaded cloister had been cleared of its debris and wild plants. The interior had become a vegetable garden, and the spring, stripped of its mint and hart's-tongue, had disappeared, confined under a wall coping. Chickens were scratching in the manure of a little courtyard nearby, which had been the steam bath and was still paved with purple rock. A lane of newly planted mulberry trees, which didn't appear to have made up their minds to adapt to the terrain and climate, led down to the new road, without passing through the former park or ruins. The owners of the Castle of Pictodru, settling into a corner of their ancestor's nest, had done their best to turn their backs on it, never needing to pass through it.

Politely admiring the way Blanche had made use of the remains of the old dwelling, Diane sighed, thinking how very differently she herself would have done it. But Blanche seemed so proud and satisfied with her arrangements, that Diane very graciously refrained from criticizing anything. The marquis and his son-in-law soon arrived for supper. The son-in-law, red and sunburned, calling his dogs, spoke in a resonant, cheerful voice, with bursts of laughter after each sentence. But no one could guess what was so amusing. The marquis was polite, as always, affectionate, unassuming, and melancholy. He greeted Diane very warmly. He had forgotten nothing of her first visit. And then he showered her with strange questions that were impossible to answer without explaining at length, as you would to a child. The good man lived so apart from the world, his horizons had grown so narrow, that, wanting to talk about everything so he wouldn't seem too backward, he revealed he understood nothing of the subject under discussion.

Blanche, more refined, and a little more polished by exposure to the outside world, suffered from her father's simplicity. But she suffered even more from the audacity with which her husband corrected him, proclaiming ideas that were even more simpleminded. She contradicted both of them with obvious disdain. Diane missed Pictordu's former solitude and wondered why she had left her father's friendly chats and the doctor's interesting conversation to listen to this tasteless trio who hadn't a brain among them.

She claimed to be tired and went to bed early in the narrow little bedroom that her hosts graced with the title of "guest room." She couldn't sleep there. The odor of fresh paint forced her to open her window to keep from getting a headache.

Then she saw that the window looked out on a small outside stairway running diagonally along the wall. It was a section of stairs saved from the earlier construction. The banister had not yet been replaced, but the night was clear and beautiful. Diane wrapped her robe around her and went down, happy to be alone, as before, and to discover the marvelous castle of her dreams. The beautiful muse that she considered her good fairy didn't come to take her by the hand to help her climb the spiral stairs standing in the empty air above the crumbled ceilings. She could not walk under the arcades which tried, in vain, to span the chasms of rubble. But in her imagination, she reconstructed the magical castle, created in the heart of this isolated area, in the Italian Renaissance style, at a time when Italy was still ahead of France in art and in taste. Once again she saw in her mind the celebrations of that vanished splendor which could no longer be reborn in its former state and which industry had already banished from the future. She met no ghosts on her walk, but she took tremendous joy in contemplating the beautiful effects of the moonlight on the ruins. She could climb high enough on the rock cliffs overlooking the castle to see the gleam of dull blue-green light in the small open space that the little river cut in the depths of the ravine. Here and there, the black shape of rocks blocking the riverbed stood out in the midst of flickering diamonds. Owls called to each other in cat-like voices, shrubs and ferns exhaled their wild perfume. A deep tranquility reigned in the air, and the branches of old trees were as still, as statuesque, as the stone ornaments on the terrace.

Diane felt the need to re-examine her short life amid this nature, which seemed to be absorbed in the meditation of eternity. She reconsidered her childhood, her moments of serious curiosity, her sickly languor, her longings for a mysterious ideal, her disappointments, her enthusiasms, her sorrows, her endeavors, her successes, and her hopes. There, she stopped; her future was vague, as mysterious as certain phases of her past. She understood everything she lacked in order to go beyond the humble limits she had accepted by coming to the aid of her father. She knew very well that beyond the career that assured her independence and her dignity there was great step to be taken. But could she ever enter into that stage of her development? Could she travel, know, feel? Could she shake off her family circle, her routine, her everyday obligations, the limits that her father could have gone beyond, but where he had stopped in order to heed the demands of a woman who only saw profit in his art?

Diane felt tied down, held back, broken by the very woman from whom she tried constantly to wrest her father's lazy, indecisive mind. Once, on the verge of lashing out at her stepmother with contempt, she had held back, since she had better self-control than her father. When she had felt ready to explode, she had heard some secret strength inside her say, "You know you must control yourself."

She remembered the moments of inner struggle and thought of her mother, who undoubtedly had bequeathed to her the secret and precious power of patience. Then, passionately, she invited this protective spirit to enter her soul to show her what she must do, just as her face had entered Diane's vision and revealed beauty to her. Must she resolutely give up the higher pleasures of the mind in order to stay with her father? Must she resist the voice of the motherly muse who had raised her up and transported her to a realm of beauty and truth in order to show her the endless road on which an artist must not stop?

She was reflecting on these things as she walked, when suddenly she found herself in front of the faceless statue, her first inspiration. She leaned against the pedestal, her hand resting on its cold feet. Then she seemed to hear a voice, which, although it came from the statue, reverberated strongly within her.

It said, "Leave the care of your future to the maternal soul that watches within you and over you. Together, we will both find the path to the ideal. Accept the present as a stopover where, even as you rest, you're working. Don't think you must choose between duty and noble ambition. The two are made to travel together, one helping the other. Also, don't think that victory over anger and long suffering are the enemies of talent. Instead of wearing it out, they stimulate it. Remember it was through tears that you found the face you were looking for, and be assured that, when you suffer valiantly, your talent and your strength grow without your knowing it. A healthy intelligence is not to be found in rest, only in victory."

Diane returned, overwhelmed by this inner revelation, and leaving her window half-open, slept as she'd never slept before.

The next day, she felt a delicious peace in her entire being. She listened patiently to the good marquis's naive comments and his son-in-law's trite remarks. She even went so far as to be in a good mood with Blanche and led her, a little against her will, to explore the ruins in broad daylight.

The doctor hadn't limited himself to point out beauty in art to his dear Diane. He had made her understand it in nature also, and he had given her ideas that made a walk more interesting. He had recommended she bring back a few rare plants native to Cévennes for him: *Reseda jaquini, Saxifraga clussi, Senecio lanatus, Cynanchum cordatum, Aethionème saxatile*. Diane looked for and found them. She gathered them carefully for her old friend. And for her own use, she reaped less precious, but still charming flowers: cliff cinquefoil; beautiful blue meadow crowfoot and gracious sailor's knot; rock soapwort, which carpeted the rocky banks of the river with its countless little pink flowers; wall erinus, which blossomed in the humid places among the ruins; and mountain buttercup, which sprinkled the terrace lawns with gold. While looking for the little flowers, Diane picked up a rather misshapen coin, covered with a thick layer of oxide, and handed it to Blanche, telling her to clean it carefully without scratching it.

"Keep it," the viscountess answered, "if you attach some value to these old worthless coins; I really don't know anything about them and I've many others I've no use for."

"Show them to me," Diane replied. "I don't know much about them, but I can tell you which ones are interesting, and with the help of Dr. Féron, who's very knowledgeable—who knows? I'm very lucky according to him. Maybe, without knowing it, you own a small fortune."

"I'll give it all to you for nothing out of the goodness of my heart, my dear Diane! It's nothing but copper, very thin gold, or tarnished silver."

"That doesn't matter! If it's valuable, I'll let

you know and pay you what it's worth."

She examined other medallions the marquis had found and thrown into a corner of the house, where they had a hard time finding them. Diane thought they might not be worthless and made it her business to have someone competent look at them. She didn't want to clean the one she had found, afraid she might spoil it, attaching who knows what superstitious idea to her personal find. She wrapped it in paper and put it into her trunk with the others.

The next day she went to watch the sunrise at the top of the mountain; she was alone and walked aimlessly. She found herself in the crevice of a boulder, facing a wonderful little waterfall that tumbled brilliantly and joyfully into wild rosebushes and silky tufts of clematis. The slanting sunlight cast pink rays on the exquisite detail of the scene, and, for the first time, Diane felt the exhilaration of color. Since only the outline of the mountain was visible against the light, she became aware of the magic world of light, more or less diffused and more or less reflected, changing from brightness to softness, warm tones to cold tones, through indescribable harmonies.

Her father had often spoken to her about "neutral tones."

"My dear father," she cried involuntarily, as if he were there, "there are no neutral tones, I swear to you, there are none!"

Then she smiled at her own passion and drank in to her heart's content this revelation from the sky and the earth, from the foliage and water, grasses and rocks, the dawn chasing away the night, the night graciously and sweetly retiring, behind its transparent veils, which the sun was trying to penetrate. Diane realized she could paint without giving up her drawing, and her heart shivered with hope and joy.

When she returned, she again stopped in front of the statue and remembered what she had felt articulated in her soul the night before. "If it's you who are speaking to me," she thought, "you taught me well yesterday. You made me understand that good resolution is better than a wonderful voyage. You told me to return, smiling, to a prison of duty; I promised I would, and already today I've made an exhilarating artistic conquest. I've done more than understand; I've felt, I've seen. I've acquired a new power, my eyes have been filled with light, and my determination has been renewed. Thank you, my dear mother, my fairy! Thanks to you, I hold the secret of life."

Diane left Pictordu to spend two days in Mende. Once home, she returned to her drawing, and, at the same time, she tried painting without telling anyone. She found some good pictures and copied them every morning for two hours. She paid close attention to her father's work. From time to time, he still painted simpering, chubby virgins for churches, but because he was a painter of some ability, he had acquired a good deal of skill. She watched what he did and what he didn't do. She learned from his good qualities and his weaknesses.

And one day, she tried to paint a portrait. She copied children and created angels. People began to notice she painted well and very beautifully, and her reputation grew. Mama Laura realized that this stepdaughter, so hated and so patient, was a goose who would lay golden eggs. She pretended to love Diane, and, lacking true tenderness in her cold heart, showed her at least respect and consideration. She made up her mind to stop speaking ill of Diane, to say she was very happy, that there was nothing she needed, not even a necessary little luxury, because Diane would very willingly go without a new dress to give Mama Laura a more beautiful new one. And finally, she made up her mind not to torment good Flochardet anymore, who, thanks to his daughter, was once again as wise and happy as he had been with his first wife.

One day, the Viscountess de Pictordu arrived, and after a thousand hugs and much beating around the bush, finally got around to asking if Diane had been able to find anything of value in the coins. She admitted that the bath pavilion had cost more to restore than she had counted on and that her husband was in a very awkward position to pay off the amount he had borrowed, small in reality, but considerable for him.

She added that she had made up her mind to get rid of the Pictordu ruins. If Diane still had an artist's lover for them, she would give them up along with all of the rocky part of the old park, for a very good price.

"My dear Viscountess," Diane replied, "if, someday, I am in the position to allow myself this fantasy, I'll wait until you are thoroughly disgusted with your ancestor's castle—but please realize that you are in no way forced to make this sacrifice. I haven't forgotten your antique coins. It took me a while to have them appraised and let others know about them. I did what I planned, and I have the pleasure of telling you there are four of real value, especially the one I found myself. I was going to write to you about the various proposals the doctor has received from museums and collectors. Since you are here, I want you to consult with Dr. Féron yourself, but rest assured that in accepting the offers such as they are today, you can earn an amount that is double what you need."

Overwhelmed, Blanche threw her arms around Diane and called her her guardian angel. She got on very well with the good doctor, who did his best to help, and she obtained her little fortune rather quickly. Blanche returned home full of joy, after begging Diane to come back for a visit.

But Diane had no further business at the Castle of Pictordu. She had absolutely no desire to possess it materially. She possessed it in her memory as a beloved and sacred vision that appeared to her when she wanted it to. The fairy who had welcomed her there had left Pictordu to follow her, and this inspiration now lived with her, whenever and wherever she went. She built innumerable castles for her, palaces filled with marvels; she gave her everything she could wish for, mountains as well as forests and rivers, stars in the sky as well as flowers and birds. Everything laughed and sang in her soul, everything sparkled before her eyes when, after working very hard, she felt she had achieved real progress and taken one step further in her art.

Do I need to tell you the rest of her life? You can easily guess what it was like, my children. It was a very noble, very happy life, very prolific in exquisite works. When Diane was twenty-five years old, she married the doctor's nephew, that excellent adopted brother who was a man of merit and who had dreamed only of her. So she was rich and could do lots of good things. Among other things, she established a studio for poor young girls, whom she instructed herself, free of charge. With her husband, she took the wonderful trips she had dreamed of and always returned happily to her own country, her old friend, her father, and even her stepmother, whom she had come to love by forgiving her. For it is a law of good natures: you become attached to what you put up with, you hold on to what has cost you a lot. Generous hearts love sacrifice, which is lucky for stingy people. There are both kinds, and apparently the latter live at the expense of the former. But in reality, those who give and forgive are loved the most by genies and fairies, those spirits who are absolutely free in their outlook and who flee from people enchanted with themselves. Fairies only reveal themselves to eyes that are wide with wonder and devotion.

The Feminist Press promotes voices on the margins of dominant culture and publishes feminist works from around the world, inspiring personal transformation and social justice. We believe that books have the power to shift culture, and create a society free of violence, sexism, homophobia, racism, cis-supremacy, classism, sizeism, ableism and other forms of dehumanization. Our books and programs engage, educate, and entertain.

See our complete list of books at
feministpress.org